Manpower planning for local labor markets

Garth Mangum · David Snedeker

Olympus Publishing Company Salt Lake City

Washington · San Francisco · Boston

Contents

331.11
M276m

List of Tables

4

5

List of Figures

Preface

This book is long overdue, since we have been promising ourselves for two years to get it written. It grows out of a long-term conviction that the primary source for improvement in the results of manpower programs must be adaptation of those programs to the needs of individuals and the realities of labor markets. We view this as only one beginning of several currently being made. Its source is basically our personal experiences, and it may suffer from that narrowness and gain from that practicality.

The text has profited from reviews and comments by Sar Levitan, Robert Taggart, Richard Arnold, Michael Kirkham, Gary Felker, Ms. Nancy ReMine, Robert McPherson, and Ms. Marty Gould. We appreciate their perceptive comments, all of which we have welcomed and considered, though not all did we adopt. The book has profited from their advice.

Publication of this book was sponsored in part by the National Manpower Policy Task Force, which is a private, nonprofit organization primarily concerned with furthering research on manpower problems and assessing related policy issues. The Task Force sponsors three types of publications: (1) policy statements in which Task Force members are actively involved as co-authors, (2) studies commissioned by the Task Force and reviewed by a committee prior to publication, and (3) studies prepared by members of the Task Force but not necessarily reviewed by other members. We are most grateful for the financial support from the National Manpower Policy Task Force, and we dedicate this book to that body in its continual effort to upgrade the quality and effectiveness of manpower policy and practice in this country.

The glossary is included because of the vast "confusion of tongues" which exists in the field and the need for some beginning to codification. It represents a multitude of compromises. Although our goal was to create a glossary that would be useful to a relative newcomer to manpower planning, some readers will not find needed listings because we felt that the particular term was in the normal vocabulary of the majority of our expected readership. Others will find their pet terms have met with cavalier treatment. Still others will not find listings for terms which by their complex nature (in our opinion) precluded simple definition. It is hoped that time and use will assist us in improving the utility of the glossary. Finally, we have relied heavily on official definitions where they are in widespread use and afford greater precision than would our altering these definitions to suit our interpretation of them. The most useful source in this regard is the "Explanatory Notes" section of *Employment and Earnings*, a monthly publication of the Bureau of Labor Statistics. Responsibility for sins of omission and commission, however, belong to the authors.

The Authors
July 1974

 1

The Case for State and Local Manpower Planning

The thrust in federal manpower policy since at least 1966 has been toward local labor market manpower planning. The advocacy may have been hidden beneath terms like coordination, consolidation, decentralization, decategorization, and special revenue sharing. But if planning is a process of attempting to identify problems and devise solutions that fit, that (along with public service employment) is what all the furor in manpower legislation and policy over the years since 1966 has been about.

There have been many stages in that advocacy: (1) early attempts to coordinate programs to see that all of them in total focused consistently and coherently on the needs of their common target groups, (2) the Concentrated Employment Program (CEP) which sought to bring all manpower programs together under one roof in census tracts heavily impacted by poverty, (3) the Cooperative Area Manpower Planning System's (CAMPS) initiation of parallel planning for interrelated programs, and (4) ultimately to the decentralization-decategorization advocacy of discretion to local elected officials to adapt program offerings to the realities of communities and the needs of individuals culminating in the Comprehensive Employment and Training Act (CETA) of 1973. But throughout the underlying driving force has been the same, and the direction has been consistent.

Every community has its disadvantaged people who have manpower needs. But what can and should be done for them depends upon the state and nature of the local economy and their

9

own personal characteristics. Nationally uniform programs can be generally applicable, but they never can efficiently meet variant needs. Employment and income for the disadvantaged has been the priority of U.S. manpower policy for the past dozen years, but that is not the only reason for labor market manpower planning. Economic development is a function of human resources as well as of natural resource endowment and capital investment. Whether and in what direction to grow in a local economy will depend in part upon the nature of the work force. Every social and technical problem has manpower requirements in its evolution. There are incentives in the labor market which lead generally in the right direction, and fortunately, most labor markets are at least viable without such planning. But if pathologies are to be avoided in the labor market and ingrained problems ameliorated, it makes sense to look ahead, decide what the community wants to be like, and take steps to make it happen.

But if planning encompasses identifying problems, establishing objectives, exploring alternatives, designing and implementing programs, and monitoring, evaluating, feeding back, and improving efforts based on observed results, manpower planning has been widely advocated but seldom done. One should not be harsh, for the trends are clearly in the right direction, and the task is not easy. In manpower programs the planning function did not precede the programs; planning was added after a sizable number of categorical federal programs had already been put into operation in local labor markets by a variety of local program agents or operators. Planning was initiated to help stem the tide of rising criticism about program organization and administration and to counter the criticism that federal administrators did not know local conditions. In part, it was a necessary attempt to shift the burden for explaining what was being done from national to local levels as a political strategem, and in part it was the recognition that the federal administrator was too far removed from the local scene to really understand local needs and programs. Planning, it was hoped, would cause program operators to correlate individual program efforts and to develop program linkages and coordination.

To say that most of what has been called manpower planning till now is in reality a somewhat more analytical approach to program administration is not to say it is not worthwhile. The analysis cannot but improve chances of program success, and the tendency is for staff described as manpower planners to want to live up to the name and explore the boundaries of their new profession. Therefore the clear tendency is to reach slowly out from the day-to-day operational analysis, which might be described as tactical planning, to the longer term, foresighted relating of action to emerging need and social goals, which can be dignified as strategic planning.

However, to call an individual a "planner" or a group a "planning council" is not to provide a format and technique for planning or to ensure competence. "How to do it" is the next required step after deciding a task should be undertaken. The Labor Department, with its responsibility for funding and putting in place the beginnings of manpower planning, has also provided the rudiments of a tactical planning technology at a level as sophisticated as, or even more so than most planners and planning bodies are capable of using. Progress, however, depends upon constantly stretching efforts beyond current capability.

This book is designed as an elementary introduction to planning manpower services for those who are the victims of pathologies in the marketplace — the unemployed, the underemployed, the poor, and the hard to employ. It is intended primarily for the manpower planning staffs funded since 1969, who have been assigned the task of developing manpower planning programs for governors of states, mayors of cities, and for county executives — a new breed who are multiplying rapidly under CETA.

One of the central premises of the book is that manpower planning, like human resource planning (of which it is one part), can and should be a major activity of local labor markets. A good manpower planning program begins with an understanding of the system by which skills are developed and jobs created, and how the two are matched in labor markets. It does not begin with federal guidelines and programs. These latter policies and resources must fit into and complement a considerable variety of activities which go on largely independent of the programs. This argument in no way lessens the importance of federal programs and guidelines. Indeed without federal initiatives, there would be neither manpower programs nor manpower planning.

From meager beginnings in 1967, manpower planning is emerging as a sophisticated and continuing activity which has implications far beyond the efficient use of federal resources. The progress achieved in this field is having an impact on health and education planning as well as on economic development planning. Present trends toward decentralization in policy administration, including larger roles for elected state, city, and county officials and their staffs, should bring local labor market manpower planning into its own. There is, however, a danger that such decentralization could have the opposite effect, unless the federal funds are accompanied by strong requirements for and support of a continuation in planning.

It is the ambition of this book to (a) set forth some techniques of manpower planning useful at the present state-of-the-art, and (b) derive some principles, provide some techniques, and identify further needs in planning technology reaching toward a more ideal but still achievable system.

In pursuit of that goal, this chapter offers definitions, a typology, and some underlying principles for manpower planning. The following chapter reviews recent experience in the field. Chapter 3 presents an overview of the role and functioning of labor markets in the economic system. The remaining chapters address "how to do it" at two levels: (1) the presently achievable and (2) that which should be pursued as achievable a little time ahead, given recommended efforts.

Why Manpower Planning?

That manpower is a vital economic resource while employment is the primary source of income and status in our society are truisms. But they do not justify manpower planning. Social energy is always limited. There is no reason to undertake planning unless lack of foresight will make things worse and a successful effort to foresee future conditions and accommodate to them or modify them can make them better. Manpower has always been a vital economic resource, and employment became the primary source of income as a consequence of industrialization. Which recent developments have made important what before was not necessary?

A new stage of economic history increasingly brings to human resources the primacy once held by natural and capital resources. In a preindustrial stage marked by investment of most human effort in some form of agriculture, fertility of the soil could be the major source of economic strength and land ownership the source of wealth and power in society. Industrialization transferred labor to the production and distribution of manufactured goods and wealth and power to the owners of industrial capacity. The first of these two periods in the United States encompassed roughly the years up to the Civil War, and the second is only now in transition to a new era yet to be very clearly specified. But for this postindustrial stage, it appears that direct human services and information processing are likely to be a focal point of employment. And in that stage human resources promise to have primacy in economic theory and fact. Emphasis has shifted from goods production to services and blue-collar to white-collar employment. The most rapidly growing occupations have been those which required the most formal education and training. Increasingly, factory and even farm were directed not by owners but by professional managers. International competition and internal prosperity have demanded scientific development and technical competence and the trained manpower to supply them. More and more, it is not one's ownership of anything other than his own talents and skills which determined one's place in the scheme of things. Human resources are in fact becoming the wealth of nations (Harbison, 1973).

All of this does not mean that natural and capital resources are no longer important. The rising productivity which has freed man, to the extent he has been freed, from drudgery has been primarily the result of more and better equipment to augment man's puny strength. Rising standards of living still depend upon increased productivity. The "energy crisis" is a sharp and belated reminder that the passengers on Spaceship Earth are dependent upon a fixed supply of natural resources. They can be discovered and developed but not created by man. But the failure to recognize these limitations and plan to enjoy the good life within these constraints was a failure of human wisdom, not of natural resources. If planning is to make the best of natural and capital resource constraints, if new natural resources are to be developed and known ones conserved, it will be the wisdom and the skill of the human resource component that will achieve it.

The economic and social changes which have put a premium on the quality of the human resource contribution have had their impacts at both ends of the manpower spectrum. Those without education and training have come to be at a competitive disadvantage as their opportunities shrank relatively and the competition from better prepared people increased. Technological, economic, and social changes isolated some in rural depressed areas and others in central city slums. Cities developed perversely with the well prepared often living in bedroom suburbs and working at white-collar jobs in central city offices. While well-paid, semiskilled production jobs migrated to the suburbs, the victims of deficient education, racial prejudice, family breakup, and a variety of other social and economic ills were trapped in central cities contiguous only to jobs for which they were unprepared or to which they had no access and to jobs which offered little attraction and low pay.

High birthrates from 1947 to 1957 gave at least sixteen years' warning of swollen labor market entry rates, but public policy failed to heed the warning. School attendance multiplied and extended; labor force participation rates shifted, with those of men declining and of women rising; technological change quickened; mobility increased. Subsequently, falling birthrates signaled declining need for education personnel, and the supply of technical- and college-trained manpower began catching up with demand, but few seemed to notice. All of this is an old story to any student or practitioner in the U.S. labor markets.

The point is that all of these developments were foreseeable but little acted upon. That inaction brought crises which were responded to by programs. Programs range from those to increase the supply of educated manpower to those to improve the employ-ability, employment, and earnings of those least able to compete successfully in labor markets. Programs with the former objectives were familiar and they worked, perhaps even to excess in some areas of highly trained manpower. The latter programs were new, the problems to which they were addressed were unfamiliar, the techniques undeveloped, the staffs inexperienced and untrained, and the objectives complex.

Operating under crises, real or imagined, government officials decided that action seemed more needed than planning. At least in the public sector and at the national level, pressures of budget cycles and elections dictated a short-run focus. Since the initiatives on behalf of the disadvantaged were federal, state and local govern-ments merely responded to administer federal resources under federal direction. At a more general level, expenditures for educa-tion and training multiplied without being planned or coordinated. Schools and colleges responded to perceived rising demand without wondering how their output related to that of all the other sources and to manpower requirements. Congress and federal agencies also responded piecemeal with incentives for expanding production of this or that type of specialist, with no attention paid to the total impact. New programs were introduced and old policies shifted without recognition of their manpower implications or the availability of staff to carry them out.

All of this transition is occurring at a time in economic history when society is becoming incredibly complex and planning has become recognized as a vital necessity. Population growth, urbanization, and technological development have made everything related to everything else. Actions of one tend to have an impact upon all. Private and social decisions are likely to bring into play long successions of unforeseen consequences. Such forces set in motion often seem almost irreversible. Where once fragmented and atomized "ad hoc-ness" was considered essential to freedom, planning is now the accepted insurance against binding strictures on future decisions. Add to all this, as the demand side of planning, the availability of massive data processing capability augmenting the potential supply of planning capacity, put the primacy of human resources together with the demand for planning as an essential social function, and there is a recipe for the emergence of human resource and manpower planning.

Gradually, a positive response has developed from this seeming chaos. Slowly but increasingly, the larger firms in private industry attempt to foresee crucial manpower needs and prepare for them, insofar as it seems profitable to do so. Government statistical agencies provide better and better data and projections as aids to personal and institutional planning. The national government attempts to foresee total employment needs and, qualified by other goals, seeks an acceptable level of employment. Policies, more than planning, determine the shape and size of programs on behalf of the disadvantaged members of the work force. However, those disadvantages are faced in labor markets which for most transactions, particularly for these workers, are local in scope.

Nationally, a manpower planning assignment has been given to state and local governments, but planning competence and a planning format are just beginning to be developed. Neither state nor local governments have had the planning assignment until CETA carried with it the discretion for them to see that plans relate to labor market needs and realities and thus has affected operations and achieved results. Now, however, decentralization of program responsibility from the federal to the state and local levels promises the discretion but not necessarily the competence for meaningful and effective planning.

Political jurisdictions are not economic entities, whereas manpower problems occur in labor markets. Federal manpower program resources are minor in contrast to the range and size of manpower problems in any economy. There, objectives may or may not accord with local priorities. And CETA represents only 40 percent of federal manpower programs on behalf of the competitively disadvantaged. The sum and substance of these considerations are:

(1) Manpower planning is necessary in a world of rapid change where human resources play a vital role.

(2) Manpower planning is scarce because of lack of expertise and discretion, but both are growing.

(3) Manpower planning should be undertaken wherever:

(a) Problems can be foreseen and avoided.

(b) Unfavorable conditions can be ameliorated.

(c) The future can be shaped in more satisfactory ways than had it just been allowed to happen.

(d) Looking ahead to objectives can allow a measurement of progress.

(4) But it cannot be done unless there are techniques, skills, and discretion.

(5) When it is done effectively, the planning will be done where the problems are; i.e., where people live, where jobs are created, and where the two match or fail to match.

Definitions and Typology for Manpower Planning

Definitions in the emerging field are not universally accepted, and one must be arbitrary in advancing terms. By "human resources" we mean all of the productive activities and potential contributions of human beings. Human resource development is an effort to enlarge upon the productiveness of people, whether in employment, in work, in art, in volunteer service, or in any other way that humans contribute to making life better for themselves or for others. Work is any productive activity undertaken to produce goods or services to benefit one's self or others, whether or not the person performing that work is paid for it. We reserve the term "manpower" for the labor market and relate it to employment; i.e., work that is employed human effort that results in income. Therefore human resource development would include all aspects of health, education, and employability development; most social welfare activities; and even such diverse social and economic functions as housing and transportation, insofar as they affect the social and personal as well as the economic productivity of people. In fact the human resource term is saved from being infinitized into meaninglessness only by its restriction to productivity, achievement, and service.

Manpower development refers to the enhancement of every human ability which contributes to effectiveness in the employment nexus. Manpower policy is a two-sided term encompassing all social decisions which deliberately affect:

(1) The use of people in labor markets as economic factors of production

(2) The ability and opportunity for people to pursue remunerative and satisfying work careers in employment

Since the concerns of manpower policy embrace its roles both as a productive resource and as a determinant of personal welfare, it is well to think of a manpower system as those forces in society which not only use people in productive ways but also create their productivity. The system must recruit people from the population pool, motivate them to productivity, prepare them for productive activity, create employment opportunities for them, match the people with the opportunities, reward them with both incomes and feelings of self-worth, and refurbish, upgrade, and replace them as economic forces, or displace them because of age. Planning is a systematic way of thinking through and designing a system to do these things.

Manpower planning includes every effort to foresee manpower problems, establish manpower goals, and design systematic approaches for avoiding the problems or achieving the goals. Though this book devotes itself to planning for public manpower policies as pursued primarily by state and local governments, perspective on that assignment may be provided through a typology of manpower planning.

Macro Manpower Planning

Conceptually at least, it is useful to think of economic planning as manpower planning, so long as its primary goal is employment. The Employment Act of 1946 implied the task of estimating the number of persons likely to be seeking work and devising policies for sufficient economic growth and job creation to absorb them. Though this is not a very explicit process, the Council of Economic Advisers always has available to it labor force projections made by the Bureau of Labor Statistics. The employment outlook is a key consideration in economic and political policy making, and despite the need to temper the employment goal with other goals, some action is always recommended.

Similarly, the federal budgeting process could be considered in part as a manpower planning exercise. Decisions to spend various amounts on defense, aerospace, atomic energy, agriculture, education, or any of the myriads of federal budgeting allocations are also decisions for sectoral allocations of manpower resources. Tax decisions are also decisions to allow or discourage private activities which allocate manpower within the private sector and between it and the public sector. Economic development activities, such as those to aid depressed areas, are in reality designed primarily to affect the spatial distribution of manpower and employment. Availability of federal aid to education influences the labor force participation of the young, just as public assistance affects the participation rates of some marginal and potential members of the labor force and Social Security benefits impact upon the participation rates of older persons. Nationally made projections of manpower requirements both aid and influence individual choice among occupations, the planning for educational facilities and other resources, and the actions of employers.

Though not the purpose of this book, the tremendous impact on manpower policy of national decisions outside the manpower policy field should be noted. Just a few examples can illustrate the impact and the economic and social failure to foresee and compensate for the manpower impact of national policy. Agricultural price support programs introduced in the 1930s were major factors in encouraging consolidation and mechanization of farms, forcing (or allowing) millions to leave the land, to migrate successfully or unsuccessfully to the cities, or to remain as the rural nonfarm poor. Medicare imposed greater burdens upon an already short supply in health occupations. Aerospace decisions encouraged large supplies of expensively trained manpower to invest their careers in that field, then abandoned them. Federal housing and highway building policies encouraged the demand for labor to shift to the suburbs, without aiding substantial portions of the supply to follow. Availability of retirement benefits continually encourage earlier retirement in a population characterized by increasing longevity, while Social Security restrictions on continued earnings discourage second careers.

These are sufficient examples to illustrate the need and opportunities for manpower planning at the national or total economy level. The need has been discussed for some years and was most recently noted in the 1972 *Manpower Report to the President*. Recommendations have ranged over a broad number of devices, a Council of Manpower Advisers, a manpower member among the three-man Council of Economic Advisers, a special assistant to the president for manpower, an intergovernmental Cabinet committee on manpower, with a primary role for the Labor Department among them. Still, policy responsibility remains fragmented with the consequence that nonmanpower decisions are made with little anticipation of their manpower consequences. Manpower considerations need not dominate, but at least there should be some focal point of recognition of manpower consequences with sufficient "clout" to get its voice heard.

Micro Manpower Planning

Much more is happening at the level of the individual business firm and, to a lesser degree, in the public agency as an employer. Firms dependent upon sophisticated manpower look ahead, relating product and sales outlooks to manpower needs and setting in place programs to get the right man in the right place at the right time. Enlightened firms also attempt to foresee declining manpower needs so that attrition can reduce otherwise excessive supplies. Most corporations at least try to look ahead at the attrition of top management and attempt to have replacements ready to take over. The number of firms undertaking such planning is relatively small but growing (Patten, 1971).

Manpower Program Planning

Little planning at the national level has gone into the variety of programs aimed at enhancing the employability and income of the poor and the competitively disadvantaged. Most were launched without clear identification of problems, explicit statement of objectives, or experiment to see if they would work. All were based on political supposition. Subsequent appropriations also have only the most casual relationship to need, being based on a variety of political judgments. At the local level, the response has been simply to accept federal funds, recruit eligible enrollees, and administer programs as directed by federal guidelines. Allocations to the state or communities from the federal level were either by formula or by politics and grantsmanship. Allocation decisions within states were ordinarily made, without guidance, by low-level functionaries.

At the state and local levels, the scene is now changing. Disturbed at the chaotic hodgepodge of programs seeking to serve the same target groups at the local level, the federal agencies did what they had not been able to do for themselves. They superimposed a coordinating mechanism among program administrators at state and area levels. From a mere interagency communications system, CAMPS in some places evolved into a real effort at manpower planning. (The CAMPS concept is discussed more fully in chapter 2.) Its major weaknesses were lack of a planning format and trained staff and the delegation of sufficient policy discretion that planning could make a difference in the allocation of funds. Passage of CETA seems to promise the discretion, and necessity is forcing the development of planning format, techniques, and staff.

Labor Market Manpower Planning

Manpower program planning has as its current focus the employability and employment needs of those individuals who find it most difficult to compete successfully for the opportunities available in the job market. It has as its goal improvement of the employability, employment opportunities, and incomes of members of those target groups. Others, perhaps most, participants in the labor market find less than optimum fulfillment and income from their working careers and could use help as recipients of manpower program planning. But resources and social energy are limited, and priorities among target groups and activities must be set.

Although manpower program planning seeks to enhance the ability of individuals and groups to compete successfully in labor markets, it does not encompass and is less than total labor market planning. A labor market is both a theoretical concept and a practical reality, but it is not a single place or event. It is conceived of as all of those ways in which those seeking to sell their labor and those seeking to buy labor services come into contact so that transactions — that is, hirings, promotions, and so forth — take place.

There are labor markets and labor markets. The term can apply to all of those who work or seek work, or to all workers in an occupation (e.g., the clerical labor market), in an industry (the construction labor market), or in a geographical area (the metropolitan labor market). The occupational, industrial, and geographical markets overlap (college professors in a national market, ironworkers in a regional labor market, and taxi drivers in a local labor market). A highly touted recent theory of labor markets related to manpower policy (the theory of dual labor markets) conceives of a primary labor market of good jobs, good pay, fringe benefits, and prospects of advancement; and a secondary labor market of poorly paid, unskilled, dead-end jobs open to the disadvantaged with an impervious wall between (Doeringer and Piore, 1971).

Clear and relatively precise in concept, actual markets are always fuzzy at the edges, and the boundaries are hard to identify. Since this book was primarily conceived for the labor markets in which manpower programs are relevant and for which manpower planning councils do their planning, the emphasis is local labor markets; i.e., the geographical area which encompasses both the residences and places of employment of most workers within normal commuting patterns. The edges will always be fuzzy as population thins and then thickens, with those commuting to other concentrations comprising other local labor markets. Political jurisdictions are hardly ever contiguous with labor markets, but standard metropolitan statistical areas (SMSAs) usually are.

A labor market must incorporate and bring together both the supply of and the demand for labor. The domain of manpower policy is generally conceived of as encompassing all supply side concerns; but on the demand side, it is conceived of as including only concern for particular employment opportunities for particular individuals (Bakke, 1969). As such it serves as a bridge between and overlaps to some degree economic development policy on the one hand and social welfare policy on the other (the social welfare concept being broader than the human resource concept, in that the former involves all factors related to the welfare of individuals and groups in society, while the latter is limited to their productive attributes and activities). The manpower planner therefore must limit his field so that it is manageable, but must be familiar with and able to relate to, contribute to, and use policies, programs, and resources outside but closely related to his field of concern. Clearly, if there is not economic activity, there are no jobs; but an array of social services and amenities is necessary to make employability possible. The manpower planner must know the economic system which creates the jobs; the employers who control them; the unions who represent the employees; the roles of the families, churches, schools, and other institutions which contribute to work values and job skills; and the institutions of the labor market which match or fail to match supply and demand.

Of course, the federally funded manpower programs for the disadvantaged are only a minor part of the monies spent upon manpower matters. The target groups of the programs are only a small minority of the actual and potential labor force. Problems range across the entire spectrum of skills and occupations on both the demand and supply sides of the labor market. A planning process similarly dedicated to improving labor market functioning would concern itself with relationships across industries and occupations, population groups, generations, and institutions. In that exercise, federal manpower program budgets would be viewed as only one important source of funding. The response would be a search for ways to fit federal programs and funds into the pursuit of labor market objectives without violating federal objectives.

In general, this book emphasizes how to do manpower planning at the level of labor markets, which are of lesser scope than state jurisdictions (though often overlapping state boundaries) but broader than the scope of cities. Also in general, the labor markets addressed are those over which a worker can range in search of a job or an employer in search of an employee, without either having to change his residence or location. It is at this level that the challenge of manpower planning lies. This is where the problems are and where the jobs must be. However, this book addresses only one level of labor market problems: efforts to improve the employability, the employment opportunities, and the incomes of those workers experiencing difficulties in competing successfully for available jobs. This by no means covers the range of labor market planning needs, but it is task enough for one volume.

Principles and Techniques of Planning

With this broad orientation, the job of the planner is to plan. And planning is an art in itself, with certain well-developed practices and techniques which are applicable to all planning, public and private, for education, health, or any set of objectives, but with adaptations to particular planning environments. Certain terms — goals, objectives, systems analysis, management by objectives, critical path method, cost/effectiveness and cost/benefit analyses, for instance — are familiar to the planner's trade wherever it is practiced. And there is a particular jargon for the particular field in which planning takes place. A goal is an end result sought, objectives are the intermediate midpoints to be achieved on the way to the goal. Strategic planning is the master plan to achieve the goal, and tactical planning devises the day-to-day program for achieving objectives. Clearly identifying goals and establishing objectives are the most critical and yet oft-neglected steps in the planning process. Both are ends, not means to an end; yet programs often get lost in pursuit of means while forgetting or never identifying ends.

Planning has been a much debated activity, function, and process in American society. For some it is regarded as an attempt by the self-appointed elite to structure a future society contrary to the evolutionary process of democracy. While for others it is a simple exercise designed to accomplish two limited purposes, first to understand and evaluate what is now being done, and then to offer to decision makers — usually elected officials or their administrators — some alternative choices for predicting and improving effectiveness and efficiency in ongoing program efforts.

This book clearly sees manpower planning in the latter role. Planning is a simple concept involving some generally agreed-upon steps and procedures, or tools and techniques. Planning can be profitably applied to almost every aspect of human endeavor and to all facets of human resource policy, such as health care, education, employment, economic development, and manpower development and utilization. Planning has gained its greatest acceptance in the American business firm, where most of the pioneering work in planning and in forecasting has been done. Planning has been and is now being applied more rigorously and possibly more effectively in physical planning for roads, airports, water and sewer systems, bridges, schools, and other facilities. Planning programs do not by themselves guarantee success. Planning is no panacea; great mistakes occur with or without planning because human vision is limited, unforeseen conditions arise, and unforeseen results emerge. But planning is the best hope for gaining greater efficiency in most forms of human activity.

It is commonplace to call America a future-oriented society, and fascinating to note that there is a new industry called "futurism." The accelerating pace of human events, the demands of modern technology, the rapidity of its change, and the ability to plan and forecast — all contribute to the rising interest in the future. Whether it is futurism that gives rise to the interest in planning or the ability to plan that gives rise to futurism is an interesting question that will not be resolved here.

Planning is gaining wider acceptance and support and is increasingly thought of as an essential aspect of rational human behavior. Increasingly, Congress writes into new laws requirements for plans and planning, although resources required for planning are not adequately provided and the guidelines for minimum requirements to assure reasonably good planning are seldom a part of the mandate. Planning must be evaluated in terms of its present and expected results and can only be justified when it contributes in a meaningful way to preventing or solving problems. There is a rapidly growing body of literature on what planning is, why it is done, and how to do it. A review of the literature on planning reveals a growing consensus that planning involves some generally accepted steps, procedures, tools, and techniques that can be adapted to a wide variety of problems. To be sure, there are some extremely complex planning models that have been developed for planning in the business firm, models that involve highly mathematical and complex systems analysis, using sophisticated computers and the highest levels of human skills from a variety of academic disciplines. There are no such models currently in wide use for social problems.

Since this book is viewed as an introduction to a particular kind of manpower planning — for the unemployed and underutilized in local labor markets — its approach to the planning process consists of relatively simple, uncomplicated models which seem to have broad application to a wide variety of problems. In the simplest terms, a planning model outlines a number of systematic and sequential steps that can be described, without making them specific to any area of planning interest. While the number and ordering of these steps are recorded differently in various writings, the content and sequence are usually roughly the same: A set of problems disturbing the social welfare is identified and given priority over other such problems. Goals and priorities among goals concerning the nature of the society desired are chosen, all reasonable alternatives for achievement of the priority goals are explored, specific objectives are established, and a program is devised to accomplish the objectives. A monitoring and evaluation system is established to determine how well the program is working to achieve the objectives. Results of the evaluation are fed back to modify and improve the effectiveness of the program.

Since some problems are more serious than others, and there is seldom the resources to attack them all simultaneously, priorities are necessary in pursuit of solutions. In general, the choice should be to pursue first those problems most likely to increase in seriousness if left alone. A goal is a long-term, broadly encompassing target, and objectives are immediately actionable milestones on the way to the goal. Useful objectives must be desirable, attainable, and measurable. No reasonable person or corporate body would pursue an undesirable objective; it is a waste of energy to pursue a solution which has little likelihood of success. Unless objectives are measurable in some fashion, there is no way to tell whether a particular course of action is bringing the objective closer or casting it away.

A necessary step in any planning program is to identify and define, in as much depth and detail as possible, the alternative courses of action which could be adopted to achieve the objectives. There is almost always "more than one way to skin a cat." The search will be for the most cost/effective solution; i.e., the solution most likely to be successful at the least cost in resources. Alternatives may involve:

(1) Choice among target groups

(2) Resource constraints

    (a) Funds

    (b) Staff

    (c) Facilities

    (d) Time

(3) Labor market realities

(4) Technically possible solutions

(5) Political realities

(6) The possible mix of services

Some selection must be made from among the alternatives, based upon criteria which designate one or some combination of the alternatives as preferable to the other alternatives. Having thus arrived at a plan of action, the planner must now put the plan into action through a program of implementation involving:

(1) An effective delivery system

(2) Resolution of political issues

(3) Human relations skills

(4) Clout to bring compliance with plans

Planning is a cyclical and continuous process, with the results of one cycle influencing what is included in subsequent rounds of planning. It is the monitoring, evaluation, and feedback function that gives a sustained life to planning and makes planning a continuing tool for meaningful policy and program management. Evaluation results are then used to reject unworkable programs or to modify others to improve their effectiveness.

Though these are almost universal steps in a planning process, their application to a particular planning endeavor will require specialized data and analysis. For instance, as later chapters will demonstrate, application to manpower planning requires among other things completion of eight data tasks:

(1) Analysis by detailed characteristics on the numbers, ages, and precise location of eligible persons needing manpower services

(2) Development of useful and accurate data on accessible job openings

(3) Development of useful and accurate information on the education and skills development process, including formal training in public and private schools and on-the-job training by public and private employers

(4) An inventory of all possible manpower services and development of the conceptual power and decision-making ability to design a mix of services to meet the needs of any target individual or group

(5) A careful identification and analysis of local delivery systems; i.e., the institutional capability and commitment to administer and manage programs and services

(6) Development of the skill, knowledge, and expertise to manage a manpower planning council which represents a wide diversity of interests in the manpower corral

(7) Identification of federal, state, and local resources and the formulation of both short- and long-run plans

(8) Development and administration of a system of program monitoring and evaluation, complete with feedback into a subsequent planning process

Now that these planning steps and tasks have been set forth in abbreviated form, it is essential to underscore one of the most important lessons to be learned about planning: the understanding of the environment within which planning takes place. It is here that planning becomes more complicated and sometimes confusing. At this point it is necessary to return again to such questions as: What is manpower planning? Or health planning? Or education planning? What is included and what is excluded in the environment of manpower planning? In the modern world, everything is related to everything else, and it is hard to tell where problems, programs, and policies begin and end. An essential precedent to planning is the drawing of boundaries or parameters around the field of endeavor and spelling out the essential characteristics of the environment or the landscape in which planning is to take place.

Thus the primary task of this book is not to describe manpower problems, or to overcome the confusion about the objectives of one or more of the manpower programs designed over the last few years to aid the disadvantaged. Rather the task which this book seeks to accomplish is to define the environment within which meaningful manpower planning can occur and to describe and understand the massive amount of work that must be done in any labor market area in order to provide the analytical and informational base upon which programs and policies can be planned.

Dichotomy in Manpower Planning

Manpower planning to meet the needs of disadvantaged workers, indeed manpower planning of any sort, is a relatively recent concern. Manpower planning in the corporation designed to have the "right man in the right place at the right time" has a long history but has only been applied on a broad scale since the 1950s. Public manpower planning designed to improve the accomplishment of the federal programs for the disadvantaged has yet to see its first decade of life. For all practical purposes it began with the initiation of the CAMPS program in March 1967. Like every other program, there were antecedents which prompted CAMPS, but the main impetus was the realization that a great many programs and policies had been initiated without the benefit of any planning. Thus planning was tacked on to a set of programs that were already functioning in a highly volatile setting. The initial goals set for planning were modest, and judging from federal actions and support, the expectation of results from planning was also modest. Looking at the results, as the saying goes, there was much to be modest about. However, like other new program efforts, planning soon started to take on a life of its own which has led to an expansionary and evolutionary development of the planning process. But key philosophical questions remain unanswered: *What is manpower planning?*

From the outset there were conflicting views of what manpower planning was or should be. The narrow view saw manpower planning as an effort to accept federal resources and develop a program to meet federal guidelines, and to make the programs work in some local environment. The broader view required that someone develop some understanding of how federal programs and resources had an impact upon a total labor market system, already operating in each community, to develop and utilize human talent. The narrow view dominated planning initially and is still the dominant mode. Increasingly, however, the manpower planning process has broadened in a number of states and communities, seeking to understand and adapt to the total environment within which manpower programs must survive and work. This latter approach is gradually emerging both in local practice and in federal guidelines.

The initial goal of CAMPS was to get operators of programs to acknowledge fully the size, scope of services, and clientele of each program and to foster the sharing of that knowledge among all or most program operators in the area covered by the plan. Equally important was the use of the planning document as a formal statement of willingness to abide by federal guidelines. From the outset, local planners viewed the planning process as a vehicle for increased federal fundings by showing greater needs or ability to implement acceptable program services. Manpower planning immediately became embroiled in all the discussions about the role of the manpower programs and their relationship to income maintenance, economic development, education, and other social policies. The application of planning thus took on widely different perspectives until federal guidelines were developed to channel planning efforts in a common direction.

State and local manpower planning remained a concept rather than a reality until federal funds were provided, beginning in June 1969, to provide staff and related resources to support a planning program in each state. Resources were made available to cities a year later, while counties came into the manpower planning picture primarily in 1973. The decisions to provide staff suddenly resulted in a small army of manpower planners in every state and in all large cities and counties. Unfortunately there were no professional manpower planners available, and hence most of the people recruited to positions as manpower planners had little or no previous experience in anything approximating a closely related field of endeavor. Because there usually was greater familiarity with administration than with planning, and more familiarity with the art of government than with economics, the tendency has been to continue to emphasize planning for administration of current programs.

The cynical have described manpower planning as spreading next year's budget over last year's programs. But with increasing experience and growing self-confidence, state, city, and county manpower planners develop ambitions to be agents of change in their labor market environments, not just responders to the directives of others and perpetuators of past practice. Each fiscal year brings a new and better set of guidelines than were available for the year before. Given a little experience and the prospects of decategorization of programs and the decentralization of administration, local planning bodies began to broaden the scope of their work, and federal guidelines began to incorporate the best of local practice. Without that ambition, effective labor market-oriented manpower planning would be a forlorn hope.

But one cannot trust that these favorable trends will continue. Planning is always a tenuous function. There is always pressure to spend money and to deliver services. The leisure and energy to look beyond day-to-day activities and the putting out of current fires in order to plan for a more attractive future often seem a luxury. Decentralization and decategorization make possible and even imply planning but do not require it. National and regional offices of federal agencies often find the concept of decentralized planning more attractive than the reality. Planning cannot continue without discretion. It implies options and varying choices among alternatives — both in objectives and paths to objectives. However, there is no good way to judge the worth of a plan except to wait and see if it works. Under categorical problems, federal monitors could tell whether prescribed procedures were being followed. They can even observe whether a plan has within it the prescribed elements. But is it a workable plan and does it fit the situation? Will it work? There may be differing judgments, but only time will tell.

Therefore the tendency will be to concentrate on procedures, on the filling of the appropriate blanks with the proper numbers, to limit discretion to ease the monitoring task. Once a plan is in place and operations under way, there is always resistance to a modified or new plan which wants to do new things in new ways. The planner may also find it difficult to sustain his commitment to planning. Most practitioners in the manpower field entered that effort with a commitment to improve the welfare of individuals. They like people and like to deal directly with them face to face. But planning is mechanistic and a paper process. It is almost by definition removed from direct contact with the target groups. It is elitist and antidemocratic in a sense. It assumes a superior knowledge and logic, which also strikes against the personal orientation of the manpower field. The manpower planner may thus experience a revulsion to planning and seek a more direct and operational involvement. Thus given these and other pressures, the life of a planning system is always tenuous. It may go on carrying the name, but the charge of "spreading next year's budget over last year's programs" was always a threat of reality.

Who Is a Manpower Planner?

Manpower planning is an emergent profession without accepted theory and techniques, entry requirements, a professional ethic, or professional society. Planning as a profession is no more than two generations old, with most of its growth occurring in the past quarter-century.

Is the manpower planner a planner applying the tools of the trade to manpower problems? A specialist in labor economics or industrial relations applying analytical abilities to solutions of labor market or work force problems? A public administrator with manpower programs as the assignment? A behavioral scientist concerned about the welfare of culturally deprived peoples? Does it make any practical difference?

The answers to these questions not only affect the way the manpower planner approaches the assignment and the tools used in search of solutions, they are precedent to answering such crucial questions as:

(1) Who is the client of the manpower planner? Is it the government body which employs him? The political leadership of the jurisdiction? Labor market institutions? The body of persons directly suffering from labor market dysfunction?

(2) Who can speak for the client? The planner? The elected official? The program administrator? The community-based organizations?

(3) What are the responsibilities of the manpower planner to the client? Professionally? Ethically?

(4) Do decisions really precede action?

(5) Can the planner really understand large-scale systems and the extent that they can be modified at will?

(6) Does the political system preempt planning?

(7) How does the planner handle equity vs efficiency questions?

(8) Is a synoptic perspective really possible?

Planning's antecedents in this country are primarily in the physical and esthetic realms, with origins which lie somewhere between the visual esthetics of the turn-of-the-century "city beautiful" crusaders and their brothers under the skin, the American utopians. From an initial push to intersperse the monotonous city grid with civic equivalents of English and Italian gardens, through the ill-fated public housing schemes of the 1950s and 1960s, the planning mainstream has been preoccupied with the visual and physical. Although late in coming to the forefront, change has begun to take place. Long before the first superblocks gave way to the dynamiter's hand in St. Louis, public policy caught up with reality, and the professional has taken a half-turn toward a people orientation. The Model Cities program was one beginning manifestation of this change. In a recent survey article, Friedmann and Hudson (1974, p. 2, emphasis added) characterized planning as:

> ...an activity centrally concerned with the *linkage between knowledge and organized action*. As a professional activity and as a social process, planning is therefore located precisely at the interface between knowledge and action.

In the context of manpower planning, it is the *planning* component which sits between the knowledge of the problems that the theories of economics address and the organization of action that is the province of administrative science. Consequently, the parent central intellectual traditions appropriate to manpower planning are the general theories of planning which deal essentially with the relationship between knowledge and action. The perspective taken in this book is that the manpower planner is a planner and that the theories, methods, and practice of planning offer more relevance to the emerging profession of manpower planning than do those of either economics or administrative science, though the manpower planner must be fully conversant with both. The three major functional components that are central to the professional practice of manpower planning are as follows:

(1) Concerns, techniques, and interpretations involving the evidence of labor market dysfunction

(2) The channels of syntheses employed to integrate evidence and develop appropriate prescriptions

(3) The techniques for implementing an action prescription for dealing with dysfunctions

The theories of economics, and more specifically labor economics and more generally demographics, offer entry points for dealing with the first component, while educational theory, psychology, sociology, political science, and administrative science address the third component. It is the second component of practice, however, which is the defining element determining the central theoretical tradition of most relevance to manpower planning.

The manpower planner must understand the economy, which responds to the needs of consumers and the demand for human inputs into production, and the labor markets, which attempt to match the two forces. And the manpower planner must also be conversant with and sympathetic to the problems of the administrator, who must turn plans into the delivery of services. While the need for planning in the implementation of manpower policies can be identified by the economists and administrators who make national and local manpower policy, they cannot extend a satisfactory theory of planning to the new manpower planners. Increasingly, the manpower planner will be required to look to the planning profession for the methods and theories needed to interface knowledge and action.

Within the body of general planning theory, this book fits into that school of planning thought generally known as the rationalist school. Advanced decision making is a central theme of rationalistic planning. Another central theme is optimization and its cousin, "satisficing." Common assumptions of rationalist planning paradigms are that uncertainty can be handled, community welfare can be reasonably quantified, the tradeoffs among multiple objectives can be systematically dealt with, and finally, decisions generally precede action, and therefore it is possible to coordinate action. The planning process we offer for manpower planning is based on these assumptions. Nevertheless, the manpower planner must become aware of other theories for dealing with the interface between knowledge and action and their possible application in the context of manpower planning.

Summary

Manpower planning is the task of looking ahead to perceive impending labor market problems and opportunities and of designing programs to prevent or ameliorate these problems. It is needed in order to "invent the future"; i.e., to influence future developments along the most desirable lines possible. It can also be used simply to measure progress.

Planners must have authority for their plans to result in action. Yet they must avoid overinvolvement in administration. Plans must encompass the whole of a problem, and most social problems are complex. Included among the manpower planner's skills must be an intimate knowledge of the labor market and manpower problems and a familiarity with the interrelationships among the total labor market decision-making system: households, intermediaries, and employers. The planner must understand the intercourse of the political system in which he operates. He must understand the planning process and have the technical and political skills of implementation.

Currently there is little manpower planning occurring at the national level and none at the regional level. There is a growing amount in the public sector, with its beginnings primarily at the state and local levels. The short-term focus of the political system is the major obstacle at the federal level. Lack of ability, authority, and resources impedes the state and local levels. The prevailing political system lacks incentives for planning. There are few decisions to make, few rewards for doing a good job, and almost no accountability. Officialdom survives more from fancy political footwork than from demonstration of achievement. The private sector has a more ready measure in its profit and loss equation and finds it harder to dodge responsibility.

There has been neither planning skills nor planning format, but this is changing rapidly. The Labor Department is responsible for whatever planning exists. Without its introduction of CAMPS, there would have been no planning. Yet the system specified an approach to planning which offered no incentives to go beyond its minimum requirements. Planning will not survive unless it leads to policy action, giving further incentive to plan; yet policymakers are often distrustful of the planners. State and local agencies generally oppose planning at first because it upsets comfortable relationships. Politicians can rarely agree on objectives, and political jurisdictions do not coincide with economic boundaries.

Despite all of those obstacles, manpower planning efforts are accelerating. The Labor Department made major progress administratively prior to CETA in giving a few jurisdictions the discretion to reallocate funding in response to state and local plans. With new legislation, at least the appearance of planning becomes a requirement, but its reality and its quality remain in doubt. Chapter 2 reviews in more detail the experiences to date before subsequent chapters develop a labor market manpower planning system.

References

Bakke, E. Wight. *The Mission of Manpower Policy.* Washington, D.C.: The W. E. Upjohn Institute for Employment Research. 1969.

Doeringer, Peter B.; and Piore, Michael J. *Internal Labor Markets and Manpower Analysis.* Lexington, Massachusetts: Heath. 1971.

Friedmann, John; and Hudson, Barclay. "Knowledge and Action: A Guide to Planning Theory." *Journal of the American Institute of Planners* (January 1974), vol. 40, no. 1.

Harbison, Frederic. *Human Resources as the Wealth of Nations.* New York: Oxford University Press. 1973.

Patten, Thomas H. *Manpower Planning and the Development of Human Resources.* New York: Wiley Interscience Publishers. 1971.

U.S. Department of Labor, Manpower Administrator. *Manpower Report to the President.* Washington, D.C.: U.S. Government Printing Office. 1972.

2
Emergence of Manpower Planning

History is often intellectually intriguing (and perhaps emotionally satisfying, if one is sufficiently selective in the choice of facts and interpretation of events), but it is useful primarily to broaden understanding of the present and to forecast the future. In 1973 CETA mandated that major decisions relevant to providing manpower services to those most in need of them be made at state and local levels. The Act culminated a consistent drive which surfaced earlier but has been the major emphasis of manpower policy since the beginning of the Nixon Administration. But there is little in the wording of the Act to identify the forces from which it emerged, any longer term agenda of which it is a part, or the direction in which manpower policy is trending.

Political administrations come and go. A policy which seems to represent the interests of the particular personnel in charge at a particular point in time does not merit the same attention and acquiescence as one which is the consequence of experience and the product of a longer term consensus. It is taking nothing away from the present Administration or from those in Congress or in lobbying activities, who shaped and brought into being a new law, to recognize that the philosophy it represents arose from long-term experience and represents a consensus often hidden beneath political arguments over specific details. Administering the Act, functioning within it, and using it as a step to desired long-term goals can be better accomplished by recognizing whence it came and keeping an eye on where it will imperfectly direct us.

The essence of the new legislation is decentralization and decategorization. Its basic impetus is the longer term goal of manpower policy and programs which have dominated a decade of effort: to enhance the employability and improve the economic security and incomes of a variety of people facing various disadvantages in the competition for jobs. The case for manpower planning at the local labor market level is amplified by considering the events and contingencies which have created the demand for it.

Nature of Manpower Programs

By 1966, the Manpower Development and Training Act (MDTA), the Economic Opportunity Act, and the Civil Rights Act of 1964 had introduced an institutional and on-the-job skills training program for unemployed persons of all ages, a residential vocational skills program for youth (Job Corps), separate work experience programs for in-school and out-of-school youth and for the adult poor, a community action program, and the beginnings of efforts to enforce equal opportunity in employment. The initiative was necessarily national. No lesser jurisdiction had the know-how or resources, and few had the interest to serve unfamiliar and often unpopular margins of the population. MDTA did require state employment services and state boards of vocational education to design, for federal approval, training projects in occupations with "reasonable expectation of employment" in the local labor market, and the community action program did contemplate putting together an antipoverty program adapted to local need. In general, however, services were nationally prescribed.

Programs did not emerge from a careful exploration of problems; conduct of research and experiment with solutions were rarely based on experience. There was imperfect knowledge, felt need, a gut feeling of what would work, political enthusiasm, and promise of total solution. With various legislators putting their own brand on special gimmicks to serve essentially the same clientele, there were soon competing federal agencies and a proliferation of programs and service agencies at the local level. Even though more programs were to be added in 1966, 1967, and 1971, the services available among the numerous programs represent a smaller number than the programs themselves: classroom skills training, limited basic education, subsidized public and private employment, minimal work experience as an excuse for transfer payments, various supportive services, placement, and enforcement of anti-discrimination measures.

Congress in 1966 hearings first began lamenting the inter-agency competition at the national level and the proliferation of programs at the local level. The Labor Department responded to that criticism in two ways: (1) by intensifying the efforts it was already making to wrest from the Department of Health, Education and Welfare (HEW) and the Office of Economic Opportunity (OEO) their hold on pieces of the manpower action, and (2) by launching tripartite federal monitoring efforts within the largest cities and a few rural areas under the President's Committee on Manpower. Three-man teams representing the Labor Department, HEW, and OEO descended on local areas to ferret out misman-agement and bring about coordination among programs.

The President's Committee on Manpower effort was short-lived because it served the purpose of rising concern for the increas-ingly restless central city minority disadvantaged. The first act of the manpower drama had been rurally oriented — the Area Rede-velopment Administration. Then with early MDTA, the supposed target was the technologically displaced in industrial communities. The Economic Opportunity Act first identified the poor and minorities as prime targets for manpower services. Enthusiasm for the "war on poverty" soon had the Labor Department declaring also that MDTA would give 65 percent of its emphasis to the disad-vantaged, even though no definition of the term existed until 1968. Involved in the changing targets was a shift of emphasis in the civil rights movement from equal access to public facilities to jobs and income, competition to the old-line Cabinet departments from the new OEO, and increasing signs of restlessness in central city ghettoes.

The Concentrated Employment Program (CEP), launched in 1967, had as its primary instigation the commitment to concentrate available funds in the central city census tracts of the most serious poverty and unrest. The "subemployment index" was developed at the same time to measure the incidence of underemployment, low wages, and low labor force participation, as well as unemploy-ment. But a byproduct of CEP, if not a major intent, was putting the variety of programs under one roof. If it wasn't possible to adapt a mix of services to individual need, at least it might be possible to have a limited smorgasbord of programs from which to choose those most nearly meeting individual needs. The new program was inaugurated by pulling the three-man federal teams from the President's Committee on Manpower coordination assignment and using them to staff the CEP concept and get it under way.

An almost simultaneous development with CEP was CAMPS, which grew from Labor Department efforts to introduce more consistent planning into the MDTA program. Initially local, state, regional, and national manpower advisory committees were part of the MDTA structure; but the local and state committees primarily defended local interest against expansion of manpower supplies, and the regional and national committees addressed only broad policy issues. There was no planning input from any level. As time passed, controversy arose over the appropriate state vs federal role in the program. Originally, each training project required federal approval, even though MDTA funds were allocated among the states according to an established formula. As a result of complaints about delays and difficulties of continuing institutional programs, Congress amended the Act, giving the states the right to undertake small projects within their allocation without federal approval. To minimize the impact of the new amendments on the existing system, the Labor Department introduced a state planning concept for these small projects. The Labor Department would provide guidelines, and each state plan would require federal approval; but once the plan was approved, the state could initiate the individual small projects throughout the year without further federal involvement.

The state planning proposal for these small contracts so appealed to the manpower administrator that he directed its use for the total MDTA program. Continuing the emphasis, the Manpower Administration won approval from HEW, OEO, and the Departments of Housing and Urban Development (HUD) and of Commerce for a CAMPS unit to consist of area, state, and regional coordinating committees. The CAMPS agreement was reached in March 1967, and guidelines were developed and sent to the states soon thereafter. The states were in turn to require local CAMPS committees to formulate joint programs to be consolidated into state plans in time for regional approval. Final approval of the state and regional plans, as well as individual projects, would remain the prerogative of the individual federal agencies.

Initial state and local reaction to the CAMPS concept was highly favorable, but disillusionment soon set in. The planning process was impaired by the fact that no one knew how much and when Congress would appropriate for manpower programs. Appropriations were rarely forthcoming until at least three months of the fiscal year had gone by, and year by year the norm came to be for most and finally all of a fiscal year to pass before some programs were funded for that year. The continuing resolution of Congress was becoming a substitute for appropriations. With each program constrained by its own budget and procedures, the area and state plans were better described as individual agency plans stapled together than as comprehensive planning documents. Complaints of the costs and administrative burdens of the CAMPS operation grew until it was necessary to request federal funds for staff support.

However, it was not these understandable and seemingly inevitable problems that disturbed local participants, but what they viewed as bad faith on the part of the federal sponsors and a lack of discretion in giving meaning to their planning efforts. The state and local committees complained that the Labor Department itself violated the spirit of CAMPS by superimposing major programs administratively without consulting the state and local units. The basic conflict between decentralized planning and national innovation was becoming clear.

Other federal agencies were giving no more than lip service support. The Departments of Agriculture and Defense and the Civil Service Commission were added as signatories but had little meaningful involvement. The Labor Department secured an Executive Order stating its primacy and requiring interagency commitments, but it was considerably weakened in the interagency clearance process. In years of budgetary frugality and with the siphoning off of the available funds to CEP, the National Alliance of Businessmen's Job Opportunities in the Business Sector (NAB-JOBS) program, and other federally dominated uses, the CAMPS committees felt they were given no meaningful decisions to make.

The Labor Department's CAMPS guidelines were so specific in program mix and enrollee characteristics that little discretion remained. A particular complaint in 1968, for instance, stemmed from federal specification of the mix between institutional and on-the-job training in each state, unrelated to the differing balances among such factors as the nature and size of industry and migration patterns. The regional offices appeared not to know what to do with the CAMPS plans when they arrived. The end product (maintained the state and local participants) was interagency communicating, not planning.

Despite its weaknesses (natural growing pains for an innovation), CAMPS met a need for communication and sparked a desire in some areas for something more nearly approaching (at first) state autonomy. State employment services had been the initial prime movers in the CAMPS activity and usually served as the secretariat, both in the state level CAMPS and the area CAMPS, which generally encompassed roughly an SMSA. Soon, however, a few governors took interest and appointed their own manpower committees or their own choice as CAMPS chairman with the intent to coordinate and even to bring into subjection the usually autonomous state manpower agencies — a move which was officially endorsed by the Labor Department in 1968. Under pressure from their states, a number of congressmen pressed for an enlarged state role and expansion of the areas of discretion and appeared to view CAMPS as a potential instrument for achieving it.

The concept of local administration was an attractive one. A few states and cities moved to establish effective planning and administering mechanisms, and federal legislation contemplated a system that would give clout to state plans — the power to affect the flow of funds. In 1969, the Labor Department offered grants to governors and in 1970 to mayors of 130 cities to staff the CAMPS committees. By 1973 every state, 126 cities, four counties, one council of governments, and nineteen Indian tribes had grants to support manpower planning staffs. The Rubicon had been crossed. There were individuals whose allegiances were to their chief elected executive in the political jurisdiction, who owed no fealty to the traditional agencies, and who had "manpower planner" as their title and assignment. It was only natural for them to want to do what their job description in essence said.

What was happening was clear in retrospect and recognizable by 1968. Though the terms were yet to be coined, decentralization and decategorization were in the wind. Nationally uniform budget allocations among programs and services did not necessarily meet the needs of individual labor markets and communities. There were those at the state and local levels who thought themselves as well qualified to make manpower decisions as the "feds." Categorical programs required the applicant to meet the requirements and accept the services prescribed by the program; it was not possible to adapt the mix of services to individual need.

Manpower policy was not unique. Limitations of national decision making were becoming apparent in many policy areas. In the last year of the Johnson Administration there were already widespread discussions of a "new federalism" (given, as the Preacher says, that "there is nothing new under the sun," copyright should go to whoever popularizes a slogan rather than to who coined it). Internally within the Labor Department there was fatigue and disillusionment with a system that made the department a signator of literally thousands of contracts and agreements which it could not monitor. The Labor Department was also in the throes of a painful reorganization.

The secretary and his assistant secretary for manpower were attempting to corral the traditionally autonomous bureaus within the department which had independent power bases in the states and in Congress. Their interest was to eliminate the bureaus and centralize authority within the new Manpower Administration. With key congressional appropriations subcommittee chairmen supporting the bureau chiefs, the governors seemed natural allies for the Secretary of Labor. Mayors had already been made painfully aware that the antipoverty program had bypassed them to funnel money into the central cities through ad hoc community action agencies, which often became the focal point of anti-Establishment political activity. Amendment to the Economic Opportunity Act had followed to give mayors power to take over the community action agencies if the latter proved too obnoxious. Now a few governors and their staffs recognized that they too had been bypassed. Not only had funds flowed directly to the cities which, according to most state constitutions, were creatures of the state governments, but even state agencies received funding and direction from federal agencies without so much as a by your leave to the governors.

A position paper commissioned by a subcommittee of the National Governors' Conference in 1968, outlining an appropriate role for governors in manpower policy, had limited influence on the governors but considerable influence on subsequent events. The paper advocated retention of the policy-making, goal setting, monitoring, and evaluating authority in federal hands, but delegated planning, program design, and administration to governors. It assumed what was becoming conventional wisdom: that American public administration had gone too far in its century-old drive to take the administration of public services out of elective politics. Now the bureaucracies were becoming too protected and unresponsive to public pressures. Perhaps putting responsibility for quality of service back on the elected official would increase accountability. Decentralization therefore would be to the governor, who would be encouraged to centralize accountability within state government to his office.

The only exceptions to statewide manpower decision making would be the largest cities, perhaps those with a million inhabitants or more, which had their own large congressional delegations. Those cities were unlikely to approach Washington through the statehouse in any case. All program categories would be abolished and replaced by a laundry list of available manpower services. The concept was that the Secretary of Labor would set national manpower goals; state planning councils (whose chairman was the governor, or an appointee of the governor, and were composed of manpower service delivery agency heads, of representatives of employers and unions, and of target groups) would establish state objectives not inconsistent with the national ones and would prepare three-year state manpower plans, updated annually. The Secretary of Labor would have plan approval and rejection authority and would monitor state programs, evaluate the results, and reward with additional funds those especially successful in meeting their objectives.

Most governors evidenced no interest in the plan, though the governor who was chairman of the National Governors' Conference subcommittee and his chief of staff returned to their home state where they inaugurated the nation's first statewide manpower planning council. Meanwhile, the paper's author was asked to serve on one of many post-election, preinauguration task forces to recommend policies to the incoming Nixon Administration. When the chairman of that particular task force later became the first Secretary of Labor of the new Administration, decentralization and decategorization became the heart of the official Nixon Administration manpower policy.

The first legislative proposal to implement the concept was authored and introduced by Congressman William Stieger

(Republican, Wisconsin) and modeled closely after the National Governors' Conference paper. It was followed by a proposal from Congressman James O'Hara (Democrat, Michigan), also prepared by a prominent academic manpower specialist of previous staff congressional and Labor Department service, to give the Secretary of Labor authority to delegate manpower decision making to any public or private organization he chose in any labor market. An Administration bill followed, emphasizing SMSAs as the appropriate decision point, providing incentive to mayors to band together in a common planning body, and leaving to the governor the "balance of state." The shift from state to city as the locus of planning probably reflected primarily the political fact that the staff of the League of Cities–Conference of Mayors had caught the scent of manpower funds while the governors were still disinterested. However, the desirability of labor market-wide manpower planning was undoubtedly in the minds of the Labor Department authors.

The next four years were to see a series of manpower reform bills all representing a growing consensus but failing to be passed because of details or peripheral issues. All gave lip service to the concept of decategorization and then preserved in one form or another those categorized programs which enjoyed the personal protection of key congressional figures or were represented by well-organized interest groups, and even added a few for the latter. Though each legislative proposal claimed to consolidate all manpower programs, they addressed themselves only to MDTA and the Economic Opportunity Act. The Wagner-Peyser Act of 1933, the manpower programs under Titles III and IV of the Social Security Act of 1935, and perhaps even the Vocational Rehabilitation Act should logically have been merged with an omnibus manpower bill. However, these were within the jurisdiction of other congressional committees, notably the powerful House Ways and Means Committee, and no success could be expected in attacking these bastions. All the proposals contained a laundry list of nearly every familiar manpower service to be provided at the "prime sponsor's" discretion.

The prime sponsor concept had been written into the Economic Opportunity Act as early as 1967, contemplating the community action agencies as the major manpower decision makers at local levels. In fact, that amendment had authorized decategorizing most Economic Opportunity Act manpower programs into community work training programs, but the Labor Department and administrators of the Act had never been able to agree upon guidelines to implement it. The concept of a state or local unit of general government as prime sponsor, with discretion both to plan and to administer manpower programs, was a universal in the manpower reform proposals of 1969 to 1973, but there were differences over the size of the units and the relative state-local role.

As noted, the first Administration bill in 1969 was written in the Labor Department and used the SMSA as the standard planning unit, recognizing the need for a labor market-wide scope in manpower planning. From there the trend was to respond to lobbying efforts by the League of Cities–Conference of Mayors by granting prime sponsorship to smaller and smaller governmental units and to leave the still largely disinterested states only the rural areas and small towns — fifty thousand population became a talked-about minimum figure. The bill, which originated in the Senate and passed both houses and was vetoed by the President in 1971 because it contained a public service employment title and had not decategorized sufficiently, used 75,000 as its major number.

In the metamorphosis in the first Nixon term, which saw the White House staff and Office of Management and Budget gradually take over most policy making from the Cabinet departments, the determination of manpower policy too left the hands of the Labor Department practitioners and tended to more ideological inputs. The decentralization notion was in accord with the extreme "new federalism" which endorsed unconditional "revenue sharing," providing reduced funds but giving full discretion to state and local governments with "no strings attached." An Administration manpower position emerged, characterized by its opponents as "put the money on the stump and run." Its 1972 election year version would have had elected officials make plans for the use of funds disbursed by formula, would have required them to publish those plans in the newspapers, and then would have allowed the Secretary of Labor to "comment" on the plans. Congress was unwilling to grant such a complete delegation of what it considered its authority. On the other hand, most Democrats and liberal Republicans were committed to public service employment as a weapon against the unemployment which had resulted from Administration anti-inflation efforts. They insisted on attaching a public service employment title to any manpower reform bill, thus assuring its veto.

With federal action stymied, a number of states and then some cities established their own manpower planning councils, usually as an expansion of the CAMPS concept and secretariat, to exercise as much discretion as possible within legislative requirements. The Labor Department's Regional Manpower Administration offices, established during the latter Johnson years and strengthened under the Nixon decentralization drive, insisted on exercising their full prerogatives, however, and those efforts at local decision making were usually thwarted. Some of the state and city manpower planners gained the ear of the assistant secretary of labor for manpower and finally won agreement to a series of pilot projects called Comprehensive Manpower Programs to go as far as possible in the decentralization-decategorization direction within the constraints of existing law (stretched perhaps somewhat beyond the limits of legitimate interpretation but without serious opposition).

During the two years it took to negotiate the Comprehensive Manpower Programs agreement, however, another election passed and further expanded the commitment to decentralization. Encouraged by an overwhelming mandate, the Administration resolved to introduce decentralization and decategorization by administrative fiat without awaiting congressional action. In essence, if a few pilot projects could be legitimately undertaken, why not blanket the country with them? Congress fumed a bit but was relatively helpless. Besides, the approach taken did not differ appreciably from what Congress had itself resolved to do. The Comprehensive Manpower Programs process retained a strong federal presence. The money was not on the stump.

By the time Watergate had weakened White House adamancy and authority had returned somewhat to the Labor Department (though still under close supervision of the Office of Management and Budget) for negotiation with Congress, the decentralization process had already progressed in substantial degree in all states and more than a hundred cities. Even before that time, in 1971, as a preliminary to the Comprehensive Manpower Programs, CAMPS was restructured to provide for state manpower planning councils under the governor, area manpower planning councils under the largest city in major labor market areas, and ancillary manpower planning boards for planning districts in the balance of state designated by the governor. And CETA of 1973 essentially endorsed, legitimized, and extended what was already in place.

The major addition of 1973 was manpower planning at the county level. The 1970 census demonstrated that two-thirds of the nation's poverty and unemployment was located in suburban and rural counties, not in central cities (one could also add that central cities tend to vote for Democrats and suburbs for Republicans, but that cynicism is not necessary for explanation). Plans were well under way to extend manpower planning grants to all counties of at least a hundred thousand population, as well as to cities of the same size, before the imminence of legislation delayed the development.

Legislation in December 1973 gave a more solid policy base to the prime sponsors and the relative roles and responsibilities of federal, state, and local governments. Though regulations and guidelines are new and changing and the usual number of anomalies must be worked out in practice, congressional intent is relatively clear. Any unit of general local government with a population of a hundred thousand or more has the right of prime sponsorship. In addition, in what he determines to be "exceptional circumstances," the Secretary of Labor has discretion to grant prime sponsorship to smaller governmental units which serve major portions of a labor market or represent rural areas of high unemployment and which have demonstrated capability to carry out their own manpower programs. When two governmental units are eligible for the same area (for instance, a city inside a county), the preference is to go to the smaller unit. All areas within the state not included within local prime sponsorships comprise a "balance-of-state" prime sponsorship under the governor's authority. Contiguous eligible units may combine into consortia, and units not eligible to be prime sponsors have the discretion to join with contiguous local prime sponsors or be served as part of the balance of state. The Act has five titles:

I Comprehensive Manpower Programs
II Public Employment Programs
III Special Federal Responsibilities
IV Job Corps
V National Commission on Manpower Policy

The first two are locally oriented, with the last three totally federal responsibilities. Eighty percent of the total appropriations are to be assigned to Titles I and II, of whose funds, 80 percent are allocated to the state and local prime sponsors by formula. The services provided under Title I have a local bias: outreach, assessment, orientation, counseling, remedial education, skills training, on-the-job training, subsidized private employment, subsidized public employment, supportive services, training allowances, and labor market information. There is no explicit provision, for instance, for relocation allowances, though manpower services are not limited to those enumerated. For Titles I and II, the Secretary of Labor retains 20 percent of the funds, but they end up in state and local hands also. Of that, 5 percent is available for incentives to combine prime sponsor jurisdictions, 5 percent is to go to governors to be used to purchase vocational education from public schools, and 5 percent is to go to the states to support state planning councils and to provide state services to local prime sponsors. Of the remaining 5 percent, priority use must be to keep any prime sponsor from receiving less than 90 percent of the previous year's funding, a "hold harmless" provision. Any remainder is to be allocated among prime sponsors at the Secretary's discretion.

Each state must have a state manpower services council to coordinate CETA activities throughout the state. State and local prime sponsors must have manpower planning councils to advise the chief elected executive of the jurisdiction who bears responsibility. Each planning council must have representatives of the client population, community-based organizations, management, labor, and general public and manpower agencies. In addition, the state manpower services council must have representation from local prime sponsors. Each prime sponsor must submit to the Labor Department regional office for approval an annual "comprehensive manpower plan." Title I monies can be used for any manpower services for the unemployed, underemployed, and disadvantaged. Title II is designated as public service employment, but it explicitly authorizes recipient prime sponsors to use the funds for other manpower services if they prefer to do so.

In addition to Title I prime sponsors, Indian tribes and areas which have experienced unemployment of 6.5 percent or more for three consecutive months are eligible to share in the 80 percent of Title II monies allocated by formula. The Secretary of Labor distributes the remaining 20 percent at this discretion.

Title III meets the political requirement to keep intact funding for certain categorical programs and organizations which have developed potent support and provides special assistance for groups such as Indians and migrant workers not amenable to service by state and local government jurisdictions. It also supports research and experiment, evaluation, staff training, and technical assistance; allows the Secretary of Labor discretion for national programs; and provides for labor market information. The Act delegates manpower funds and responsibilities to the Secretary of Labor but requires consultation and approval by the Secretary of HEW when education and institutional skills training are involved.

Title IV supports and regulates the Job Corps; Title V calls for a new National Commission on Manpower Policy, consisting of Cabinet officers and public members, ostensibly independent of any of the federal manpower agencies and answerable to the President and to Congress. Because Titles III, IV, and V together are assigned only 20 percent of total CETA funds, national programs under CETA are far below previous levels (CETA replaces only MDTA and the Economic Opportunity Act). The Wagner-Peyser Act, the Work Incentive Program, and other manpower aspects of the Social Security Act, the vocational rehabilitation and vocational education programs, and the Health Manpower Act were left out of the decentralized and decategorized manpower process — some because it was felt politically unwise to challenge the jurisdiction of powerful congressional committees and some because they were pressured to or had major additional components not directly related to remedying the employment handicaps of disadvantaged, out-of-school youth and adults. At any rate as Table 2-1 indicates, CETA encompasses no more than two-fifths of the manpower funding and action, $2 billion out of $5 billion. The total manpower budget proposed for fiscal year 1975, considering inflation, represents an approximate 30 percent reduction in total resources from the peak in 1975.

The Act will undoubtedly have many ramifications which will only appear from experience. For purposes of this chapter's review of manpower planning experience, its most pertinent portions are:

(1) Preference for local political jurisdictions, regardless of whether they encompass labor markets, but with some encouragement for them to act conjointly

(2) A limited federal role in supervising Title I and Title II activities

(3) No requirement for, but no opposition to planning in the broader context advocated by this book

(4) Little disturbance of present planning efforts and extension to other jurisdictions of what essentially presently exists in several states and cities

(5) A compass of only 40 percent of the total federal manpower funding for the disadvantaged

Crucial Variables from State and Local Manpower Planning Experience

Given that history, there are lessons to be learned from the limited experience to date. The CAMPS effort suffered initially, not only because it was new and its participants were inexperienced, but because it was a toothless tiger easy to ignore. It was at the outset a useful communications device by which agencies could learn what others were doing. However, it had no power to reallocate funds among agencies and programs, and even when agencies at a state or local level agreed voluntarily to reallocate, they were usually forbidden by legislation or by the Labor Department regional offices to do so. The CAMPS assignment originally was not to plan but to communicate and coordinate in the administration of federally funded and controlled programs. However, staff were hired to work for organizations with "planning" in the title. They began to think of themselves as planners and wanted to do planning. Federal CAMPS issuances required a "plan" involving a listing of program resources and identification of target groups in a "universe of need" (UON). Gradually the more aggressive exploited whatever opportunities were given them, and planning experience began slowly to accumulate. Geographical allocation of program funds and evaluation of results were in no conflict with law or federal directives and tended to receive the most staff attention.

Federal manpower agencies for years had had available to them a route to decategorizing and increasing the planning discretion in manpower programs, which they were unable to exploit because of their own interagency conflicts. As noted earlier, amendments to the Economic Opportunity Act in 1967 authorized

Table 2-1
Federal Outlays for Manpower Programs
(Fiscal years 1961–75; millions)

Program (Agency)	1961	1965	1969	1970	1971	1972	1973	1974 (est.)	Budget Proposal 1975
TOTAL	$235	$798	$2,297	$2,546	$3,173	$4,375	$4,952	$4,808	$4,831
I. Skills training									
Institutional training:	4	237	614	614	800	930	782	728	786
MDTA (Labor)		180	248	260	340	406	358	183	171
Job Corps (Labor)		37	235	144	187	188	188		
Concentrated Employment Program (Labor)			52	59	64	64	52		
Work Incentive Program (Labor)			25	65	86	118	71	49	50
Social services: education, training (HEW)		10	34	50	73	93	58	41	61
Model Cities (HUD)				2	11	15	18	18	7
Indians (BIA)	3	9	18	26	27	31	28	26	28
Community action (OEO)	1	1	2	4	5	5	3		
Offenders (Justice)				3	4	5	5	6	5
Upward mobility (HEW)					(<0.5)	5			
Community development training (HUD)			(<0.5)	1	1	1	1	2	1
Comprehensive Manpower Assistance (Labor)								404	462
On-the-job training:	2	34	209	280	376	437	492	512	594
JOBS (Labor)			42	86	123	127	104	78	
Jobs optional (MDTA-OJT; Labor)		33	65	50	54	68	73		
Work Incentive program (Labor)			1	1	2	4	33	44	45

Concentrated Employment Program (Labor)	2		3	4	4	5	6		
Public Service Careers (Labor)		2	27	48	23	18	17		
New Careers: PSC funds (Labor)			15	21	16	30	27		
New Careers: CEP funds (Labor)			26	31	32	2	2		
Indians (BIA)	2	2	2	2	1	1		1	(<0.5)
Model Cities (HUD)	4	10	10	9	5				
Veterans (VA)	241	245	199	124	117	87	49	2	2
Comprehensive Manpower Assistance (Labor)	302	132							
Vocational rehabilitation:	864	803	725	683	600	494	403	110	66
Vocational rehabilitation (HEW)	770	715	636	599	523	441	363	96	54
Veterans (VA)	94	88	88	84	77	53	40	14	12

II. Work support

In school:	456	357	360	459	347	263	248	100	
NYC: In school (Labor)			73	80	65	58	61	10	
NYC: Summer (Labor)			220	297	204	136	121	87	
Vocational work study (HEW)		6	6	6	4	2	4	3	
Stay-in-school (various)	36	36	35	49	42	78	28		
Summer aides (various)	26	26	26	28	32	39	34		
Comprehensive Manpower Assistance (Labor)	394	289							
Postschool:	638	1,011	1,302	898	271	220	234		39
NYC: Out-of-school (Labor)			118	125	95	98	106		18
Concentrated Employment Program (Labor)			48	59	59	70	56		
Operation Mainstream (Labor)			82	75	69	42	37		21
Work Experience (Title V; HEW)	21	21	21	11	10	1	26		
Foster Grandparents (Action)	27	25				8	8		
Work Incentive program (Labor)	29	29	15	9	6	1	1		

Table 2-1 (continued)

Federal Outlays for Manpower Programs

(Fiscal years 1961–75; millions)

Program (Agency)	1961	1965	1969	1970	1971	1972	1973	1974 (est.)	Budget Proposal 1975
PSC-STEP (Labor)					23	48	15	15	6
Model Cities (HUD)				2	8	13			
Public Employment Program (Labor)						559	1,005	631	
Older Americans (Action)								(< 0.5)	3
Comprehensive Manpower Assistance (Labor)								290	552
III. Labor market services									
Job placement:	129	204	339	372	412	421	543	542	529
Employment service (Labor)	126	200	298	331	370	371	431	428	424
Community action outreach and placement (OEO)		1	22	21	20	21	16		
Food stamp work requirement (Labor)						8	14	17	19
Indian mobility (BIA)	3	3	4	5	5	6	6	6	6
Veterans assistance centers (VA)			1	1	1	3	4	4	4
Project Transition (Defense)			14	14	15	13	15	13	
Work Incentive program (Labor)							59	75	76
Antidiscrimination:			10	19	35	43	57	75	91
Equal Employment Opportunity (EEOC)			9	12	16	21	28	40	53
Federal contract compliance (OFCC)			1	1	3	4	4	5	6
Other (various)				6	16	18	25	30	32

	26	42	96	141	187	320	433	501	584
Employment-related child care:	26	42	96	141	187	320	433	501	584
Work Incentive program (HEW)	15	24	4	15	27	32	41	45	46
Social Services (HEW)			52	71	89	204	267	305	330
Public Assistance (HEW)	11	18	40	53	62	71	110	137	202
Model Cities (HUD)				2	9	12	14	14	5
Other supportive services:							48	58	71
Work Incentive program (HEW)							48	50	51
Migrant workers (Labor)								9	21
IV. Administration, research, and support	8	32	144	143	146	184	209	220	219
MA administration (Labor)	4	12	73	72	75	84	100	115	110
MA research and evaluation (Labor)		2	9	6	8	13	17	15	17
MA experimentation and demonstration (Labor)		11	19	17	16	20	14	14	14
MA technical assistance (Labor)			8	6	8	10	17	15	15
MA store and local planning (Labor)				5	7	17	17	22	22
MA market information (MA; Labor)			21	23	20	24	25	25	25
Labor market information (BLS; Labor)	4	7	9	9	10	10	12	14	17
OEO research and demonstration (OEO/Labor)		(<0.5)	5	5	3	5	7		

NOTE: Details may not add to totals because of rounding. Some data are based on agency estimates.

SOURCE: U.S. Office of Management and Budget. From: Sar Levitan, Garth Mangum, and Ray Marshall, *Human Resources and Labor Markets: Labor and Manpower in the American Economy* (New York: Harper & Row, Publishers, Incorporated, 1972), Table 16-1. (Revised by the Center for Manpower Policy Studies, George Washington University, March 1, 1974.)

consolidation under community prime sponsors of all those manpower programs funded under Title I-B of that Act: Neighborhood
Youth Corps, Operation Mainstream, Special Impact, New Careers, and Foster Grandparents. However, Labor Department–
OEO cooperation and agreement was needed and never achieved.
Instead, the Bureau of the Budget (now the Office of Management
and Budget) provided by indirection and accident the most important leverage for the early state and local manpower planning
efforts. Congress in the Intergovernmental Cooperation Act of 1968
encouraged a system for intergovernmental coordination among
federal assistance programs which led in 1969 to the Office of
Management and Budget's circular A-95. The result has been 450
area-wide clearing houses across the country, consisting of councils
of government, substate regional planning commissions, and area
planning districts. Not only did the staffs of these units facilitate
interagency communication and planning, all state agencies
requesting federal funds were required to receive clearance through
the governor's office, providing a handle for coordination and for
influencing the content of the proposals for any aggressive governor
who preferred such participation. A-95 contained no enforcement
and, as often happened, governors failed to make use of it. However, it was from this provision primarily that some of the earliest
state manpower planning councils gained their limited clout to
influence the actions of state and local manpower agencies.

   With decentralization very much in the air but not a legislated
fact, a few states and cities began independently to organize and
start their own manpower planning activities. The major determinant of where and who was usually the accident of the personal
interest of influential persons. The states of Utah and North and
South Carolina, the cities of New York, Albuquerque, and Chicago,
and Dade County, Florida, were some of the earliest movers. They
fought political battles, experimented, experienced some failure,
tried again, and learned and failed once more in the usual trial
and error process. From these activities came a body of experience
and a beginning of communication across the country among
individuals with related interests. The federal agencies, committed
by Administration policy but restrained by existing law, were
somewhat ambivalent but generally encouraging. Federal regional
offices were somewhat reluctant, perhaps because state and local
discretionary action reduced their authority and made their jobs
more difficult.

Since the Emergency Employment Act and its Public Employment Program (PEP) originated in a public service employment title of a vetoed comprehensive manpower bill, decentralization to state and local governments was the hallmark of its administration. Both interest in and experience with manpower funding and programming were enhanced.

Finally, after three years of negotiation, the Labor Department in 1973 added nine Comprehensive Manpower Programs with state and local government: New Hampshire; South Carolina; Utah; SMSAs in Seattle, Washington, and Omaha, Nebraska; Albuquerque, New Mexico; Hartford, Connecticut; Dade and Monroe Counties in Florida; and Lucerne County, Pennsylvania.

From the CAMPS and the Comprehensive Manpower Program experiences and from those jurisdictions which have undertaken manpower planning on their own without Comprehensive Manpower Program designation can be drawn a set of crucial variables which seem to have determined relative success and failure and which offer lessons to new participants on the manpower scene (Sawyer, 1974).

Executive Involvement

It is the basic premise of the decentralization concept that manpower policy and program will be both better attuned and more responsive to the needs of local labor markets and those groups and individuals suffering disadvantages in job market competition if responsibility rests with the chief elected executive of the relevant governmental jurisdiction. Whether this will prove to be true will be read from experience. Pilot experience is supportive; but then those jurisdictions which entered manpower planning at their own volition are likely to have been the most responsive, as well as the most aggressive and innovative, insofar as manpower activities are concerned.

When, in general, is an elected executive — governor, mayor, county commissioner, or county supervisor — likely to be responsive to manpower needs, and how important is it that he be? Responsiveness can be expected when the potential beneficiaries of manpower efforts are politically organized and vocal. Many politicians will be responsive to manpower needs out of sheer concern for the welfare of the victims of labor market pathologies. The political responsiveness is a universal motivation, and the force most to be relied upon. Yet those state and local political bodies who led out in decentralized manpower planning appear to have done so more often because their chief executive or influential members of their staffs were convinced it was the right thing to do. There was rarely political pressure for them to do so or political reward for doing so well. For them, in general, the political risks were greater than the potential political gains. This picture probably changes when decentralization is the order of the day and it is known that the political executive who seeks to avoid manpower responsibilities has turned down control over substantial federal funds. Nevertheless, to assure political responsiveness, manpower target groups, or those concerned for the welfare of those groups, will have to look to their own organization and political potency.

Experience in the Comprehensive Manpower Programs and other pilot experiments indicates that involvement of key staff of the chief elected executive and access to him by that staff are crucial variables in successful state and local manpower planning. For the innovators in the field who led rather than followed federal initiative, these two variables were vital. Typically, initiative came from staff who convinced the executive and used his influence to overcome local agency opposition and persuade federal officialdom. Manpower programs as originally structured bypassed established state and local political processes. Funds from MDTA flowed directly to state employment services and state boards of vocational education without involving governors. Economic Opportunity Act programs were more deliberately designed to bypass not only local political structures but state and local governmental agencies. The assumption was that established institutions were disinterested or incapable of serving the poor, and a new set of institutions by, of, and for the poor were needed. The Work Incentive Program also relied upon state bureaucracies rather than elected officials. And PEP arrived after decentralization commitments were made and was the first manpower program deliberately placed in the hands of elected officials.

With that history, state and local agencies, answerable primarily to themselves and to the "feds" for manpower program funds and activities, were often reluctant to become answerable to the more direct presence of governors, mayors, and their staffs. Nevertheless, governors generally had enough avenues of clout that they could not be ignored by state agencies, and mayors had the Economic Opportunity Act amendment prerogative to intervene with community action agencies.

Typically, manpower initiatives, before CETA, have been the personal undertaking of key staff assistants to a governor or mayor. The only requisite was their personal persuasiveness and their influence upon their principals. Where manpower planning has emerged at a county or council of governments level, there were more decision makers to persuade. How deeply chief elected officials needed to be involved has been a function of how aggressive the planning effort was. Where no more has been attempted than the CAMPS-type interagency communication, such involvement was not important. But it is a truism that equals cannot coordinate equals. Ultimate differences not resolvable by negotiation can only be settled by a superior power or through advance agreement on some form of binding arbitration. Planning which is likely to challenge vested interests or make substantial change in established patterns will require access to a higher power.

It is not realistic to expect an elected executive to involve himself on a day-to-day basis with manpower policy or planning decisions. The politician's first concern, as with anyone else, is survival: "Don't get me in any serious political trouble." After that the priority is: "How can I do good and get credit for it?" With the multitude of issues of concern to a jurisdiction and its constituency, manpower issues will seldom have high visibility and priority. However, so long as the manpower staff can use the chief executive's name and authority and then can deliver his direct intervention when the "crunch" comes, executive involvement is real and adequate. This has been the case in every pilot state and local manpower planning effort which has attempted meaningful change and has been successful in it.

Agency Administrators

In some cases, the heads of state and local manpower-related agencies — such as the state employment service, state boards of vocational education, the Office of Rehabilitation Services, the state Office of Economic Opportunity, welfare departments, community action agencies, and so forth — have been members of manpower bodies. In other situations, they have not been members, but the manpower planning councils have been advisory to them or they to the councils. As in the case of executive involvement, the decisive factor determining whether such membership is appropriate and needed seems to be the ambition and aggressiveness of the manpower planning body. Regardless of the extent of executive involvement and the degree of clout available to the planning council, the heads of established agencies, especially those of long standing, generally have an extensive array of politically potent supporters with vested interests in the status quo. Achieving policy changes on issues central to the interests of such agencies without their acquiescence is difficult. That is particularly so over a long period of time, since a characteristic of any bureaucracy is durability. The more politically oriented executive with pluralistic responsibilities soon must turn his attention to other matters, and unwelcome change is stifled in the day-to-day operation of a public agency. Experience seems to be that if major change is desired in the assignment of an agency or in its modus operandi, its agreement or acquiescence in those changes will be required. Therefore, it must be party to the decisions which direct such change.

An additional advantage of involving agency heads in the manpower planning process is that it forces their attention to the manpower program practices of their own agencies. Particularly if manpower is only a part of an agency's responsibilities, that part may be delegated to lower level staff and rarely reviewed. Having to respond to the queries of other planning council members concerning an agency's actions has forced many an administrator to be aware as never before of the performance of his or her own staff.

Clout

Planning without implementation is a meaningless exercise. The history of city planning, for instance, is lettered with beautiful multicolored maps representing the fruitful imaginings of planners who knew what would be good for a city but who had no influence on its decision makers. The need for executive and agency administrator involvement is primarily a source of clout to turn plans into realities.

Sources of clout used by successful manpower planning organizations have varied in structure and by circumstance. The Office of Management and Budget's A-95 directive, giving governors the right to review and clear all proposals passing from state to federal agencies, has been an especially effective one when used for that purpose. Other executives have used various forms of budget control. Prior to the passage of CETA, some governors' and mayors' offices had managed to get themselves designated as the official responsible for a number of the programs, then subcontracted them to the agencies for delivery of services. In the latter case, competitive contracting, generating competition among public and private agencies, has been a rarely used possibility. Under CETA, the elected chief administrator of an office and the manpower staff representing that office have the ultimate source of clout — the power to reallocate monies and change service delivery assignments. The only limits are the political repercussions which may result. The degree to which this clout is exercised with state manpower services councils and prime sponsor planning councils under CETA remains to be seen. Experience only dictates that for planning to be meaningful and effective, there be some such potent source. Clout is unnecessary only when there is no intent to disturb the status quo.

Separating Planning and Administration

It has become abundantly clear through the limited experience to date that any organization confronts difficulty when it attempts to combine responsibility for broad strategic planning with day-to-day operation of programs and the delivery of services. The myriads of day-to-day decisions absorb immense amounts of time and energy. Since agencies represented on the planning council have various administrative responsibilities, defensiveness arises when tactical, as opposed to strategic, types of decisions are under consideration. An organization can rarely be objective in monitoring and evaluating its own activities. Even where it does achieve objectivity, its impartiality is always suspect. To specify a course of action, assign it to a subordinate entity, and then "hold their feet to the fire" for effective service delivery is a more comfortable approach and seemingly the only tenable position over the long run. It has been suggested that one of the major advantages in the decentralization of manpower responsibility is that it removes the "feds" from direct responsibility for the effectiveness of manpower programs and places them in a position to monitor, evaluate, and direct improvements in the quality of services. The

same principle is no less important between planners and administrators at state and local levels.

Labor Market Planning Scope

Once a jurisdiction seriously undertakes manpower planning,
it soon becomes apparent it is concerned with far more than the
administration of a discrete array of federally funded programs
known as manpower. A wide range of social and economic institutions impinge upon the employment process. A whole variety of
social, educational, and other services over a lifetime determines
employability. The manpower function itself forms an interface
between social welfare problems and economic development
interests. Those who have been employed long in manpower planning soon recognize the need to encompass in the planning process
the geographical scope over which most of the community's work
force live and are employed — the employing establishments, the
full range of service agencies, and all resources available which can
contribute to the solution of manpower problems.

Staff Competence

Staff competence clearly separates the successful from the
unsuccessful in manpower planning. Unfortunately that factor
appears to be largely accidental at this point. The need for preser-
vice and in-service professional staff training programs is gaining
increasing attention. The Division of Manpower Development and
Training in the U.S. Office of Education has been the leader in
recognizing and seeking to meet in-service needs through its Area
Manpower Institutes for the Development of Staff (AMIDS). The
University of Utah conducts a professional master's degree program
at various sites around the nation to train administrators and planners for manpower programs. A handful of other universities
supplies a similar preparation in their own localities. The Labor
Department has announced a series of institutional grants to support universities in building their capability for professional staff
training and technical assistance, and training contracts have been
let. The National Governors' Conference, the League of Cities–
Conference of Mayors, and the National Association of Counties
each have manpower staffs who have made significant contributions

to upgrading the quality of the manpower staffs of their constituencies. Still a tremendous training task lies ahead.

Experience suggests that staffs need independence as well as competence. Those manpower planning bodies have been most effective which have protected their staffs from the pressures of particular agencies.

Miscellaneous

Other crucial variables emerged in some jurisdictions but have not become general, usually because they require sophistication which develops only with time and experience. These can be briefly summarized:

Management through the budget denotes an emphasis upon cost effectiveness, upon measuring client success according to the increase in employability and incomes derived from manpower services, and manpower program success according to the economy with which specific increases in client employability and incomes are obtained. Viewing the budget as the primary manpower planning document requires support information which has not been available, to this point, in most jurisdictions. Prime sponsorship will allow budget analysis to proceed with the availability of information from contractors to planning bodies on the characteristics of those serviced, services provided, and costs per unit of services.

A *process orientation* focuses upon comprehending manpower development as a series of discrete processes. Four staff competencies derive from analytic skills and are suggested as critically important elements in the planner's bag of tools. These are: (1) occupational accessibility, (2) allocation modeling, (3) production scheduling and evaluation, and (4) program information and monitoring. A few jurisdictions have begun to develop expertise in occupational accessibility and geographical allocation models, but the latter skills are more rare. Later chapters introduce possible approaches to these processes.

Public member advocacy entails the active support, particularly of client members, to ensure their full participation in the planning dialog. Attractive as is the concept that recipients of programs should plan for having their own needs met, experience has been that client members are generally appointed in token acknowledgment of federal guidelines or political necessity. Little is effectively done to solicit their involvement, and they ordinarily lack the sophistication to make their presence felt politically. Only where minority organizations are forcefully militant does there seem to be a meaningful influence on policy decisions.

Status of Labor Market Manpower Planning

The history of state and local manpower planning suggests three conclusions:

(1) Today, CETA is the fruition of strong long-term pressures toward decentralization and decategorization in manpower policy and represents a widespread consensus. It can be accepted as an idea whose time has come rather than the temporary ideological preference of a particular political party or current administration.

(2) It represents only a portion of manpower resources, and a major challenge will be linking into the labor market planning process the totality of the manpower action.

(3) A base of experience exists from which a "code of good practice" can begin to develop, but that base is very limited in relation to the total universe of planning to be done. An immense task of dissemination and training lies ahead. In the short run, the responsible federal agencies will be totally absorbed in bringing to a minimum level of competence those with no experience or past commitment. Those who would push their competence beyond the minimum will largely be left to do their own pursuing.

The result over time will be a wide range of competence and commitment, but the alternative is a continuation of nationally prescribed programs unadapted to local conditions and with a minimum of monitoring and evaluation. The world will remain imperfect, but there is hope for marginal improvements.

Reference

Sawyer, James E. *Crucial Variables for Manpower Planning.* Salt Lake City: University of Utah, Human Resources Institute. 1974.

3
Role and Functioning of Labor Markets

If manpower planners are to plan in a labor market context, they obviously must understand at least the rudiments of the economics of labor markets. A labor market is not to be thought of as being like a supermarket. It is a concept which refers to all of those ways in which sellers of labor (workers) and buyers of labor (employers) come into contact so that transactions (hirings, firings, promotions, transfers, and so forth) can take place. Since manpower policy has two goals — (1) satisfying and remunerative working careers for people, and (2) efficient use of available labor in producing the goods and services needed by society — the manpower planner might conceive of himself or herself as representing all actors in the labor market drama: workers, employers, various intermediaries, and the public. However, most manpower planners operating in the public sector at state and local levels have a narrower assignment: Improve the employment and income of those suffering the greatest disadvantages in the competition for jobs within the labor market. Such a planner is less plagued by inconsistent objectives, but any improvement in the lot of the target populations will likely occur in the labor market. Its overall workings must be understood for any manpower plan to be practicable.

In addition, the only manpower solution to the problems of poverty, unemployment, and underemployment is *jobs*. And jobs are created in labor markets by the interaction of supply and demand forces . . . a process the manpower planner must understand to do the job. Manpower is the interface between social welfare and economic development, and the manpower practitioner must be conversant with both.

Actors in the Labor Market

Myriads of individuals representing numerous institutions make decisions impinging upon the labor market and determining its ability to supply incomes and allocate labor. But for simplicity, these can be reduced to households, employers, and third-party intermediaries. Each have varying and numerous objectives underlying and determining their decisions, but these too can be simplified into the most important and most determining ones.

The household's primary objective is income to support its desired standard of living. Individuals within the household will have other subsidiary objectives. For those who are employed or intend to seek employment, status, identity, and other satisfactions (or dissatisfactions) may emanate from the work role. But for the household as a whole, these are likely to be far less important than income. The extent and kind of labor force preparation, who and how many choose to participate in the labor market and at what age they enter and exit, the choice of occupation, and more are primarily household decisions.

For a private employer, the maximization of profit is a valid simplifying assumption. The businessman may not avidly pursue maximum profit, but all other things being equal and given a choice between more profit and less profit, he can be depended upon consistently to choose the former. The demand for labor is a derived demand, that is, no one hires labor for its own sake but for the productive services it can provide. The demand for it is derived from the demand for the goods and services it can produce. Therefore if the labor market decisions likely to lead in the direction of greater rather than lesser profits can be identified, the private employer's choices can be predicted with reasonable accuracy.

The motives of the public employer are more complex, but public approval and favorable votes are the generally sought currency of the governmental sector. The public demand for labor is still a derived demand and depends upon the willingness of the taxpayers and users of public services to pay for them. If one can predict from which labor market actions public approval and votes are likely to come, prediction of public employer choice becomes feasible.

The third-party intermediaries in the labor market are many — public and private employment agencies, unions which represent the workers, schools which educate and train them, community services agencies which influence their employability and access to work, and regulatory agencies which enforce minimum wages and labor standards are only a few. There are also acute environmental factors external to the labor market which influence its processes and results: housing patterns, transportation systems, communications media, the law enforcement system, political parties, religious organizations and beliefs, social mores, cultural standards, and so on. Each institution can be analyzed, its objectives generalized, and its probable directions of choice predicted.

Unless the manpower planner understands the labor market environment and can analyze and predict the probable decisions and actions of each major acting group or institution as interrelated with those of other actors, sensible and helpful manpower plans are unlikely.

Some Labor Market Concepts

A basic vocabulary, with understanding of the concepts involved, is another requirement of manpower planning. Some of these are discussed below.

Labor Force Participation Rates

The population is the basic source from which the supply of labor must be drawn. Those in the population who are neither working nor looking for work are considered to be out of the labor force, while the labor force consists of all of those who are either working or actively seeking work. The number of all of those sixteen years of age and over who are in the labor force, as proportionately related to the total population of those sixteen and over and not institutionalized, is known as the labor force participation rate and is shown as:

$$\frac{\text{Labor force}}{\text{Population 16 and older}} = \text{Labor force participation rate} \quad (1)$$

Labor force participation rates, of course, can be and are developed for subcomponents of the labor force such as age, sex, and race.

Unemployment

To be employed is a reasonably precise concept, but unemployment needs a definition. Put simply, the unemployed are all of those who are without employment and who are actively seeking it. There is a widespread mistaken assumption that the unemployment rate emerges from counting all of those registered for work at the public employment service. There is in fact a measure near to that — the insured unemployment rate — calculated from the proportion of the work force who at any point in time are drawing unemployment compensation. The insured unemployment rate can be obtained but has nothing to do with the rate commonly referred to as the unemployment rate. That is obtained from the Current Population Survey. Census takers monthly approach a nationwide sample of households and ask in effect: "How many live here who are sixteen years of age or older? Of those, how many were employed last week? Of those who were not employed, how many actually sought work last week?" That latter number, inflated to represent all households in the nation and applied as a proportion of the civilian labor force is the national unemployment rate. The total of those working plus those seeking work is, of course, the civilian labor force. Adding those in the nation's military forces constitutes the total labor force, or:

$$\text{Employed} + \text{unemployed} = \text{Civilian labor force} \qquad (2)$$

The manpower planner concerned with local labor markets will find the national unemployment rate of little use in planning. However, state departments of employment security have developed formulas for making state and local estimates of unemployment, based on the national data. Either at census time or through a special survey, a ratio is developed between measured unemployment locally and the then current local unemployment insurance data and the national Current Population Survey figures. This formula is then employed as the national rate moves up or down until opportunity for a new benchmark occurs.

Population Projections

The number in the labor force is the major dimension of the supply of labor. The other two considerations are the quality of the available labor and the proportion of their available days, weeks, years, and lifetime they are prepared to work. Since the population is the basic source from which the labor force is drawn, the manpower planner must be in part a demographer — a student of population trends. This skill would have allowed the manpower planner to forecast during the 1930s that its low birthrates heralded a minimum of new labor market entrants in the early 1950s and, among other things, a relative short supply of mid-career executives during the 1970s. It would also have made it possible to foresee, when the postwar baby boom began in 1947 and continued through the 1950s, that youth unemployment would be a serious problem from 1963 through the early 1970s and would diminish thereafter. The heavy demand for schoolteachers during the 1950s and 1960s, along with medical personnel and other occupations related to rapid population growth, would have been better foreseen. Knowing that U.S. birthrates had trended downward from 1957 to 1967 and then had persisted on a low plateau approximately equal to the 1930s thereafter (Figure 3.1), the alert manpower planner with skills in demography could have foreseen the likelihood of surpluses of teachers during the 1970s if the colleges of education did not slow their output. At the other end of labor force participation, with lengthening life spans, that planner/demographer would recognize the likely increased interest in post-retirement careers, an increase in political power among the aging, and rising demand for those occupations which service an aging population.

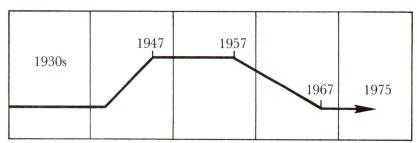

Figure 3.1. Birthrate Patterns in the United States, 1930 through 1975

Changes in Labor Force Participation Rates

Understanding population trends is the first step, but only one step, to understanding and predicting the available labor supply. What proportions of that population under what conditions will choose to offer their services in the labor market? Significant — and in historical terms, even radical — changes have been occurring in labor force participation rates. The U.S. labor force participation rate was 54.8 percent in 1940, 58.9 percent in 1947, and 61 percent in 1972, relatively little changed. But the participation rate of women in 1940 was only 26.6 percent, compared to 31.8 percent in 1947 and 43.9 percent in 1972. The relative overall stability was a consequence of the pattern of male participation rates — 82.6, 86.8, and 79.7 percent, respectively. But the rates for males 25 to 44 years of age hardly changed, holding at more than 95 percent throughout those years. The declining overall participation rate for men was a consequence of longer stays in school and earlier retirement.

The pattern for women was more interesting — in 1940 teenage girls entered the labor force, remained until marriage, and left to become homemakers throughout their lives. After the Second World War, a fluctuating pattern emerged (Figure 3.2). Girls entered the labor force, remained until the first child was due, left until the last child was in school, returned to the labor force, and remained until retirement a few years earlier in age than men. Now, year by year, the indention at the apex of the fluctuating (solid) line smoothes out as women have fewer children and are less likely to quit work when they become mothers. Yet during these years, while the participation rate for married women was doubling, the rate of single, widowed, and divorced women hardly changed. There are other interesting patterns: Nonwhite females have a higher participation rate than white females, while the relationship is the opposite for males. Education, family income, rural and urban location, community mores, the industry and occupation mix of the community all have their influence on labor force participation rates.

The annual *Manpower Report to the President* is an excellent source of national data on labor force participation rates. State and local rates may depart radically from national averages. The decennial census is the basic source for state data. The state em-

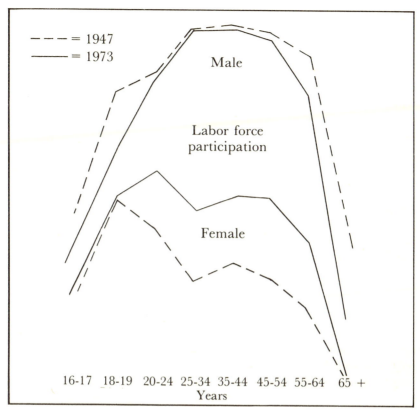

Figure 3.2. Comparison of Male and Female Labor
Force Participation in 1947 and 1973

ployment service can and should be responsible for sub-state data
on a year-by-year basis between censuses.

Elasticity of the Labor Force

Of particular significance to the manpower planner is the
elasticity of labor force participation. How do members of the
population respond to the demand for labor? The question was
raised during the Great Depression but never answered. If times
are bad, does the labor force expand as other family members seek
jobs to maintain family income when the primary worker loses his
or her job or works only part time? Or does the labor force shrink
as discouraged workers, having lost their jobs and having no success
in finding others, stop looking? The question arose again during the

prolonged but lower level unemployment of 1955 to 1963 and was answered during the falling unemployment of 1964 to 1969 and its rise again in the early 1970s. The discouraged worker hypothesis won out. Particularly with the availability of public assistance and other income maintenance sources, the tendency is for those with the most marginal of labor force attachments — teenagers, women, and some minority group members — to leave the labor force as demand falls. Then they come flooding back as jobs become available. In the recovery of the 1960s, it took two new jobs to bring unemployment down one count as workers became available from outside the labor force as well as from the unemployment pool.

Given that teenagers, women, and minorities are now a larger proportion of the total labor force than in the past, bringing unemployment down to preferred rates becomes that much more difficult. It is for this reason that some in the national Administration and the economics profession argue for giving up the old 4 percent national unemployment target which prevailed during the Truman, Eisenhower, Kennedy, and Johnson years and settling for 4.5 percent or 5 percent. Most manpower experts are reluctant to acquiesce in the lowering of sights because they are more aware than most of the human costs involved. Nevertheless, it must be admitted that the old national target is now more difficult to attain.

Hours of Work

Labor force participation rates account for the periods of life during which persons either have jobs or seek them. Therefore lifetime work patterns — periods during schooling before labor force entry, periods out of the labor force for further schooling, child rearing or other reasons, and retirement — are accounted for. Not accounted for is the amount of time people choose to work when they have jobs. With women and youth a larger proportion of the labor force, there are more persons who prefer to work only part time. As goods production becomes a smaller portion of total employment, there are also more jobs in retail sales, health occupations, and so on, where the employer is comfortable with or prefers part-time workers. Some part-time workers on the other hand may prefer full-time work but not be able to find it. Holidays, vacations, length of the workday and workweek are other important quantitative factors.

Labor Force Quality

Qualitative factors pertaining to the work force involve health, motivation, education, training, and accrued skills. They affect both the productivity of the worker and the occupations for which the worker is qualified. However, supply and demand in the labor market are never independent of each other. It has already been shown that the jobs available in the labor market (demand) are a major determining factor in the number of persons who offer themselves for work (supply). Similarly, the relative tightness of the labor market — the state of demand in comparison to supply — affects the quality employers demand of those they prefer. If demand is high, employers will "make do" with the quality of manpower available. If their needs are not so pressing, they will insist on higher quality manpower simply because they can get it. A major manpower role emerging in the past few years has been the job developer whose assignment in part has required that he or she convince the prospective employer to accept a reasonable match between job requirements and worker capability, rather than pursue unnecessary qualifications because they could be had. In keeping with these cyclical fluctuations, job development may be effective when demand is high, with training to improve basic employability more appropriate during periods of high unemployment and low worker demand.

Not only do the employer's demands affect the quality of the supply he or she requires, the nature of the available supply affects production processes and therefore the qualitative nature of demand in the long run. For instance, in the U.S. economy where a relatively well-educated labor force has been available, engineers have developed a technology which assumes and requires a fairly sophisticated work force. Engineers and employers in other countries have learned to man a sophisticated technology with illiterate workers because they had no other choice. The manpower planners should not assume that the labor supply must of necessity always accommodate itself to the demand or vice versa. An accommodation process will occur which they must understand and to which they must adapt. In general, since the demand for labor is a derived demand, customer demand determines what is to be produced, but the available labor supply will be a major determinant of how production is to be accomplished. The manpower practitioner who represents marginal workers must help them accommodate to the processes developed for the majority or must influence employers to treat these clients differently. Either way, the job can be done only by understanding the system.

Productivity and Economic and Labor Force Growth

The number of people required to meet a certain level of demand will be determined by their productivity measured in output per man-hour. That in turn is in part determined by their health, education, skills, diligence, and motivation and in part by the effectiveness with which they are managed and the tools and equipment with which they are supplied.

At the total economy level there is an important relationship between the total output of the economy (gross national product) and the pace at which it grows (economic growth) and the rates of labor force growth and productivity increase. Over the past decade, the U.S. labor force has increased at the average rate of 1.7 percent per year. At the same time, output per man-hour has been growing at an average rate of 2.8 percent per year. The gross national product had to grow at least 2.8 percent per year, on the average, just to keep *employment* from going down. With a 2.8 percent growth rate producing stable employment, the economy had to grow at an additional 1.7 percent in its output of goods and services to offer jobs to the new labor force entrants. Thus economic growth had to average 4.5 percent per year just to keep unemployment from rising. Faster growth was necessary to bring unemployment down. And this had to be real growth, not inflationary growth in dollar expenditures only. It is the amount of goods and services purchased which creates jobs, not the amount of dollars spent.

Conversely, of course, the economy could not grow faster than 4.5 percent in real terms, on the average, without pulling unemployment down, since this is the measure of the increasing productive capacity of the economy as well as its employment needs. For example, the economy was able to grow more rapidly than 4.5 percent in real terms during 1964 to 1966 as unemployment was being brought down from 5.7 to 3.8 percent. From that point on, the excess demand turned into inflation. In more recent years, inflation has eaten up too much of the economic growth to turn it into real production of goods and services and bring down unemployment.

The same principles apply at the local labor market level. The labor force grows but rarely contracts, except by outmigration. The locality may or may not share in national productivity growth, but the chances are it will. Jobs will be created only by expenditures to purchase goods and services; productivity and the price level will determine the amount of employment any particular amount of expenditure will generate. However, local labor market planners will rarely have the data on economic output and productivity to allow them to project employment from that vantage point. Alternatives which make more effective use of data more likely to be locally available are suggested in chapter 6. Nevertheless, understanding the way in which supply and demand interact with job creation and the employment process is a necessary part of the manpower planner's skills.

Demand for Labor

Largely by way of reiteration and as a basis for understanding unemployment and wage phenomena, a summary of the process of job creation and the determinants of the demand for labor may be useful. Once again, the demand for labor is a derived demand, derived from the demand for the products labor can produce. The level of that demand is determined by the purchasing power available to consumers, investors, and government decision makers and the extent to which they choose to use it. Consumers and investors have available not only their past accumulations of funds and their current income but their credit — their borrowing power — as well. State and local governments are dependent upon their tax revenues and their borrowing power. The federal government has the unique ability to create purchasing power and can use its powers to tax, spend, and determine the money supply and interest rates to encourage or discourage spending.

A decision of all to spend tends to create jobs and employment, and the opposite, to contract spending, jobs, and employment. If one group of spenders decides to reduce its contribution to total purchasing power, another can offset that move by accelerating and enlarging its spending. The federal government, particularly, has this responsibility for "compensatory fiscal policy." Or it can reduce taxes or lower interest rates to allow or encourage more private spending. However, when conditions are ripe for it, some of the spending may be siphoned off into inflation without creating jobs. The federal government can reverse its compensatory policies to reduce spending and inflationary pressures, but only at the cost of slowing or stopping job creation.

Total spending as related to the price level and to output determines the overall level of employment but says nothing of the industries and occupations in which they occur. The industries in which the jobs will be created depends upon the particular goods and services which consumers, investors, and governments choose to buy. The product or service purchased determines the industry, and the technology of production determines what the occupational mix will be: construction products (construction workers), manufacturing (assembly workers, machinists, and so forth), insurance (salesmen and clerical workers).

Some industries are fixed to particular locations by raw materials, transportation systems, or other factors, and purchases from each industry allocate jobs to its locality. The effectiveness of certain companies can also determine the locations to which purchases and jobs will flow. Other products and industries are ubiquitous and not limited to particular localities. Relative success in competition (or in avoiding competition) determines which companies will succeed and offer jobs.

Allocation of Labor by the Wage Structure

Traditionally the wage structure has been assumed to be the mechanism by which available labor was allocated among its alternative uses to that use which was of highest priority to consumers. Wages are the price of labor and, like all prices, are set by the interaction of supply and demand. A high demand for products leads to a high demand for labor and to higher wages to attract more labor. A scarcity of supply also tends to raise the wage, resulting in expansion of that supply from new entrants, retrained persons, and those with transferable skills who offer to apply them in higher paid employment. But the higher wage also discourages use of the scarce labor, therefore rationing it.

Of course, relative wages are not the sole determinant of the occupational choices young people make as they choose their careers, that reentrants to the labor force make, that the unemployed choose if they have alternatives, or that motivate employed persons to shift to new jobs. Availability of openings is the first criterion. Location, working conditions, and other factors are important. Nevertheless, when all other considerations are equal, most people will choose a higher paying to a lower paying job. The result is usually a net flow of labor toward the higher paying jobs — thus the manpower allocation process: Increased consumer demand sparks higher prices and attracts new and expanded firms. Their labor requirements lead them to push up wages, thus attracting workers to the expanding activities.

Many factors are involved in employers' ability and willingness to pay various wage rates and workers' acceptance of them. But the result is a wage structure in most labor markets which generally results in about the right amounts of labor in the right jobs and places to get the community's work done. The mechanism is not perfect, but considering the complexities, the paucity of controls, the comparative freedom of choice, and the usual lack of information as to available workers and jobs, the relative effectiveness and efficiency are more remarkable than the errors. This wage-induced labor allocation process has numerous implications for the manpower planner. For instance, demographic trends forecast a declining labor force growth rate into 1985, and economic growth must slow unless productivity accelerates radically. Unless consumer and investment spending slows accordingly, further inflationary pressures will be added to current ones. Worker demand for wage increases above those which employers are willing to pay will cause grave allocation problems. In addition, the mix of alternatives for manpower programs will be affected — training, dropout rates, and placement in low-paying occupations in periods of inflation.

Not only is there a wage structure of established and changing relations among the pay scales of various employers, there is also an internal wage structure within each establishment. Employers not only must attract workers, they must retain and motivate them. For people working together, there must be a general acceptance of the differences in pay among them to keep them reasonably satisfied. There must be sufficient differentials to reward workers for accepting greater responsibility. This system, too, will rarely be perfect but must be effective enough to keep the wheels of industry and employment rolling. The manpower planner's job is to facilitate and improve the efficiency of the labor market and to intervene on behalf of the victims if the labor market fails to provide adequate employment and income opportunities for many. However, understanding of labor market realities must be a prerequisite if well-intentioned intervention is to help more than hurt.

For instance, a legislated minimum wage is always a tempting solution by legislators to the income problems of the working poor. They have jobs and are willing to work. Why not just require employers to pay a wage sufficient to boost the family out of poverty? But a minimum wage law does not require employers to raise their levels of pay. It only forbids them to hire anyone at less than the minimum. Before becoming an advocate for higher minimum wages or broader coverage, the manpower planner must be convinced that the result will in fact be a larger total wage bill, rather than the loss of even the low-paying jobs. One can argue that there is a wage below which it is socially better not to be employed; but one who argues this case must be prepared to argue for some form of income maintenances to replace the lost wages. Policy prescriptions are anybody's prerogative, but manpower planners are obligated by the very title of their position to be able to foresee the long-range impacts of their recommendations.

Labor Mobility

The notion of a wage system as an efficient allocator of labor presupposes worker mobility. Not that all workers must be willing to drop what they are currently doing and move to a new job and even a new residence when a more favorable package of wages, working conditions, and other perquisites appear. However, enough persons are assumed to be, and usually are sufficiently mobile that changes in wages and other offerings can motivate enough movement to meet society's production needs. Whatever their mobility limitations, American workers are among the most mobile in the world.

Labor mobility has many facets. Interindustry and inter-company mobility occurs as opportunities open and close. A great amount of mobility occurs within companies as workers are transferred or promoted. Workers move among occupations, usually more reluctantly when their current occupations involve considerable training and specialization, less reluctantly if the change does not require abandoning "human capital" invested on one's self.

Such occupational shifts may be up or down and may occur within an individual's working lifetime or between generations. In a recent national longitudinal study, it was discovered that three out of five men 45 to 59 years of age were working at jobs of higher socioeconomic status than those in which they began their working careers (Parnes *et al.*, 1970, p. 127).

From parent to child, the intergenerational mobility is considerable, but the moves upward are usually short — two or three steps up the occupational ladder, with college education the major leverage for such change (Blau and Duncan, 1964, p. 420). The undereducated and members of minority groups still find their occupational mobility most restricted. About one in fourteen Americans move across county lines each year, with about half of these migrating to another state. Within county moves, one in six changes residence each year. Moves of the past have been first from other counties to this, then farm to city, and now inner city to suburb. Many moves will involve a combination of industrial, occupational, and geographical mobility, with a great deal of social and personal pain in the process. Typically, those most in need of new opportunities will be the most reluctant to move or will face the greatest obstacles to moving. The greatest obstacles to desirable mobility are the lack of information concerning alternatives, lack of self-confidence, and lack of access to available jobs.

Since the manpower planner's objective is to facilitate the workings of the labor market in order to improve the workers' employment options as well as the allocation of available labor in accord with society's priorities, a more than cursory understanding of the role of labor markets and the obstacles to their effectiveness is a necessary tool of the trade. As noted above, to attempt policies and programs not in accordance with the workings of the labor market may be foreordained to failure. Sometimes short-range objectives will conflict with long-term goals, but that should only occur with the planner's having full realization of the consequences. For instance, suppose an entry-level occupation suffers from extraordinarily low wages. The likelihood is that workers will tend to avoid this job, and unless the demand for the product or service is declining, the wage may tend to rise. However, if a manpower program undertakes training or subsidizes entry into that occupation in some way, wages may be kept low. Workers may enter the occupation under the encouragement of the program, be placed (giving the program favorable marks), and then leave because of the low wages, only to be replaced by a continuing series of program enrollees.

A Typology of Labor Markets

The general understanding of labor markets vital to the local labor market manpower planner includes familiarity with various kinds and aspects of labor markets. Knowledge of job growth, replacement needs, and job vacancies is essential to manpower planning but of little value to manpower program target groups unless they can obtain access to these openings. Even though planners are not personally responsible for placement, they need to understand the nature and working of labor markets; the recruitment, selection, and hiring practices of employers; the role of various labor market intermediaries; the sources of information; and the obstacles to job access.

As the first paragraph of this chapter stated, a labor market is not an institution like a grocery supermarket, but a concept which includes all of the ways, places, and techniques by which potential employers and employees come into contact and hiring transactions take place. The concept can be applied to a particular industry, an occupation or set of occupations, job seekers of prescribed characteristics, or a place of any geographical scope. Characteristics of various classifications of labor markets are essential to understanding the problems and chances of gaining access to the jobs within them.

Geographical Scope

Labor markets may be international, national, regional, or local in scope, depending upon the product market, the technology, the scarcity of skills, the training required, and the information channels. For instance, engineers, scientists, college professors, and business managers, among others, tend to participate in a national and sometimes international labor market. Those in some construction crafts, characterized by high skills and infrequent construction of the type in a certain locality (for instance, pipefitters in an oil refinery), move about in regional markets.

Most workers are employed within daily commuting distance of their homes. Labor markets overlap geographically by occupation, industry, and location. However, there is in general a metropolitan area which encompasses most of the comings and goings between home and work of most workers. Areas of more sparse population comprise "gray areas" between the metropolitan labor markets from which neighboring workers may commute in various directions and are the nearest thing to labor market boundaries. The concept of the SMSA emerges from this reality. More significant for manpower programs has been the concept of ghetto, central city, suburban, and rural labor markets.

Internal vs External Labor Markets

Many large business firms and some public employers follow the practice of filling higher level job openings primarily by promoting from within, hiring new workers only at the bottom of the promotion ladder. Other employers hire from outside for a variety of jobs and promote from within for others. Those transactions such as promotions and transfers which occur within the employing establishment are described as an internal labor market.

The point of access at which the employer hires from the external labor market is known as the port of entry. Manpower planners must address their efforts to gaining access for their clients through these entry points. To train for an occupation which is not accessible through a port of entry, for instance, would be a waste of resources and a disservice that frustrates the trainee.

Private vs Public Labor Markets

Approximately 81 percent of the nonagricultural jobs in the U.S. economy are provided by private business firms. About 28 percent of all nonagricultural jobs are regulated to some degree by rules agreed upon through collective bargaining between management and unions representing their employees. Most large employers follow more or less formalized personnel practices in recruiting, selecting, hiring, promoting, and otherwise dealing with their employees. Smaller firms may act with total informality.

Most jobs with units of government are now covered by merit system regulations. Advancing persistently through various levels of government since the 1880s, these rules are designed to guarantee to the public competent public servants and to limit the "spoils system" whereby winning politicians reward their supporters with public jobs. Admirable as this incentive may be, these formalized rules tend to rely heavily on educational credentials and written tests as entry ways into public employment and often inadvertently set up hurdles difficult for disadvantaged workers to surmount. Since the result is often to select overqualified persons who do not remain in the jobs, the result is often poorer, not better service. Reforms opening merit system jobs to potentially qualified disadvantaged workers are widely advocated but little achieved. The manpower planner will need familiarity with the various types of private and public labor markets.

Primary and Secondary Labor Markets

Spreading throughout the manpower literature in recent times has been the concept of the secondary labor market as an explanation of the persistence of unemployment, underemployment, and poverty among disadvantaged workers. There exists, it is alleged, a primary labor market of good jobs — well paid, providing job security, fringe benefits, and advancement opportunities — available to workers who share the broad norms of race, education, life-style, and location. There exists also a secondary labor market of dead-end, poorly paid, insecure jobs which have little value to workers, resulting in high turnover, sporadic employment, and low incomes. Workers may reject such jobs as often as employers may avoid or dispense with these workers. An allegedly impervious wall, it is charged, blocks secondary workers from the primary market. Remedial manpower programs consisting of skills training, basic education, and work experience are described as useless because they do not help break through the wall. Only job restructuring, subsidized employment, or antidiscrimination enforcement can crack the primary market for disadvantaged workers.

The concept is a useful one, despite the fact that labor markets cover a continuum of conditions, rather than fall into two neat categories, and workers do move upward into better jobs and downward into worse ones. The concept can help the planner keep clearly in mind that not just an immediate job but above-poverty income, employment stability, and income security — a satisfying working career — are the objective for disadvantaged workers as well as their more advantaged counterparts. To provide target groups with jobs already available to them or to perpetuate their poverty in lowly paid dead-end jobs is no gain. Understanding labor markets may identify routes of access to meaningful jobs.

Casual vs Permanent Employer-Employee Attachments

In most industries (notably manufacturing; communications; some types of transportation; public utilities; finance, insurance, and real estate; government employment; and so on), it is assumed that a worker, once hired and serving a probationary period, will continue as a permanent employee of the firm, accumulating seniority and pension rights and moving up a promotion ladder inside an internal labor market. In construction, maritime occupations, agriculture, and sometimes in trucking, retail trade, and service industries, the employment relationship is more likely to be a casual and temporary one. The individual accumulates no job security or guarantees of promotion, retirement, and other fringe benefits.

Where the casual employment has been organized by unions as in construction and maritime jobs, fringe benefits and protection of job opportunities are provided on a multiemployer basis through collective bargaining. Where that is not the case, as with migratory agricultural labor and many lower level service trades, the workers have only the legal protections provided by government, but no political power with which to expand these. The extreme in casualness is the contact between worker and employer, which results in a few hours or days of work with immediate payment in cash and no further contact.

Householders may know someone available as a handyman or domestic. In most large communities an informal casual market emerges and becomes recognized and used by a variety of participants for their own purposes. For instance, the corner of Georgia and Eastern Avenues in Washington, D.C., is the boundary line between the District of Columbia and the Maryland suburb of Silver Spring. More importantly, it is the farthest point one can ride in public transportation without paying an additional fare. Each morning District of Columbia residents ride to that corner. Householders, small contractors, and other potential temporary

employers drive up to the corner in automobiles and pickup trucks
to single out likely looking prospects. Whether cleaning a house,
trimming up a yard, or putting in the day on a construction job,
the worker is paid in cash at the end of the day at rates which
emerge by common consent, and the employment contract is ended.

To facilitate these labor market needs, the public employment service provides casual labor offices in most cities. Some
unions have attempted to regulate and offer protection to such
workers by providing a hiring hall, fixing wage rates, and rationing
jobs on a rotation basis. In recent years a new phenomenon has
emerged on the scene — temporary help agencies which employ
the individual, often providing many of the perquisites of steady
employment, and then sell those services to employers who need
only occasional and part-time help.

Organized and Unorganized Labor Markets

Typically (unless workers have an unusually high level of
scarce skills), good wages, fringe benefits, job security, and advancement opportunities depend upon some form of employee organization, whether in labor unions or professional associations. At times
the threat or possibility of organization can be effective in gaining
some of the same sorts of perquisites. Preparing workers for unpro-
tected markets may improve their income and employment security
over their previous situation, but they are left vulnerable to the
whims of the economy and their employers. Craft unions — those
which usually represent specialized-skill workers employed in
relatively small-scale industry — attempt to control or participate
in the hiring process, thus seeking to control the supply sufficiently
to push up wages and other perquisites of employment. These jobs
become more attractive but generally harder to gain access to,
though at least there is a formal channel through which to be
admitted or refused.

Apprentice programs and union hiring halls become typical
ports of entry into these occupations. Industrial unions, on the
other hand, typically represent all or most of the employees in any
particular establishment. However, they generally leave hiring
policy and practice to the employer but insist on representing the
employees once they are hired. Planners have some obligation to
seek, among the achievable alternatives, those employment sources
likely to be of greatest long-run advantage to their clients. Since

unions generally enhance the attractiveness of jobs but may make entry more difficult, manpower planners and practitioners must understand and accommodate to or confront these practices in ways which are in the best interest of their clients.

Specific vs General Skills

The job content and skill requirements of occupations vary widely. Some involve only simple repetitive activities, learned easily in a short time by any reasonably intelligent and adept person. Others require high degrees of specialized skill. Some require only the normal abilities, mental and physical, held by almost everyone. Others have requirements so specialized that only substantial training or experience will bring the individual to acceptable productivity. People's abilities are infinitely varied. Employers naturally want the best trained, most experienced, and most productive employees possible, but must take what they can get. Therefore requirements to get and hold a job will vary widely because of the state of competition in the job market.

Every employer has the choice of recruiting and hiring people with the requisite skills or hiring those who have the potential for obtaining such skills and training them. The tendency is to choose according to what has the greatest advantage in terms of costs and returns. In general, the first choice would be to hire those already experienced, unless the feeling is that:

(1) The employer can do a better job of training without it being too costly

(2) The wage differential between an experienced and an inexperienced person is large

(3) The experienced people are at an age that the employer considers it advantageous to the firm to hire, train, and retain younger people

(4) The experienced people are not readily available

In general, most employers would prefer to shift training costs to public institutions or other employers if possible. Employers will provide training only if:

(1) They mistrust the training ability of other training institutions

(2) Training is low cost

(3) Their needs are sufficiently specialized that other institutions cannot provide the necessary training

The availability and costs of hiring vs training will depend upon the nature of the job. Some skills are best and most economically obtained on the job and others in training institutions. In general, classroom or institutional training is preferable if:

(1) There is substantial intellectual, as contrasted with manual content to the skill

(2) The skills have broad application to many employers

(3) There is an important safety element making it dangerous to have untrained people learning on the job

(4) The job content is complex and varied, making it preferable to teach all of the skills in a "mock-up" situation rather than depend upon the vagaries of work assignments to cover the full range of scales

On-the-job training will tend to be preferred if:

(1) The skills are limited and easily learned

(2) They are frequently experienced on the job

(3) Training will not interfere with production

(4) The job content is such that it is difficult to duplicate in the classroom

(5) Expensive and specialized equipment duplicative of that found in the workplace is required

The relative availability of job access and preferred entry route will depend in part upon such factors. For many skills, the most logical training process would be a coupling of initial classroom training with subsequent on-the-job training. However, the first is generally the responsibility of the schools and the latter of the employers. Only in the limited number of "co-op" programs in secondary level vocational education have the two got together to pool their relative advantages and capabilities.

Channels of Recruitment

Given the growth and replacement needs of occupations, the problem emerges of ascertaining access to jobs for those for whom it is the planner's objective to plan. The problem has essentially three dimensions: (1) getting information to the job seekers and employer, (2) bringing the job seeker and the potential employer into contact, and (3) achieving agreement between them on the requirements of the worker and the job, and the conditions under which hiring will occur. Performing these tasks is not the responsibility of the planner, but understanding their realities and the likelihood of closure is.

It is a truism of labor market studies that most job information is spread informally by word-of-mouth and most matching of available people and available jobs takes place informally as information is spread by family and friends and by incumbent employees. Numerous intermediaries exist in the labor market: company personnel offices, union hiring halls, professional and trade associations, public and private employment services, community action agencies, and so forth. Discrimination by employers on the grounds of age, sex, racial and ethnic origin, education, and the like, is a reality of the labor market which must be accommodated, circumvented, or confronted. Workers and potential workers have their own convictions about the kinds of jobs they are willing to accept and to stick with once obtained, depending upon alternatives and their own economic circumstances. Employers control access to jobs unless unions have and use the power to wrest that unilateral control from them. Other intermediaries can only supply information or act as agent of the employer or employee. Occasionally and on some issues, public agencies may have intervening authority prescribed by law. All other intermediaries lack power in the labor market. Planning must include incorporation of and response to these realities.

Knowledge of legal requirements, employer and union practices, available tools for gaining information and access, and the relative competence of the various public intermediaries is a planning capability. It is the planner's job to determine what job opportunities are and will become available for whatever target group the plan encompasses, to determine which would be available to individuals in that target group under what conditions, and to advise program administrators on routes to those jobs and probabilities of success.

Labor Market Pathologies

In part, manpower programs have their origins in the failures of labor markets. That is, there are not enough jobs to absorb all of those seeking work, the job-matching mechanisms do not bring workers or employers into contact, or one or the other of them has misconceptions which lead to rejection of the job or the worker. At times, however, it is the very fact that labor markets do work which creates the need for manpower programs. The expectation is that a well-operating labor market will place the best available employee in the best job available for him or her. But company personnel departments are generally set up to screen out those not likely to be good employment risks. Unions and professional associations have a better chance of maintaining job control if they have within their memberships the most qualified workers in the labor market. Employment services have traditionally been expected to provide the best applicant to fit the employer's job order. But what of those screened out? For those screened out for objective reasons related to their productivity, the manpower program answer is to improve their skills and competence. For those suffering from prejudice in the hiring process, the need is to reform institutions and open access on objective grounds.

Unemployment, underemployment, low incomes, and labor shortages are the major pathologies to which labor markets are subject. The definitions and causes of these pathologies most manpower practitioners will undoubtedly know, but review of them may be appropriate.

Unemployment and Underemployment

Underutilized manpower resources can be divided into four distinct categories: (a) the unemployed, (b) persons outside the labor force who want or need work, (c) persons who are working fewer hours than they would prefer for reasons beyond their control, and (d) persons employed at jobs that are below their actual or potential skills. There are no data or even careful definition for the fourth category, though it must be large. Examples of the incidence of the first three under various economic conditions are given in Table 3-1.

Table 3-1
Demand for Jobs
(Thousands)

Category	1967	1971	1973
(a) Unemployed	3,008	4,993	4,304
(b) Outside the labor force, but wanting to work	4,698	4,404	4,460
(c) Part-time work or reduced workweeks, economic reasons	2,163	2,675	2,519

Unemployment has already been defined as the condition of being without but actively seeking employment. Its causes can be classified as cyclical, frictional, seasonal, and structural. Cyclical unemployment is the general unemployment resulting from inadequate, overall economic activity consequent to periodic slowing in the rates of economic activity. Figure 3.3 charts unemployment rates for the total economy for the past thirty years. It is this cyclical unemployment resulting from deficient total demand for goods and services which determines nationally *how many* are to be employed and unemployed. Other factors determine *who* is to suffer the unemployment. It is also this overall unemployment which is amenable to federal government fiscal and monetary policies which affect the total amount of spending. And it is primarily against this cause of unemployment that unemployment compensation is aimed.

Seasonal swings in economic activity — in outdoor work such as construction and agriculture, in retail sales affected by weather and by holiday seasons such as Christmas and its depressed aftermath, in education with its long summer "vacations" — result in alternating periods of slack and tightness in labor markets. Seasonal unemployment is so regular and foreseeable that a seasonal

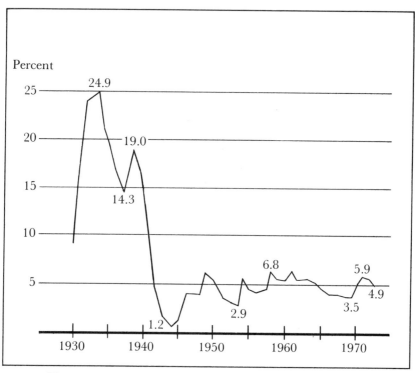

Figure 3.3. U.S. Unemployment Rate, 1930 to 1973

factor is introduced into national unemployment data to abstract from their effect in measuring the national economic health.

Frictional unemployment results from temporary difficulties in matching available workers with available jobs. It arises mainly from lack of knowledge of job opportunities and of the availability of workers, and is marked by relatively short duration. Some frictional unemployment is an unavoidable consequence of free choice in labor markets, but the amount can be lessened by improved information flows and placement assistance.

Structural unemployment is a more complex phenomenon than either seasonal or frictional unemployment and arises from basic changes in the composition of labor demand and failure of labor supply to accommodate itself to new market conditions. For instance, cutbacks in the space program, the decline of railroads and coal mining in earlier years, the relocation of New England textile mills in the South — all left skilled workers stranded in labor surplus areas and needing new skills or relocation to more promising areas. All of these causes of unemployment may of course combine, interrelate, and overlap.

Most unemployment — particularly frictional — is of relatively short duration, about 50 percent lasting less than five weeks. Longer term unemployment of fifteen weeks or more — usually cyclical or structural in origin — on the other hand is usually no more than one-eighth to one-quarter of the total. However, given the dynamics of the labor force and labor market, even that small proportion represents a lot of people. For instance, in 1972, the most recent year for which such data are available, the civilian labor force averaged 86.5 million, but 98.3 million persons worked or sought work sometime during the year. Likewise, 4.8 million persons on the average were unemployed during the year, but the total number who experienced unemployment was 15.3 million. A total of 4.8 million persons experienced fifteen weeks or more of unemployment during that year, 1.9 million were unemployed for more than half the year, and two million sought jobs at some time during the year but did not at any time find work. Only 57 percent of the labor force was employed full time for the full year.

The factors which determine the level of unemployment are impersonal economic forces, but who the unemployed are is highly personal. Of 1973's unemployed, two out of five were in that situation because they had lost a job, one out of six because they had voluntarily quit a job, and 45 percent were searching for a job upon entering or reentering the labor force.

The incidence of unemployment is concentrated by age, race, sex, education, and location. Teenagers typically have unemployment rates three times the average level of all unemployment. Black workers experience double the unemployment of the average of the labor force. If we combine the two groups, we find that black teenagers typically experience six times whatever the prevailing unemployment rate, and since women experience higher unemployment than men, black teenage girls may have an unemployment incidence of as high as 35 to 40 percent. Unemployment rates for the Spanish-surnamed are similar to those of blacks, while three-quarters of those who live on Indian reservations may be without jobs. And these are average national rates. Those for rural depressed areas and central city ghettoes may be two or three times the average. College graduates, for 1972, averaged about 2 percent unemployment, compared to 4 percent for high school graduates and 8 percent for those with some high school but without diplomas. Rates for laborers are typically five times greater than those of professional and technical workers and double those of craftsmen.

Poverty

Low incomes are an obvious consequence of unemployment, but this is not the only cause. In 1972, there were 5.1 million families with incomes below that designated by the Social Security Administration as representing poverty. Some were there because workers in the family experienced sporadic or extensive unemployment. For other families the problem was an aged or disabled family head or a female family head burdened with child-care problems. In one million families the family head worked full time, full year and still could not earn sufficient income to raise the family above the poverty level. After all, employment full time for a full year at the federal minimum wage would result in an annual income of $3,200, whereas $4,300 is required to lift an urban family of four out of poverty.

Careful consideration must be given by the manpower planner to the causes of poverty because only from those causes can cures be postulated. An old issue in manpower policy is: For those experiencing unemployment, underemployment, and low incomes, is the basic cause inherent in the individuals (their lack of skills, their health, or their motivation) or in the institutions of the labor market (which may impose barriers for certain people and groups that the others do not confront)? In the first case the prescription would logically be "change the people"; in the latter, "change the institutions."

Similarly, labor market solutions are appropriate only for those who can reasonably be expected to compete for jobs. These solutions hold little cure for poverty of the aged and are limited for the disabled. Labor market solutions for female family heads may involve child-care and other supportive services. Between 1960 to 1969, the number of poor in the United States declined from forty million to nineteen million. However, only those families whose problems had been the unemployment and low wages of the family head emerged from poverty. Those families with aged and disabled heads of household made no progress, and the number and percentage of female-headed families among the poor actually increased.

Disadvantagement

Following the passage of the Economic Opportunity Act in 1964, manpower policy attention focused more narrowly on those who were poor in particular instead of on the unemployed in general. Manpower programs took as their target the "disadvantaged," and it was necessary to formulate a definition of the term. The one that emerged — persons who are both poor and without satisfactory employment, plus being under 22 years of age, over 44, a high school dropout, a member of a minority group, or handicapped — was useful for evaluating the extent to which a program was attempting to give priority to those most in need of help. It is not useful as an indicator of causes of unemployment and poverty or for a prescription that will cure. Persons are not poor or unemployed because of their skin color, for instance, but maybe because some employers choose to discriminate against their race. It is not youth, though it may be inexperience, which is a handicap. As chapter 1 points out, the manpower planner is obligated to find tools of analysis which are useful in identifying problems and proposing and evaluating solutions. One cannot settle for convenient pigeonholes which are useful for filing but not for serving.

The "Employment and Earnings Inadequacy Index"

Unemployment statistics, widely used as a measurement of economic health, are in fact a measurement of the use of human resources, not of the economic and social welfare of the work force. They count who wants to work, not how many need it. An appropriate measure of economic welfare would combine all of the labor market measures which account for inadequate income, unemployment, underemployment, low wages, and the discouraged job seeker. Levitan and Taggart (1973, pp. 19-27) of the George Washington University have constructed such a measurement. Called the "Employment and Earnings Inadequacy Index," it lists:

(1) All of the unemployed

(2) Those discouraged workers who want work but are not actively seeking it because previous search has convinced them that no jobs are available for them

(3) Family heads and unrelated individuals who work full time, full year without earning above the poverty threshold

(4) Those with less than poverty income because of intermittent employment

(5) Part-time workers who would prefer full-time work but cannot obtain it

From these are subtracted all full-time students, those 65 years of age and older, working wives and other relatives in husband-wife families, and all of those otherwise included in families above the mean income for families. The remaining deprived persons are considered as a ratio to the sum of the entire labor force, plus discouraged workers.

The Employment and Earnings Inadequacy Index is new and not yet well known and accepted, but it points up a crucial measurement need not met by any accepted statistical method. As an example of the application of this index, in March 1972, there were 5.2 million persons (6.1 percent of the labor force) listed as unemployed, generally considered to be an accurate index of the number and proportion of the available labor force not being used. The Employment and Earnings Inadequacy Index at the same time gave 11.5 percent (involving 9.9 million persons) as the figure, a contrasting measurement of economic welfare.

Labor Shortage

A manpower planner charged with contributing to the overall health of the national or a local economy, as well as the welfare of its disadvantaged citizens, would be as concerned for unfilled jobs as for unemployed people. Relative scarcity of labor does occur and may slow economic growth, spark inflation, deny needed goods and services, and bottleneck the demand for supportive workers whose jobs are attached to those occupations in short supply. However, given the generally high levels of education and mobility among the American work force, it is difficult to identify substantial numbers of jobs standing vacant or demanded goods and services not produced. More likely is the modest strain of "getting by" with less than desired competence or "making do" with a different mix of people and machines or alternative mixes of skilled and not-so-skilled people.

After the Second World War, the U.S. economy found itself with a persistent situation of starting from behind and chasing a moving manpower target. Depression and war had reduced opportunities for education, training, and experience. Technological developments during the war applied to civilian production had given a new sophistication to production methods. Hot and cold wars kept up the drive for more sophisticated weapons of defense and destruction. Population and concepts of adequate education and health care rose rapidly. Therefore, for some 25 years the nation was constantly straining to keep its supply of professional, technical, and skilled manpower rising as rapidly as demand. There never were serious bottlenecks, though there was pressure on educational institutions to expand their capacity and perhaps some restraint on the quality of services provided.

Then in the early 1970s, slowing of birthrates, cutbacks in aerospace priorities, and a business recession, all occurring simultaneously, flattened growth trends in the demand for highly educated manpower just as demand and supply were coming into equality. Except for teachers and perhaps physicists, rising unemployment proved temporary, but national labor shortages now seem to have disappeared except in some medical occupations, and supply is rapidly catching up there as well. We are producing more educated people than the labor market requires by standards of the past. However, the response of the labor market to the changing supply situation has been for employers to raise educational requirements simply because people with educational credentials are more readily available, and for wage levels to rise less rapidly for those groups than would otherwise occur. Unemployment is a rare experience at the higher levels of education. What occurs is a bumping back process, with those at the tail end of the line always taking the competitive rap.

A general equality between demand and supply nationally and surpluses in some educated fields, however, do not mean that labor shortages will not occur locally. For instance, the sudden turnabout in the demand for coal after years of decline and automation has created shortages requiring recruiting and training efforts throughout coal-producing areas.

To the local labor market manpower planner, labor shortages may occasionally pose obstacles to new or expanding industry. More often such shortages will offer opportunities for the training and placement of unemployed and underemployed people. Since, generally, spot shortages are more likely to occur in low-level jobs that few are willing to take and jobs requiring long or expensive training, there is a challenge to identify employment opportunities and arrange training and access to promising working careers. Chapter 6 suggests a pathway between these extremes by identifying occupations of stable or growing demand and desirable wages and working conditions which attract a supply of workers at or below their absorption potential.

Labor Markets and the Manpower Planner

It is the role of the labor market to place those who seek workers in contact with those who seek jobs. Most of what occurs in the labor market happens from the unguided interrelationships of thousands and millions of potential employers and employees. No planner has the scope of control to be able to plan the entire labor market. The planner must be satisfied to act at the margin, changing things that can be changed, tinkering to make small improvements here and there. There is only so much staff time and so much social energy. The labor market manpower planner's task is to identify those pathologies that can be cured with available resources and knowledge. To do so, he or she must understand labor markets and their role and structure, the plight of those most in need of help, the resource base available, and the techniques which give promise for alleviating the observed pathologies. These insights are the purpose of this book.

References

Blau, Peter M.; and Duncan, Otis Dudley. *The American Occupational Structure.* New York: John Wiley & Sons, Inc. 1964.

Levitan, Sar; and Taggart, Robert. "Employment and Earnings Inadequacy: A Measure of Worker Welfare." *Monthly Labor Review* (October 1973).

Parnes, Herbert; *et al. The Pre-retirement Years.* Volume 1. Manpower Research Monograph No. 15. U.S. Department of Labor, Manpower Administration. Washington, D.C.: U.S. Government Printing Office. 1970.

U.S. Department of Labor, Manpower Administration. *Manpower Report to the President.* Washington, D.C.: U.S. Government Printing Office. Various years.

4

The Manpower Planning Process

Preceding chapters have made a general case for state and local manpower planning, traced the forces bringing it into being, and provided an overview of the role and functions of labor markets. Subsequent chapters get into the specifics of how to do labor market planning on behalf of the victims of labor market pathologies. This transitional chapter provides a general framework for planning to tie together and give sequence and perspective to those which follow. Chapter 1 provided definitions and simplified steps in the planning process. Now it is time to get into more detail as to who should plan for whom, with what resources and to what ends. The philosophy of this book and this chapter is that (1) labor market pathologies are endemic, but significant marginal improvements can be made with adequate and effective effort, (2) constraints are everywhere, but the case where no degrees of freedom are available for the exercise of discretion is nonexistent.

The Who of Manpower Planning

It is worthy of note that the demand for state and local manpower planning did not emerge from CETA. Rather, it was the demand for such planning which was the impetus behind the passage of the Act. Similarly, the decision to place responsibility for manpower decision making upon state and local elected officials had two motives: (1) their familiarity with the local scene and its needs, and (2) the accountability which allows the populace, if it cares to do so, to reward or punish with the ballot good or poor performance. A number of public agencies in the community could possibly meet the first criterion, though most seem too absorbed in their own programs to garner general knowledge. The political form of accountability is available only through a staff responsible directly to the chief elected official. The accountability will be effective only if enough of the citizenry are concerned with manpower and if the actual and potential recipients of manpower services are organized for political potency.

Planning occurs at a variety of levels. Chapter 1 noted the difference between strategic and tactical planning, the first being the establishment of broad social goals and the latter, the specifics of how to achieve particular objectives contributing to accomplishment of the goals. It is appropriate that those elected to represent the people's interests be responsible for strategy decisions. Generally, of course, a legislature establishes priorities among the problems to be addressed and sanctions or directs general approaches to problem and solution. The executive may request or prod the legislature into that action. Once the legislative endorsement is given, the executive has the responsibility of implementation, turning legislative language into more specific goals or objectives and assigning an agency or staff to commence planned delivery of services.

The manpower planner stands as intermediary between the policy makers and the services delivery agency. The planner may alert the policy makers to problems and facilitate policy choices. However, it is the fixing of intermediate objectives on the way to the policy goal and deciding on a program to accomplish these objectives which are the essence of that tactical planning function. It is after the planner has designed and won agreement to a program relating client needs to available services in preparation for accessible jobs that those charged with service delivery responsibility take over, leaving monitoring and evaluation to the planners. Thus planning evolves through stages when policy makers are made aware of population and labor market needs, are confronted with options and set priorities among goals, and are exposed to and choose among alternatives. Beyond this stage explicit programs must be designed, operational guidelines established, and existing or new operating agencies assigned the task of implementing the programs. Operational guidelines must in turn be translated into management directions and staff duties. Program monitoring and evaluation encompass and proceed at all of the policy effectiveness, operational efficiency, and managerial self-evaluation levels. The manpower planner may be involved singularly or simultaneously in any of these stages and levels as researcher, adviser, operations planner, or managerial monitor, to the confusion of the planner, the policy makers, and the operator, unless the varied roles are clearly defined and recognized. What that role is at any instant will undoubtedly affect the planner's perceptions and judgment. Greater clarity will emerge from recognition that the planner's role is to identify problems, pose policy options, devise alternative plans, and become involved in operational and organizational objectives, but that decision making is not the planner's prerogative. Planners may in fact make policy and operational decisions, but when they do so, they function as policy makers or program operators, not as planners.

As noted in chapter 2, strategic manpower planning is best undertaken by a staff reporting to the chief executive but with involvement of the heads of agencies which will be charged with delivery of services, as well as representatives of target groups, employers, and the labor community. In general, the nongovernmental representation has not been too meaningful, except to give an air of respectability to the effort. Yet real inputs are possible if the labor, management, and minority members take the effort seriously and in truth represent and have credibility within their groups — and if they are taught how to function effectively in their roles, a teaching process which then can and often will be used against the teachers. Under CETA, of course, these planning organizations will include the state manpower services councils, and a state or local planning council will be available in each prime sponsorship.

There are many ways of staffing the manpower planning function. Staff can report to the chief executive or to his designee. Or the staff can be subject to the planning council as a corporate body. In general, the experience appears to have been better where staff remain somewhat independent of the council members and have clear and direct loyalties to their chief executive. They may tend to develop an adversary relationship with agency staffs, and council members may feel helpless and unserved; but at least loyalties are clear, and the staff can escape from being pressured from a variety of agency interests. The state planning staff can identify problem areas, propose geographical allocation among target groups and mix of services for the balance of state, and monitor and evaluate programs for the prime sponsors. Staff of prime sponsors have the same relationships and assignments to their councils and council members.

With the staff reporting to the chief executive of the jurisdiction, the councils become truly advisory, with executive responsibility for strategic plans clear and undivided. The agencies chosen to deliver specific services are responsible for the tactical or operational planning and can be held accountable for their performance by the planners exercising executive power.

Steps to Planning

The strategic planning assignment in the public sector commences after a legislature, representing in the broadest sense the voice of the people, provides a charter through passage of and appropriation for a bill. Essentially a legislative charter passes through three formative stages:

(1) Substantive committees shape a bill and shepherd it to passage.

(2) Appropriations committees determine the resources to be assigned to the bill and often amend its intent in the process.

(3) In the federal system, departmental regulations and guideline writers frequently bend its intent toward their predilections as they interpret the "intent of Congress."

However, the state or local manpower planner need not be a pawn of national legislators and administrators ... considerable discretion remains in the manner in which regulations are interpreted and applied, in whatever aspects of the program are emphasized, and in the interrelationships among federal, state, and local programs and priorities.

Such discretion is especially apparent in CETA. The predilection of Administration proposals was "no strings attached," and Congress added few restrictions. Title I and II monies can be used for any manpower purpose, so long as Title I preference is given to those most in need of assistance. A locality can establish its own priorities and pursue them without challenge, so long as the procedural requirements of plan formulation are observed.

More freedom is provided when planning is expanded beyond the narrow compass of CETA. For reasons of congressional jurisdiction, the "Comprehensive Act" encompassed only MDTA and the Economic Opportunity Act, and left outside that legislation the Wagner-Peyser Act, the manpower aspects of the Social Security Act such as the Work Incentive Program, unemployment insurance and employment service financing, vocational rehabilitation, adult basic education, manpower undertakings of Model Cities, health manpower, post-secondary vocational education, and other programs, depending upon one's interpretation of manpower boundaries. Each of these programs is in itself relatively restricted. But the jurisdiction which can agree among all of its constituent units to marshal resources in pursuit of a common goal or agenda can relate them in highly innovative ways. The permutations and combinations are almost endless.

The technical assistance guides provided for prime sponsors by the Labor Department are substantial and helpful, but they provide guidance primarily in the planning and administration of CETA. The planning unit that wishes can go far beyond those guides in the marshaling and direction of multiple resources.

Every planner has his or her choice of the order in which planning steps are implemented, but all traverse essentially the same set of steps. If one plans only for direction of a particular program, one begins with the goals of that program and plans for their achievement. If a wider and less specified goal is endorsed, a prior step is necessary. A sequential set of steps is discussed below.

Step 1. Establishing Manpower Policy Goals

Congress declared the purpose of CETA to be "to provide job training and employment opportunities for economically disadvantaged, unemployed, and underemployed persons, and to assure that training and other services lead to maximum employment opportunities and enhance self-sufficiency." The manpower services, target groups, and program objectives are rather clearly prescribed. However, broad scope is left for a state or community to establish its own broader manpower policy goals, subsuming CETA under it. As chapter 1 averred, manpower policy in the broad sense pursues: (1) rewarding working careers for people, and (2) optimum development and efficient use of manpower resources.

At a point in time, economic development or manpower solutions to the energy crisis or career preparation for youth might take higher priority than the remedial and disadvantaged manpower concerns expressed by CETA. Yet CETA could be planned and administered in such a way that it would contribute to those higher priorities.

Social philosophy must play a preeminent role in goal setting. In general, the values placed on self-sufficiency and material standards of living in American society suggest a high priority for efforts to improve the employment status and income of those facing the most serious disadvantages in the competition for jobs. However, application of that priority cannot be determined without an inventory of the major manpower and labor market pathologies that impinge upon the community. They may be poverty, unemployment, labor shortages, or lack of skills; or they may be loss of human resources through drugs, alcoholism, and crime; inadequate preparation of labor force entrants, and so forth.

Having been presented with a list of pressing labor market pathologies, elected officials and those who advise them must choose the goals of manpower policy. The manpower planner can serve best by suggesting alternatives and illustrating their relationships to unclearly expressed public preferences.

Suppose then, for the sake of illustration, that there is a goal statement emanating from broad community consensus to bring the disadvantaged out of poverty and establish self-sufficiency among all of those now with earned incomes below the poverty level. This brings us to the next step.

Step 2. Identifying Barriers

Having chosen a broad community manpower policy goal, manpower staff must then identify the specific barriers which impede its accomplishment: Why does the problem exist? Who and how many are its victims? What is the magnitude of its social costs? Who, if any, has vested interest in continuance of the problem? What is the evidence that the barriers exist? What is known of its nature and magnitude? What data are required to answer these questions? To what extent does the problem exist? What other data systems are required? What has been tried in the past to alleviate the barriers? What worked and what didn't? And, most important of all, to what extent do the barriers appear to be inherent in the shortcomings of the people themselves and to what extent in the shortcomings of social and labor market institutions? Must we change the people or change the institutions, and to what extent?

Step 3. Examining Alternatives

Nothing but frustration and waste can come from considering solutions which cannot work. The manpower staff must probe issues such as: What are the alternative approaches which might be effective in overcoming the barriers and achieving the goals? What are the required social and technical skills for each? What are the relative resource and social costs? What are the tradeoffs between money and time in the solution? What are the foreseeable byproducts and consequences of each approach? What are the likelihoods of unforeseen consequences? What is the political climate? Which solutions can win the necessary political support? What is the range and source of resources available to address the various alternatives? What are the probabilities of marshaling them? In exact dollars and numbers, what will be the budget and the staff available for a specific period of time?

Step 4. Setting Objectives

Goals are by their nature broad and ill-defined. In effect, they paint a picture of how one would like some aspects of the world and society to look. They offer little guidance for an implementable program, nor do they measure the progress toward the goal. Objectives are best thought of as specific milestones on the way to a goal. To be useful they must be desirable, realistic, achievable, and measurable. Why pursue an objective which, once achieved, would make a situation no better or would cause ills worse than those for which a cure is sought? Why pursue an unrealistic goal which cannot be achieved? As a milestone, an objective has no value unless one can measure progress toward it. How far have we come? Are our efforts moving us in the right direction? How far have we yet to go? Are there ways of speeding progress? At what cost?

With elimination of that portion of poverty amenable to labor market solutions as the manpower goal and given the resources available, bringing x families of y characteristics above the poverty line by z date is an example of an appropriate objective. If persons have been identified whose poverty is labor market related, if there are jobs which can become available and services which can provide the access, if the numbers are realistically related to the budgets available, and if the staff is sufficiently knowledgeable for the planning and operation, then the objective is desirable, realistic, achievable, and measurable.

Step 5. Designing and Implementing a Program

Having examined the alternatives and set appropriate objectives, the planner must now design a program and put it into effect. From the vantage point of the strategic planner, this consists of designating a target group, deciding upon an appropriate mix of services to meet these needs, and choosing and assigning one or more agencies or organizations to deliver the prescribed services. To the tactical planner at the agency level, it consists of working out the logistics for facilities, staff, budgeting, administrative controls, and so forth, and for recruitment and service of the clients. To the program administrator, the assignment is to do what the planners have only designed.

Step 6. Monitoring and Evaluation

No plan can foresee all eventualities. Estimates of relative effectiveness and costs of alternative approaches are, at best, judgments based on experience in never identical circumstances, and often in simple best guesses. Administrators and staff are never of the desired competence; nor do they work often (or for very long) at peak efficiency. Performers are rarely the most objective judges of their own performance. Continuous monitoring is necessary to identify weaknesses and strengths. Only evaluation can assess results and compare achievements of alternatives. The question for evaluation is not merely, "How well was it done?" but also

"At what cost?" Monitoring without evaluation has no measure of achievement. Evaluation without monitoring may know *what* but not *why*.

Monitoring and evaluation are needed at several levels in a manpower program. Program administrators monitor and evaluate their own performances for immediate reform. Strategic planners monitor and evaluate whether they have chosen the right mix of services and the most effective delivery of services. The funding sources monitor and evaluate whether effective use is made of public funds.

Step 7. Feedback and Modification

Manpower programming is not a one-time thing. Labor market pathologies and individual barriers are too large in magnitude to conceivably be conquered. Individuals can be aided in overcoming the labor market barriers confronting them. There will be sufficient numbers who are unserved and unservable, and new entrants and others will take the place of the successful. Total numbers needing services may even be reduced at times, though economic and social conditions outside their influence or those of the manpower fraternity are major determinants of the number. The problems will not go away.

Monitoring and evaluation make their contribution by "feeding back" information on relative success and failure and suggesting modifications which may make programs more effective or replace them with alternatives. The manpower task is continuous, though changing, and so must be the manpower services system.

Good Practice in Manpower Planning

The manpower planner is ultimately faced with making decisions about which alternatives to present to policy makers. Manpower plans are logical packages of financial, administrative, allocative, and policy decisions. They aim at solving problems directly, indirectly, immediately, and over longer periods of time. Prior to constructing the planning package, the planner should: (a) understand the nature of the problem to be addressed, (b) know how much leeway exists in allocating resources, (c) ascertain the real alternatives available, and (d) have a reasonable grasp of the probable impact of various choices on the problems being attacked. Data and data manipulation are tools that assist the planner in achieving this knowledge.

Planners should take extreme care not to use more complicated techniques than are required or justified to solve the planning problem. The same caution holds for data; never use more data or more sophisticated manipulation techniques than are required for the information desired. Both limitations require judgment on the part of the planner. Many planners have the tendency to try to purify their information — to make everything 100 percent correct — and to attempt to plug all the slots in the rows and columns of their planning data tables. This attitude not only wastes precious time and resources but usually results in poor plans, since planners who approach their work in this manner have not grasped certain fundamentals about economic decision making. If the gains are not greater than the costs, and other courses could have been taken where the reverse was true, then incorrect decisions have been made.

If planners spend their time using complex planning techniques, detailed data, and complicated data manipulation processes, and obtain no better plans or no increase in "output" (e.g., more people employed) than would have been the case had they used simple techniques and data, they have wasted planning resources. Moreover, they have probably designed plans more complicated than necessary and thus created the danger of achieving fewer desired objectives than would be otherwise possible. With these cautions in mind, planners should work their way through the steps below. This discussion will concentrate upon the quantitative aspects of the process.

At the outset, the planner will want to gain a firm, but not too detailed picture of the relevant supply and demand factors and the elements affecting them. Keeping in mind that manpower programs deal with employment and unemployment problems, planners will want to know the total amount of employment, particularly in the general categories in which there is unemployment. This means that, for example, the planner will not bother gathering data on such occupations, but will want to know whether employment has been rising, declining, or remaining relatively constant over recent years; whether there are seasonal elements to unemployment; whether there are large and peculiar charac-

teristics to employment (e.g., one or two employers dominating
the relevant part of employment); whether there are any obvious
large changes on the horizon, such as firms planning to leave the
area, federal contracts about to be granted, important construction
or development programs likely to bring an expansion of the labor
force and so on; and whether unemployment appears to be concentrated among a particular segment of the population or spread
among many groups. These are all demand characteristics and
should be approached at this stage from a nondetailed point of view.

On the supply side, planners will want to know the extent of
unemployment and underemployment, recent trends in these
quantities, easily identifiable sources of their expansion during the
coming year (the planning period) and in the next several years.
A glance at particularly significant characteristics of both the employed and unemployed (special skills, extreme closeness or distance
from existing jobs, age, sex, or minority domination) will be important. In addition, the extent of union organization and the relation
of unions to workers and employers may provide some initial
insights.

For these initial pictures of the supply and demand factors,
the planner can obtain information from the local employment
service (information *normally* distributed from a local office); from
the Labor Department's Bureau of Labor Statistics *Employment
and Earnings* (published monthly); from the Commerce Department's publications *County Business Patterns*; from discussions with
bank officials, members of chambers of commerce, large employers,
union officials, city planners in related areas of housing, transportation, and economic development; and from members of prospective client groups.

Next, planners should know how much they can actually do
with the total resources available. It makes no sense to plan for the
utilization of resources that are already locked into ongoing programs or committed to not-yet-started projects, when there is no
possibility of altering these. These commitments should be put into
the plan as "givens" or starting points, or as constraints; and the
planners should understand how such factors will affect the alternatives over which they do have control. At some early point in the
planning process, planners should clearly understand just how
much flexibility they have in designing the plan. They should

concentrate their subsequent effort on planning for the use of those resources for which decisions have not already been made.

Knowing the resource constraints, each planner should now return to supply and demand analysis to gain a detailed understanding of relevant specifics. The degrees of freedom now understood will partially dictate what kinds of resources are available for attacking problems, and the planner will spend time finding out details about those areas which can realistically be altered or examined. For some cities this will constitute many problems, but for others, only a few. At this point planners should determine the minimum commitment necessary to design a planning package. That is, they want to understand the problem(s) to the extent required to work out effective paths to their solution. To accomplish this, they must return to the information gathered in the first round and focus on the disaggregation (a breakdown into more detailed sections in order to better understand their specifics) of the more relevant variables identified in the first "look." The peculiar characteristics of the area's problems will determine which details should be sought.

If demand exists, or is expected in the near future, for skills not present among the unemployed, planners will want to know which skills are required, who requires them, whether they are rigid requirements, or if there is some job description that might be altered without changing what the employer really requires. They will want to know what period demand is expected to increase and by how much; what the skills level of the unemployed is compared to that demanded; if there are any barriers to acquiring new skills; what the existing sources of obtaining required skills are; if there is any tradeoff between classroom and on-the-job training; and if the unemployed are willing to acquire new skills. In this case the planner seeks knowledge that will help in understanding why unemployment exists and whether there seems to be any reasonable prospect of reducing it by changing the supply characteristics. It is probable that this direction will *not* significantly reduce the problem and that at least for the immediate (several years) future, the problem has to be attacked from the demand side by linking manpower programs to other city and state plans and encouraging decisions to maximize additional employment possibilities.

In another instance, a planner might face a highly complex supply and demand situation. There might be widespread and rising unemployment cutting across many groups — minorities, various occupations, women, or migrants. Demand might be changing in character — large federal employment disappearing but new firms entering and others expanding. Inflated wage rates could be causing automation in many firms. Local bureaucracies could be antagonistic to employment programs. Some of these elements reduce the degrees of freedom available to the planner, and it should be recognized from the outset that to design plans requiring cooperation that would not be forthcoming and institutional changes that simply would not occur is futile. Thus the planner does the best possible job and concentrates efforts on those areas where a reasonable chance of making progress exists. These will be the areas of detailed diagnosis — even if not those areas encompassing most significant employment problems. In general, the more complex the situation facing the planner (situation in the sense of those areas where it is worthwhile to plan), the more complex planning models he or she will have to use and the more sophisticated will be the data requirements.

In all cases where it is possible to use published or already collected data, they should be used, even if there are deficiencies. Data should not be used if they are unreliable (knowledgeable sources should be consulted), and no amount of sophisticated data manipulation can make good data from bad. When data do not quite meet the needs of planners, they could contact other possible sources and make small changes to get what they need. Planners should attempt to get the original sources to make the changes (this is usually possible only at the local level). Much published material is also often available. Many published works involve the collection of data not used in final publication, and many studies are never published. Local chambers of commerce, colleges and universities, consulting and marketing firms, and large industries and service industries (insurance, banking, and the like) have such studies. This is particularly true for more aggregate information such as the output, employment, and investment trends and prospects for an area. It is a universal problem that people often ignore or are uninformed of work relevant to their own, and unnecessary duplication takes up a massive amount of scarce human resources. Various people and groups who are involved in the overall manpower planning process may be more than willing to become involved by securing information required by the planner. Plan-

ners should gather and maintain all relevant information sources —
through subscriptions, or through local library collections as a
service to the community in this field — and keep themselves and
their staffs up to date.

Planners will sometimes find that existing information is
simply not sufficient for what is required, even taking the limited
view that only minimum information will be sought. Data creation
then becomes necessary, but the planner should do what is necessary. If existing data can be extrapolated (e.g., by taking a simple
average of several past observations and using this for the present),
and one is reasonably sure that the figure obtained is 80 to 90 percent correct, then this should be used. If a "proxy" variable can
be used with confidence, it should be used. For example, one may
want to know the expected rate of increase in employment in
a particular manufacturing industry over the next year but cannot
obtain the figure. However, a good estimate of the expected rate
of increase in *total* manufacturing employment for the area may be
available, and the particular industry being examined may be
a significant proportion of that total. The rate for the total can
then be used as a proxy for the particular. On the other hand, the
planner may want to know what proportion of the unemployed
and underemployment in the area is black. A figure may be available for the black population and the planner may be tempted to
use that proportion as an unemployment proxy. This would not
necessarily be correct, since it may be that the rate of unemployment for the black population exceeds its total share of the
population.

Surveys are a way of obtaining some kinds of data, but they
should be simple. Information could be obtained by telephone
from several employers representing most of the demand. If a more
formal survey is to be conducted, the questionnaire should be
designed carefully and then tested on persons not involved to see
that it is understandable, that it can be carried out by those conducting the survey, that it produces the precise knowledge desired
(i.e., vague questions which create difficulty in interpretation of the
answers should be avoided), and that it seeks information which
actually exists in standardized form. In this case, it is worthwhile
to think ahead several years and anticipate some planning problems and directions so that information can be gathered in the
same survey. It is usually true that the quality of the information

received decreases as the number of surveys increases. Professional assistance will aid in selecting samples when the survey is not total in coverage.

A large number of questions and many respondents will probably require a computer to sort out answers. This should be arranged for before the questionnaire is formulated. Computer personnel can help arrange questions for conversion into computerized symbols, can assist in formulating questions that will provide the information desired, and can point out "bonus" information possibilities from the computer not obvious from the survey questions. Computers may also be useful in sorting already available data. Planners should gather what is available, get a rough idea of what they want to know, and consult a computer-knowledgeable person about what might be secured by feeding data into a computer, keeping in mind that results must be worth the effort.

Finally, planners should always look toward the future. Some problems are too complicated to be fully analyzed or effectively attacked in the planning period in which they are currently observed. Other problems may be on the horizon and should be contemplated beforehand so that action can be prepared. Therefore the planner should, insofar as possible, inject a perspective into the plan longer than the typical one-year planning cycle and begin thinking in two- and three-year terms, even though the planning budget period remains an annual one. In other words, the planner should plan for two to three years and implement for year one. This makes additional sense when the length of most skills training programs is considered. Next year, the planner should revise the second and third years of his three-year plan, add a fourth year, and implement year two. Thus planning becomes a process of looking ahead with continuous revision.

The Specifics of Planning

With this planning process as the broad framework for action, remaining chapters get down to the nuts and bolts of labor market manpower planning: How are those in need of manpower services to be identified and their needs determined? How can the local labor market planner find and influence accessible jobs? What is the process of skills development, and how can it be influenced? What is the full range of available manpower services, and how

labor force despite the need for a job is a starting point for defining need. But the raw numbers have little to say about the reasons for or nature of the need. For example, not all the unemployed are equally in need; some clearly have skills and resources such that their stay in the ranks of the unemployed will probably be very short and painless. Others will suffer a great deal and remain unemployed for substantial periods. Both groups are not equally in need of manpower services, nor do they need the same services.

Even if there was available an adequate typology for determining the severity of the experience of individuals caught in labor market dysfunctions, the necessity would remain of categorizing them by personal characteristics which influence their service needs and priorities. Are they men or women; old or young; rich or poor; black, brown, or white; heads of households or single individuals; married, divorced, or single; blue collar or white collar; manufacturing or service workers? How many are single, white, poor, young, unemployed men? The problems involved in making more precise estimates of the demographic characteristics are substantial.

Beyond knowing what has happened to a somewhat precisely defined population subgroup, the planner must still determine the factors which account for the particular subgroup's labor market experience. Are they skilled or unskilled, and in what areas? What levels of education characterize the group? What role does discrimination play? How many have transportation-related problems, medical problems, physical or mental handicaps? Are there enough jobs even if they have the right skills and other handicaps were eliminated?

Even tentative answers to these questions do not come easily. The data sources are fragmented and the available methodologies not particularly elegant. These problems are further compounded by the time frame in which manpower planners need to work. Estimates of need must be made for a future period. Need in that future planned-for period will be affected by the economy at that point in time, by basic demographic trends and shifts such as migration and population bulges, and by what manpower programs are doing in the current period.

The manpower planner is faced with a complex and difficult task in the estimation of the need for manpower services. Yet the task cannot be avoided. A competent analysis must assess the need for services in terms that facilitate decisions as to who should be served and what services should be provided. The remainder of this chapter tries to describe some of the concepts and methods that will help state and local manpower planners with this task.*

Universe of Need Methodology

The most widely used technique for estimating the demand for manpower services is the Department of Labor's universe of need (UON) method. State employment services prepare annual UON estimates which establish parameters of service need for states and substate employment service administrative areas against which the annual "plans of service" are developed. The UON takes a target group approach that is conceptually consistent with the historical development and operation of manpower programs. Although the UON approach has both negative and positive attributes, it deserves thorough examination as the only systematic approach to the estimation of manpower services need used on a wide scale in the United States.

The Approach

The basic intent of the UON approach is to make an unduplicated estimate of the total number of individuals who could benefit from manpower services sometime during a given year. The UON classifies persons in need on three basic dimensions: labor force status, income, and "disadvantagement." Labor force status is indicated in estimates of the unemployed and the underutilized. The underutilized estimate is subdivided into three additional categories: (1) those employed part time for economic reasons, (2) those employed full time, but with family income at or below poverty level, and (3) those not in the labor force but who "should be." The poverty classifications used in the UON estimates are: (1) the poor, (2) the near-poor, and (3) the nonpoor. The poverty classifications are based on the Social Security Administration's poverty index. The disadvantaged are defined as members of poor households who lack adequate employment and who additionally

---

*This chapter will not replow ground already adequately treated in the Labor Department's *Handbook for Manpower Planners*. Complete publishing information will be found in the references at the end of this chapter.

with actual measurement. Information is costly and while it is probable that states and localities will increasingly commission local surveys and mid-decennial census, the estimator's art will generally continue to come at a price more acceptable than that of the census taker. The fact that the planner deals with the future also limits the usefulness of measurement. By definition, the future is estimated and not measured. Consequently, the state and local manpower planner should carefully study the UON methodology. It provides a reasonably current and defensible gross estimate of needs, and with more attention to calibration of the methodology to provide more demographic detail and operationally meaningful qualitative descriptors, the basic UON approach could be a useful tool for state and local manpower planning.

Transitional Techniques

In preparation for transition to CETA, Manpower Administration guidelines suggested analyses beyond the simple use of the employment service-produced UON tables. The revised approach suggested that the planning area population be classified by race, sex, age, labor force status, educational attainment, income levels, and several specific target group indicators. The objective of this approach was to develop estimates which were more useful in designing an appropriate mix of services than was the UON methodology. Data for the suggested analysis were provided for each planning area in the form of *Summary Manpower Indicator* and *Detailed Manpower Indicator** packages. These packages are produced by means of a computer program designed to process the 1970 census tapes. Instructions for using the indicator packages were incorporated in volumes I and II of *Handbook for Manpower Planners* prepared by the Census Bureau for the Labor Department. Both the handbook and the packages were first available to planners during the fiscal year 1973 planning cycle. While these materials have many limitations, they have helped to standardize the data base available to state and local manpower planners. Further work under way at the Census Bureau is being directed toward methods for updating census materials and developing additional data on the assessment of the need for manpower services.

---

*Also prepared by Lawrence Berkeley Laboratory. See references.

Despite the greater availability of census data in more usable form and the recent updating of the employment service UON methodology, little real impact has yet been made on the actual operation of manpower programs. The present manpower planning process still largely ignores decisions about whom to enroll and why. Age, race, and income guidelines are used to screen in and screen out applicants who, within those broad categories of eligibility, are enrolled basically on a first come, first served basis. The result has been a nightmare for operational planners and has hindered rational and efficient job development. Program operators are faced with the problem of meeting an almost endless variety of enrollee interests, aptitudes, and needs. Rational planning is most difficult under these circumstances.

Planning tools, which group prospective clients by the specific types and degrees of service needs they have in common, are needed. The incidence of barriers to employment for these homogenous groups must be identified and the barriers related to specific employment requirements. The planner should identify which barriers are amenable to modification by what services. Resources can then be allocated to services in proportion to the incidence of the relevant barriers in the group to be served. These tasks require an overall construct which relates the population to the labor market and overcomes the use of static measures in what is actually a very dynamic environment. The stocks and flows model is such a construct.

Stocks and Flows Model

The state or local manpower planner should begin the analysis of the need for manpower services with an understanding of the dynamics of how population and labor market changes interact. A stocks and flows model is a basic conceptual tool for analyzing populations for manpower planning purposes and offers a sound analytical framework for data collection and analysis.

A stocks and flows model is an abstraction of reality that attempts to organize observations and simplify highly complex systems thus to facilitate analysis and suggest causes and effects of systemic malfunction. Human systems are characterized by a variety of states and transitions. A stock is simply an identifiable condition at the beginning or end of a time period. A flow is simply

of participants who are unemployed. The changes in each stock are a function of the flows in and out of the stock. Equilibrium in the stock over time requires that the gross flows out be balanced by the gross flows into the stock. Because most of the stocks have multiple inputs and outputs, change or equilibrium of the size and characteristics of persons in a particular stock from one period to another can be caused by several different combinations of inflows and outflows. For example, let's assume that the stock of employed persons at the beginning of period 1 was 200,000, with 250,000 at the beginning of period 2. If we limit our examination to the time series, we know that employment increased and little more.

Employment changes in response to demand changes in the product sector. However, the resultant size of the stock of employed persons can come about from a wide range of different combinations of flows in and out. In Figure 5.2 we can see that flows in and out of the employed stock are as follows:

(1) Flows into employed stock (origins):

    (a) New potential workers

    (b) Unemployed

    (c) Of working age but not in labor force

(2) Flows out of employed stock (destinations):

    (a) Death and outmigration

    (b) Unemployed

    (c) Of working age but not in labor force

The increase in the employed stock from period 1 to period 2 could have been caused by any of a very large number of combinations of changes in the flows. For example, the total flows in could have remained stable while the total flows out decreased; total flows out could have remained stable while total flows in increased; total flows out could have increased while total flows in increased at a faster rate. Similarly, the analyst could postulate a number of other component flow changes that could result in the increased employed stock. It is also easy to see that the effect of different combinations of flows resulting in similar stock *sizes* can have substantially different implications in terms of the size and characteristics of the populations potentially in need of manpower services.

While a great deal of developmental work must be completed before stocks and flows models can be widely applied to local manpower planning environments with any degree of precision, it is certain that the potential these models offer for analytical synthesis and prescription will generate considerable interest among manpower planners.

Starting Points for the Description of Stocks and Flows

There are very little hard data on flows between major stocks available in most local labor market areas. Symptomatic and partial data (such as unemployment insurance operating data and turnover statistics) are available, but their relationship to actual total flows remains largely unknown. In contrast, a great deal of data on the size and composition of key stocks are collected on a regular and uniform basis. In addition, competent population studies employing the cohort survival method are increasingly available in most large urban labor areas. Consequently, the description of stocks is the most reasonable starting point for the local manpower planner.

A first step toward developing detailed analyses of the composition of key stocks is to disaggregate the existing employment service UON estimates. The disaggregation can provide useful breakouts with minimal effort, and the derived figures can sometimes be used as control totals for later analytical use. Disaggregation of the UON requires access to the "Worksheet for Estimating the Universe of Need for Manpower Services in a State or Labor Area," developed by the employment service staff in making the UON estimates for the planning area. (These worksheets are not normally provided to manpower planners with the UON.) The worksheets provide a step-by-step guide and permit further analysis of the UON, as well as a disaggregation of its major elements. In categories for which no data are available, a residual figure can often be derived by subtracting other known or estimated subelements from the parent population.

While the UON worksheets provide a good base for a more detailed analysis of the need for manpower services, a certain amount of care is required. For example, the UON methodology is designed to produce an estimate of the total number of different

then develop more precise information on the groups where specified characteristics suggest priority treatment. Estimates would
be developed on other groups as time becomes available. For
example, the planner's first breakout might show that in the base
period, only 5 percent of the unemployed were nonpoor, and were
25 to 44 years of age. Seeing this, the planner might choose to
develop the detailed estimates on other groups before returning
to this group.

Estimating Individual Data Cells

When the manpower planner has defined the structure of the
cross-tabulations desired, he or she must then focus attention on
attaching reasonable estimates to each data cell. One basic technique employed in this work involves using known proportions to
allocate control totals to relevant estimate components. Care must
also be taken to keep cross-tabulations within the parameters of
known data. For example, where education levels are known for
a population by age but not by sex, the planner might choose to
allocate education levels by sex, based on the relative sizes of the
male and female cells, but within known age group levels. Both of
these principles can be simply illustrated. Estimating the unknown
data from the known proportions is a standard technique used in
UON analysis. For example, suppose that the planner has made an
estimate that there will be two thousand poor, unemployed, white
males, aged 45 to 64, in the local labor market during 1974. To
program for this group, the planner might need an estimate of how
many of the two thousand had attained specific levels of education, measured by years of school completed. From census figures
the planner knows what the educational levels of the group were in
1970. He or she could then develop a reasonable approximation
of the educational attainment of the expected 1974 population of
unemployed, poor, white males, aged 45 to 64, by applying the
1970 census proportions. Table 5-1 illustrates this process.

Information Sources for Barriers Data

Systematic analysis of characteristic work experience and
employment barriers data is essential to serious UON analyses in the
local labor market. Sources of quantitative data on the work experi-

ence of specific groups are not uniform or systematically collected. Consequently, the state or local manpower planner must be flexible and inventive in his or her collection, manipulation, and use of barriers data. The most difficult problem for the local manpower planner in this regard is the identification of barriers data suitably cross-classified for relevant subpopulations. For example, considerable work experience data are available by age, sex, and race. However, very few sources provide barriers data by age, sex, race, and education level. Data with *potential* for barriers analysis are not uncommon in most state and local planning areas, and the manpower planner should begin to assess this material. The listing below gives some suggested data sources:

(1) Detailed census tabulations

(2) Manpower program and employment service applicant files

(3) Individual counseling records

(4) Individual employability plans

(5) Interview schedules from previous local household surveys

The design of manpower service delivery systems appropriate to the needs of the local population requires a sound assessment of the employability barriers of the population to be served. The ability to estimate the incidence of significant barriers in specific subpopulations is an important manpower planning competence. The remainder of this chapter examines the potential for using client assessment data in the estimation of employability barriers.

Table 5-1
Estimated Education Attainment of Unemployed,
Poor, White Males, 45 to 64 Years of Age
(1970 and 1974)

Years of School Completed	1970		1974 (est.)
	Number	Percentage	
Less than eight	600	40%	800
Eight to twelve	750	50	1,000
More than twelve	150	10	200
TOTAL	1,500	100	2,000

Integrating Program Assessment Data into the
Analysis of the Universe of Need

Estimating the numbers of disadvantaged, unemployed, underemployed, or poor in various demographic classifications is only the first step in estimating the UON for manpower services for a local planning area. Before delivery of services can be planned and budgeted, one must estimate the relative probability of the existence of specific handicaps or barriers to stable and satisfactory employment within such groups. For example, from a group of unemployed, Spanish-surnamed males over 45 years of age, with less than an eighth grade education, how many are likely to lack English language skills? How many will have had limited job experience? What levels of work skills will have been developed within the group? How many will have serious health problems?

Little is known currently about the relative incidence of barriers to stable employability within population subgroups. However, data are available on particular barriers for those individuals who have been served by manpower programs. The individual assessment of manpower clients requires accurate information about the aptitudes, skills, attitudes, personality traits, and life work histories of manpower enrollees. This information is collected through a variety of means, including paper and pencil tests, interviews, work samples, biographical data forms, and observation. The potential exists for the use of such individual assessment data in making estimations of handicaps or barriers within entire population subgroups, but substantial effort is still required to develop usable techniques.

The most serious problem encountered in the projection of such data is the fact that traditional methods of assessment are quite inappropriate for use with the seriously disadvantaged. Newer, specially designed methods are coming into use, but they have yet to be adequately tested for validity. Some methods of assessment have been designed for specific local purposes, such as the assignment of individuals to training programs geared to specific labor market opportunities, but their data may lack flexibility for more general estimating purposes. The state-of-the-art in assessment tools for use with disadvantaged persons in manpower programs suffers from a condition of fragmentation. Nevertheless, some form of individualized assessment of service needs is inescapable, whether done by a formalized system or casual judgment. To identify or develop an orderly and consistent system for making such assessments, the planner must be aware of the various methods under use or experimentation, the rationale behind their usages, and their limitations and problems relative to manpower planning purposes.

Existing Assessment Tools

The General Aptitudes Test Battery (GATB) of the U.S. Employment Service is the oldest of the widely used individual assessment tools. It has been in operational use since 1947 and is one of the best validated and most carefully researched psychometric tests in existence. Particularly important is its close integration with the *Dictionary of Occupational Titles*, which is the most comprehensive taxonomy of the American job market available. The GATB is also the most widely used manpower counseling instrument. It measures aptitudes in nine areas — general learning ability, verbal aptitude, numerical ability, spatial perception, form perception, clerical aptitude, motor coordination, manual dexterity, finger dexterity — through use of eight paper and pencil measures and four measures involving apparatus.

The GATB was designed for testing individuals of sixth grade educational level or better. It does not have great utility for a more disadvantaged population. Disadvantaged individuals may have severely limited reading and arithmetic abilities. They may also have little experience with "classroom testing" situations and may associate test taking with failure. These factors may cause their GATB scores to suffer, yet these handicaps to test performance may or may *not* be factors that would affect their job performance. Also, many of the occupations used in the GATB may have little meaning or applicability to disadvantaged test takers.

The GATB along with other standard paper and pencil tests, including the strong vocational interest bank, the Minnesota Vocational Interest Inventory, and personality tests such as the Edward Personal Preference Schedule, have been criticized as manpower assessment tools because they reflect middle-class attitudes and life experience which may be quite foreign to the disadvantaged. In fact, the great majority of traditional aptitude, interest, and personality instruments seems to share certain characteristics that limit their utility with seriously disadvantaged populations. Even where such tests may be valid, they do not alone provide the planner with enough information about the individuals to project barriers to stable employment beyond those involving lack of skills, aptitudes, or general interest in various occupational areas.

The Nonreading Aptitude Test Battery (NATB) was designed to overcome some of the problems encountered by the use of the GATB for assessment of the disadvantaged. It is available presently in operational form and, subject to the results of validity testing in process, may become a valuable alternative to the GATB. A translated version of the NATB is being devised for chicanos with limited reading skills in English or Spanish. At present NATB scores are interpreted in relation to GATB normative data by the use of conversion tables. However, the precise relationship of test variables between these two test batteries remains unknown, as does how closely NATB scores reflect actual aptitude for the type of jobs for which disadvantaged manpower clients are usually trained. Unlike many of the adaptations of standard tests for those with little reading skills, the NATB is designed for adult use and not adapted from children's material often considered foolish and insulting by disadvantaged adults.

The "work sample" approach to assessment of job-relevant characteristics of disadvantaged individuals has attracted attention in recent years, though the technique has been in use for assessing the physically handicapped for more than forty years. Work samples represent activities or components of activities abstracted from job tasks; consequently, they are nearer the reality of work than paper and pencil tests designed to measure the same ability. Work samples are usually designed to include entire sets of standardized tasks corresponding to real job activities, and they may be used to predict trainability for particular types of jobs. Occupational areas are selected, particular jobs analyzed to identify their functional components, and work sample tasks devised that will represent some or all of these activities.

The Institute for the Crippled and Disabled published the "Tower System" in 1959. It is now one of the best known systems, consisting of 110 work samples in fourteen broad occupational groups: clerical, drafting, drawing, electronics assembly, jewelry manufacturing, leather goods, lettering, machine shop, mail clerk, optical mechanics, pantograph engraving, sewing machine operation, welding, and workshop assembly (Comray *et al.*, 1973, p. 55).

Job performance factors such as speed, accuracy, mechanical aptitude, and personality variables are assessed. In addition to estimates of the present skills-learning potential and training needs of clients, information about attitudes, interpersonal relationships, attendance and punctuality, frustration tolerance, and personal grooming and hygiene is collected. Thus the tower system provides valuable data beyond job aptitudes and skills that can be used to infer a profile of personality characteristics which may have positive value for determining barriers to stable employability.

There are, however, drawbacks to the use of the tower system for assessment of disadvantaged manpower clients. Both client and rehabilitation workers have been enthusiastic about the value of the work sample experience and the data it gathers. However, the method was designed to test the ability of the physically handicapped to perform various tasks. Applicability to the disadvantaged and to the nonphysical aspects of employment has not been clearly demonstrated. In fact, one major study of the tower system's practical utility indicates that tower scores in general were not as successful in predicting *vocational* successes as were ratings of clients by training instructors. There is also the difficulty of implementing the system in varying facilities and the expense involved in running each client through a five- to seven-week assessment process.

In 1963 the Jewish Employment and Vocational Service of Philadelphia created the first work sample evaluation battery specifically designed for use in assessing manpower service needs of disadvantaged persons. Its work sample consists of 28 basic assessment samples of varying levels of complexity. The sample represents ten worker trait group arrangements of occupational categories listed in the *Dictionary of Occupational Titles*. Approximately a third of the range of job activities listed in the dictionary are included. The evaluator observes and appraises the clients' performance throughout the work samples and records data on the work sample sheets and the daily behavior impressions form. The concluding work sample evaluation report describes the clients' skills levels, work habits, personal grooming, and interpersonal relationships in work environments. The information is to be used by the clients' counselors as an input for vocational decision making, but could also be valuable data for the development of profies on handicaps to stable employability within various population groups.

Tests with control groups seem to indicate significantly more placement of longer duration and fewer referrals to job openings per successful placement among clients participating in the Jewish Employment and Vocational Service work sample. Some reasons that have been suggested for its apparent value are:

(1) The work sample is much more related to actual job skills than pencil and paper tests, particularly for clients with limited reading ability.

(2) The work sample tasks do not generate as much fear and anxiety in disadvantaged clients as pencil and paper tests, and provide greater motivation to perform by providing a simulation of actual work experience.

(3) The work sample approach is more comprehensive than traditional tests and integrates a range of activities related to actual job performance.

As early as 1972, 35 manpower centers had adopted the Philadelphia program. It offers training and consultation to local manpower agencies interested in constituting work sample evaluation centers. Technical assistance is given to counselors making training decisions, and follow-up assistance is available to center staff in modification of techniques to fit local labor market requirements. The Philadelphia approach holds much promise as an assessment tool but is not yet in wide use. Here again, costs and special facilities required are a drawback in many localities, and the approach is primarily effective in assessing the capability of the handicapped to perform physical tasks.

Singer/Graflex, a commercial manufacturer of training and instructional materials, has developed a vocational evaluation system which makes creative use of audio-visual technology. This system uses an audio-visual machine with sound-tape cassettes and filmstrips to present programmed instruction for ten work samples in the following areas: basic tools, bench assembly, drafting, electrical wiring, plumbing and pipefitting, carpentry and woodworking, refrigeration, soldering and welding, office and sales clerk skills, and needle and sales skills. Task areas are coded to the

Dictionary of Occupational Titles. A standard package includes performance instructions and occupational information regarding jobs within the occupational cluster, using pictures of on-the-job situations. Those taking the exams can pace themselves. The work sample evaluations assess only their performance. Normative data on the Singer/Graflex system are presently being collected; little evidence of validity currently exists. On the positive side, the technique is not costly and appears to be extremely flexible to local needs.

The Biographical Information Blank offers another method for assessing disadvantaged manpower clients. It uses life history data to predict work adjustment. It includes many typical biographical questions as well as items concerning attitudes and value judgments. Nine major areas are covered: home and family, high school, work and military experience, present responsibilities, work and income needs, adaptation to environment, life goals, self-image, and organization of time. Much of the data may be verified objectively. It is also felt that since there are no right or wrong answers in any traditional sense, clients with negative experience may feel less threatened by this than by other "tests." The Biographical Information Blank can be scored by clerical personnel using scoring keys. Separate scoring systems have been adapted for males and females from particular ethnic groups.

This testing system (developed by Richardson, Bellow, Henry & Co., Inc., in 1970) has been used for predicting length of participation in the Job Corps and for predicting job tenure among employment service applicants. It is designed for clients with fourth to sixth grade reading ability. Preliminary test results on the predictive validity of the system are positive. However, predicting the success of a particular client in a manpower activity already chosen is quite different from identifying those available manpower services most likely to meet planning needs in predicting the incidence of certain types of barriers to employability in particular population subgroups. The Biographical Information Blank has great promise, for it seeks to identify from actual experience psychological and social, as well as physical and mental, barriers to employment. However, much remains to be done before it can become a really useful tool for predicting the needs of client subpopulations for specific manpower services.

Additional Steps in Assessment

Many other methods are used for adapting aptitude, attitude, and personality tests for use with disadvantaged manpower clients. A simplified vocabulary, extensive use of pictures, and decentering techniques are common adaptations. The major problem facing the planner who wishes to use assessment data for estimating the incidence of barriers in population subgroups is the lack of any consistent or cohesive approach to assessment of individual manpower clients.

Again, the state-of-the-art in assessment tools for use with disadvantaged persons in manpower programs suffers from a condition of fragmentation. Part of the reason of course is that different assessment tools have been developed with different uses in mind. Some are used only for counseling purposes; others are for placing clients into training programs. Some are used for predicting program or job success. Many attempt to serve all of these purposes. None has been designed specifically to assist the planner in estimating the incidence of barriers. Some are obviously better suited than others to this purpose. However, even among the most promising new assessment methods, large-scale validations have thus far been scarce. Assessment tools must be validated under varying circumstances in various types of labor markets with different subgroups of the disadvantaged if they are to be useful in the planning and administration of decentralized manpower programs. At present, the state-of-the-art permits few well-supported generalizations based upon assessment data. As promising assessment tools are administered to larger groups of manpower clients, a data base for improved projection should emerge.

Tools developed for nationwide use must also be *sufficiently flexible* to meet the needs and conditions of local areas. If sponsoring agencies could set appropriate guidelines, flexible multi-use techniques would be more likely to emerge. One suggestion is to "require" those administering newly funded research and development projects to include in their proposals plans for the dissemination and cross-validation of findings so that new assessment techniques can filter down to users in manpower agencies more quickly. New instruments must be created with provision for flexibility so that they can be used by local program planners.

Another suggestion is an increased liaison between the Labor Department and the Social and Rehabilitation Service of HEW to ensure more systematic dissemination of the results of vocational rehabilitation research to manpower researchers and practitioners. Many valuable methods have been developed in the assessment of the physically and mentally handicapped. These methods have relevance to some degree for culturally or economically handicapped persons in that the key concept of low employment probability provides much common ground. In addition, the Social and Rehabilitation Service is now directing more attention to the disadvantaged. As the funding and monitoring agent for CETA, the Labor Department has the responsibility to perform a leadership role in coordinating ongoing research and getting newly validated methods into practice. Finally, the manpower planner and practitioner can only use whatever is available to make reasonable judgments about the employment barriers confronted and the services most likely to be effective in meeting the UON.

References

Comray, Andrew; *et al. Methods of Assessing the Disadvantaged in Manpower Programs: A Review and Analysis.* In *Research and Development Findings.* No. 14. Washington, D.C.: U.S. Department of Labor, Manpower Administration. 1973.

Institute for the Crippled and Disabled. *Tower: Testing, Orientation and Work Evaluation in Rehabilitation.* New York: Institute for the Crippled and Disabled. 1959.

U.S. Department of Commerce, Bureau of the Census. *Current Population Reports.* Series P-20, -23, -25, and -60. Washington, D.C.: U.S. Government Printing Office. Various years.

U.S. Department of Labor, Manpower Administration. *Detailed Manpower Indicators for . . . .* Berkeley, California: Lawrence Berkeley Laboratory. 1973.

_____. *Dictionary of Occupational Titles.* Third edition. Washington, D.C.: U.S. Government Printing Office. 1965.

_____. *Handbook for Manpower Planners.* Volumes I and II. Washington, D.C.: Manpower Administration. 1973 and 1974.

_____. *Summary Manpower Indicators for . . . .* Berkeley, California: Lawrence Berkeley Laboratory. 1973.

6
Framework of Analysis:
II. Accessible Jobs Account

The goal of manpower programs on behalf of disadvantaged persons is clear and uncomplicated, though its achievement is difficult: Improve the employment stability and earnings of each enrollee. Preparing workers who are out of the labor force for participation in the labor force, placing and retaining the unemployed in jobs, and upgrading the opportunities of those working in unsatisfactory jobs are objectives leading to that goal. Thus the manpower planner assigned to develop programs to achieve these objectives for individuals and groups must know how to identify, measure, project, analyze, and gain access to jobs which are on an occupational and skill level attainable by manpower clientele.

To do so, planners must understand the demand for labor by industry, by occupation, and by location, and also the dynamics of the labor market in which both industries and occupations either grow or decline. In addition, planners must be able to relate the dynamics of the labor market to the economic outlook for the labor market, the region, and the nation. They must know and understand the meaning and limitations of all the data sources concerning present and future job opportunities and be familiar with the requirements and routes to access. A primary responsibility of the manpower planner is to translate an economic outlook into manpower terms and then apply these terms to a local labor market setting.

139

Understanding the National, State, or Local Economy

It is a truism already stated in this book, but with implications not always recognized by the manpower planner, that the demand for labor is a derived demand. It is vitally important that the manpower planner grasp the significance of this concept and its force. Derived demand not only controls the majority of jobs in the economy, it also controls the accessibility of job opportunities. In turn, any manpower program must cater its program style and mix to be compatible with the nature and state of the economy.

No one buys labor for its own sake but for the services it can provide. Therefore the manpower planner must have some knowledge of economics, particularly the rudiments of economic growth and development, to understand the process of job creation as it relates to the economics of the labor market. It is another truism that jobs are created only by the expenditure of money for the purchase of goods and services. With one minor exception, but an important one to manpower planners, these expenditures are motivated solely by the demand for the product of labor, not for labor itself. The exception is when government undertakes a job creation program explicitly to provide job opportunities for groups who are not finding adequate opportunities in the normal labor market. Operation Mainstream and the Public Employment Program are examples. The primary objective was jobs for the disadvantaged and the unemployed, respectively. In both programs productive work was done and useful services provided. The departure from the normal was that the employment was the objective and the services provided were byproducts. The test of this ordering of priorities is that in neither of these programs, or others like them, were the consuming taxpayers willing to pay the price for the services themselves.

Jobs of course are supplied by employers who, with the noted exceptions, are not in the business of supplying jobs. The private business firm is interested in producing and profitably selling goods and services desired by its customers. Public agencies are organized and supported by taxpayers who by political consensus have agreed to tax themselves to obtain desired services. Between the private profit-seeking institution and the public agency is an array of private not-for-profit organizations which either attract contributions or sell services thought by their supporters to be worthwhile. Manpower planners must understand this system and how it works and be able to tap into it to meet the job needs of their target groups.

When we consider the vast and complex nature of national and local economic structures, it would seem that the manpower planner must be one part economist, one part demographer, and one part soothsayer to be able to piece together the information required to structure and direct manpower programs. The remainder of this chapter is oriented toward how a planner might identify those occupations that would be best suited for his or her clientele. The flow chart in Figure 6.1 represents one method a planner might use in organizing the necessary labor market and occupational data into a workable form so that the appropriate analysis may be done accordingly. The following discussion centers round the various inputs to this procedure, describing their sources, backgrounds, and uses. It is hoped that this will provide the planner with some direction as to what kind of information is necessary and also a "feeling" for the data that are developed.

There are in the American economy perhaps twelve million private business firms. There are, of course, in addition to the federal government and the fifty states and six territorial governments, more than 81,000 local governments, each with its myriad departments and bureaus. The twelve thousand private nonprofit organizations are a relatively small but growing number.

To make sense of this complex of large and small producing and employing units, the Office of Management and Budget has developed a book called *Standard Industrial Classification Manual* (SIC) that contains codes which cover the totality of firms and categorizes them by a prescribed set of common characteristics. The number and variety of jobs are even greater and more complex. The Labor Department's *Dictionary of Occupational Titles* and the Census Bureau's *General Social and Economic Characteristics* classify these into manageable categories. Each of these classification systems is described later in this chapter.

Since jobs are created by the expenditure of money to purchase goods and services, the number of jobs at any one time is a function of the amount of spending. Four factors are involved: (1) the amount of purchasing power available to consumers, investors, and governments, (2) the extent to which they in aggregate choose to spend their available purchasing power, (3) the price

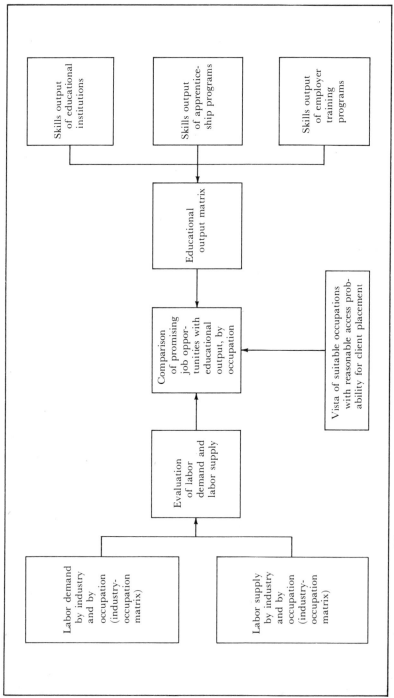

Figure 6.1. Suggested Procedure for Identification of Suitable Occupations for Client Placement

level which determines the amount of product or services purchaseable with available funds, and (4) productivity or output per man-hour, which determines the amount of labor required for the particular level of spending. The federal government, with its fiscal taxing and spending powers and its control over the money supply, is in a position to influence greatly the amount of spending and therefore the number of jobs the economy creates. State and local governments lack control of the money supply and are more limited in their ability to tax and in the extent of their borrowing power. With the extent of interstate commerce and the national and international flows of expenditure and products, state and local governments have little control over the short-run destinies of their economies. They must react to the vagaries of the national and, to a lesser degree, the international economy.

However, even though they cannot control what happens, they can foresee economic trends and adapt to them. The manpower planner cannot be an expert in everything. It would not be a wise use of time to make projections of economic activity at the national, regional, or local level. There are already ample national forecasts by federal agencies and private institutions, such as large banks and business periodicals. Regional federal reserve banks make regional forecasts, and the larger banks, universities, and state employment services publish local forecasts for most areas in the United States. The stock in trade for the manpower planner is to know where these forecasts can be obtained and what they mean in manpower terms.

Not only the overall level of economic activity but the mix (i.e., the industries which will grow and decline and the occupations which they will affect) will be of concern to the manpower planner, also the age structure of the present labor force and the labor turnover rates by industry and occupation. These will determine the numbers and kinds of jobs becoming available by opening up existing jobs as well as the emergence of new jobs. Recruiting, selecting, hiring, and training practices of employers, along with the characteristics and the capabilities of the job seekers, will tell manpower planners who of the target groups of concern to them will have access to how many of what kinds of jobs. The information system by which employers recruit and job seekers find jobs — and the availability of jobs and workers is made known — must be

understood by the manpower planner in order for him or her to
foresee job availability, to plan programs, and to aid client groups
in finding desirable employment. Each of these considerations
must be kept in mind as the planner goes about building a suitable
occupations model.

Where Are the Jobs? The Industry-Occupation Matrix

Since the demand for labor is a derived demand and jobs are
created by the purchase of goods and services, one must look first
to the product rather than the labor market to determine where the
jobs are or will be. Because there are millions of different products
and services provided by our complex economic system through
millions of workers, firms, and institutions, government analysts
have grouped the firms in the private sector of the economy into
categories by major products or services. In an era of integrated
and conglomerate multiproduct establishments this is not easy, and
some arbitrary judgments are necessary. Nevertheless, the SIC
manual should be a frequently used tool of each manpower planner.
Since industry boundaries change with the development of new
products and decline for old ones, the manual is revised periodically, with the 1972 edition being the most recent.

First, an alphabetic designation, *A* to *K*, signifies the broadest
category, such as division *D*, manufacturing. The major activities
within each division are identified by a two-digit designation, such
as major group 20 to major group 39 in manufacturing, division *D*.
For example, transportation equipment manufacturing is major
group 27. Third and fourth digits define further levels of industrial
detail; e.g., group 371 (motor vehicles and motor vehicle equipment) and industry number 3711 (motor vehicle and passenger
car bodies).

More than 35,000 jobs have been identified and are listed and
classified in the *Dictionary of Occupational Titles*. This document also
has its own classification system. Jobs can be classified by many
alternative criteria. Since the dictionary was developed by the
Labor Department primarily for matching job applicants with job
orders in the employment service, its classifications are according
to the job content and the education and skills required. It is a

nine-digit code. The first digit, which can be from 0 to 9, represents the nature of the job in broad terms such as:

0 or 1	Professional, technical, managerial
2	Clerical and sales
3	Service
4	Farming, fishery, forestry, and related
5	Processing
6	Machine trades
7	Benchwork
8	Structural work
9	Miscellaneous

The second and third digits more finely describe the occupational group such as 82 (electrical assembling, installing, and repairing occupations) and 824 (occupations in assembly, installation, and repair of lighting equipment and building wiring). The second set of three digits designates whether the occupation deals with data (fourth digit) or things (sixth digit). Thus 824,281 is a mine electrician (mining and quarrying) occupation which is described as "analyzing data, usually does not work with other people and involves precision." The third set of three digits is an extension of the first set of three and provides further industrial detail.

However, this system is unnecessarily complex for merely counting the number of persons employed in broad occupational categories. The Census Bureau records employment by occupation in ten broad categories: professional, technical, and kindred; managers and administrators; sales workers; clerical and kindred workers; crafts and kindred workers; operatives; transport equipment operators; laborers; farm workers; and service workers. Each category can be broken down into numerous subcategories.

When either current jobs are to be identified or future ones projected, it is easier to find and identify industries than occupations. Using the SIC and Census Bureau classifications, one can construct an industry-occupation matrix, with industries on one axis and occupations on the other. The Bureau of Labor Statistics has prepared and maintains such a matrix for the American economy, which provides profiles of four hundred occupational categories within ten broad groups in two hundred industries. Table 6-1 is a sample of one page of an extensive matrix (U.S.

Table 6-1
Percent Distribution of Industry Employment, by Occupation
(1970 and projected 1980)

Occupation	Office Machinery		Miscellaneous Machinery		Electrical Machinery		Transportation Equipment		Motor Vehicles and Equipment	
	1970	1980	1970	1980	1970	1980	1970	1980	1970	1980
Clerical and kindred workers:	18.77%	15.68%	12.96%	11.40%	14.17%	13.74%	12.09%	10.03%	10.45%	8.14%
Stenos, typists, secretaries	6.49	5.84	3.45	3.27	4.77	4.82	3.05	2.79	2.45	2.33
Office machine operators	0.91	0.99	0.82	0.92	1.05	1.46	0.56	0.61	0.66	0.72
Other clerical, kindred workers:	11.38	8.85	8.69	7.21	8.35	7.47	8.48	6.62	7.33	5.08
Accounting clerks	0.41	0.33	0.50	0.30	0.50	0.50	0.40	0.38	0.49	0.48
Bookkeepers, hand	0.37	0.19	0.42	0.31	0.29	0.30	0.10	0.09		
Bank tellers										
Cashiers	0.09	0.08	0.03		0.06	0.05	0.05	0.05	0.06	0.05
Mail carriers										
Postal clerks										
Shipping, receiving clerks	0.51	0.33	1.07	0.99	1.04	1.11	0.53	0.46	0.58	0.53
Telephone operators	0.13	0.11	0.11	0.11	0.16	0.17	0.10	0.08	0.10	0.06
Clerical and kindred (nec*)	9.86	7.82	6.57	5.51	6.30	5.34	7.30	5.57	6.10	3.96
Sales workers	4.65	3.51	1.80	1.69	1.46	1.59	0.59	0.55	0.72	0.60

*Not elsewhere classified.

	14.38	11.00	28.38	28.13	16.18	16.20	26.10	26.81	20.44	19.32
Craftsmen, foremen, and kindred:										
Construction craftsmen:										
Carpenters	0.33	0.31	1.08	1.23	1.03	1.11	5.38	6.47	1.53	1.70
Brickmasons and tile setters	0.06	0.06	0.16	0.09	0.12	0.11	1.28	1.38	0.17	0.19
Cement, concrete finishers			0.02	0.04	0.02	0.03	0.05	0.05	0.03	0.03
Electricians	0.18	0.14	0.58	0.68	0.72	0.74	1.76	2.10	0.89	0.95
Excavating, grading machine operator			0.01	0.01		0.01	0.02	0.03	0.01	0.01
Painters and paperhangers	0.01	0.01	0.03	0.04	0.03	0.04	0.34	0.34	0.06	0.04
Plasterers			0.01	0.01			0.01	0.01		
Plumbers and pipefitters	0.08	0.10	0.22	0.30	0.12	0.14	0.97	1.40	0.36	0.46
Roofers and slaters			0.04	0.05	0.02	0.04	0.01		0.01	0.01
Structural metalworkers							0.92	1.15		
Foremen (nec*)	2.19	1.76	4.32	4.22	4.43	4.24	4.20	3.99	4.02	3.79
Metalworking crafts, exc. mech.:	5.48	4.40	17.75	17.72	5.57	5.57	9.20	9.27	7.94	7.82
Machinists and related occupations	2.99	2.14	11.88	11.59	3.04	2.82	4.44	4.07	2.88	2.77
Blacksmiths, forgemen, hammermen	0.01	0.01	0.11	0.10	0.03	0.03	0.11	0.10	0.10	0.11
Boilermakers			0.02	0.01	0.01	0.01	0.19	0.22		
Heat treaters, annealers	0.09	0.07	0.33	0.33	0.06	0.05	0.15	0.13	0.16	0.12
Millwrights	0.05	0.04	0.25	0.25	0.19	0.17	0.39	0.38	0.69	0.67
Molders, metal, exc. coremakers	0.06	0.05	0.52	0.52	0.22	0.24	0.14	0.10	0.12	0.05
Patternmakers, metal, wood	0.38	0.40	0.24	0.21	0.33	0.40	0.40	0.38	0.40	0.35

*Not elsewhere classified.

Table 6-1 (continued)

Rollers and roll hands	0.05	0.04	0.03	0.03	0.02	0.03	0.02	0.02	0.03	0.02
Sheet metal workers	0.07	0.06	0.56	0.55	0.46	0.63	1.34	1.59	0.38	0.41
Toolmakers and diemakers	1.78	1.60	3.80	4.14	1.21	1.20	2.03	2.29	3.17	3.32
Printing trades craftsmen:										
Compositors, typesetters	0.19	0.15	0.10	0.11	0.10	0.12	0.06	0.06	0.02	0.02
Electrotypers, stereotypers	0.08	0.07	0.03	0.02	0.05	0.06	0.02	0.03	0.01	0.01
Engravers exc. photoengravers	0.07	0.05	0.03	0.03	0.02	0.03	0.01	0.01		
Photoengravers, lithographers	0.02	0.02	0.01	0.02	0.01	0.01	0.01	0.01		
Pressmen, plate printers	0.02	0.01	0.01	0.02	0.02	0.02	0.02	0.02	0.01	0.01
Transport and public utilities craft:										
Linemen and servicemen	0.01	0.03	0.02	0.04	0.54	0.82	0.03	0.03	0.03	0.05
Locomotive engineers	0.01	0.03	0.01	0.02	0.54	0.82	0.01	0.02	0.02	0.04
Locomotive firemen			0.01	0.01			0.01	0.01	0.01	0.01
Mechanics and repairmen:	5.11	3.61	3.37	3.03	3.16	3.03	5.47	5.67	5.29	4.85
Airplane mechanics and repairmen			0.03	0.05	0.05	0.08	1.78	2.28	0.03	0.06
Motor vehicle mechanics	0.03	0.03	0.10	0.06	0.02	0.02	1.36	1.29	3.12	2.97
Office machine mechanics	2.86	2.23			0.02	0.03	0.14	0.15		
Radio and TV mechanics					0.25	0.30	0.05	0.05	0.01	0.01
Railroad and car shop mechanics			0.01	0.01						
Other mechanics and repairmen	2.22	1.34	3.23	2.90	2.82	2.59	2.14	1.89	2.13	1.81

SOURCE: Bureau of Labor Statistics, U.S. Department of Labor, *Tomorrow's Manpower Needs*, Vol. IV revised (Washington, D.C.: U.S. Government Printing Office, 1971), p. 46.

Department of Labor, revised, 1971, p. 46). The matrix requires: (1) data for total employment by industry and the occupational composition of industries, and (2) annual employment data which allow examination of changes in occupational patterns by industry.

Unfortunately, this national industry-occupation matrix is of little help locally. The local manpower planner needs knowledge of the employment structure in labor markets of interest to his or her clientele, the rate at which job openings are becoming available in those labor markets, the requirements for entry into those openings, and the outlook for all of these variables over a near-term future; say, three to five years. Such data become generally available only from the decennial census and are soon outdated. The source of the base period matrix is currently the 1970 census. It is also the base used by the Bureau of Labor Statistics to project future manpower requirements.

Responding to this need for updating, developers of the national industry-occupation matrix have augmented their data with those from the Current Population Survey which surveys a national sample of households by personal interview each month, as well as from a variety of other sources. Unfortunately, the national industry-occupation matrix, though prepared and maintained by the Bureau of Labor Statistics, is not regularly published. It was most recently revised and published in 1971 as *Tomorrow's Manpower Needs.*

Efforts are now being made to establish programs similar to the national industry-occupation matrix at the state level. Beginning in 1970, the Labor Department in conjunction with state employment security agencies began an occupational employment statistics program which at present involves only 26 states. The primary objective of the program is to produce a state industry-occupation matrix system through a mail survey which gathers employment data from a sample of nonagricultural firms within each of the states. This survey information includes such items as the total number of workers employed by occupation, the total number of apprentices in specially designated occupations, and the total number of scientific and technical workers employed primarily in research and development. Each of the cooperating states and the District of Columbia have developed, or are developing, an industry-occupation matrix system covering at least two hundred and four hundred occupations. Then by using the 1970 census as the main data base, each state employment security agency can update its matrix from the most recent occupational employment statistics and also prepare substate estimates. This state industry-occupation matrix would then be tied into the national program, thus providing another source of updating the national system.

National implementation of this program is expected in 1974. However, the occupational employment statistics system is not yet standardized among the various states involved in the program. While the states are using the matrix concept as the primary tool, there is some variation among the states as to which industrial and occupational classification system they are applying to the matrix. For instance, some state employment security agencies are using the *Dictionary of Occupational Titles* and SIC classification systems, while others are using the census industrial and occupational system. The intent is to resolve any differences into a standardized form. A number of states has preceded the national system, and others are operational as a result of the national industry-occupation matrix effort. Planners can determine from the research and statistics unit of their state departments of employment security whether theirs is one of the pilot states.

It would be generally unwise for the state or local manpower planner to spend the necessary time and energy to measure employment and project future requirements. Once more, the requisite skill is to know where the data can be obtained and to have sufficient understanding of techniques to judge the validity of the data and projections. The appropriate locus of responsibility for measurement and projection of manpower requirements, employment opportunities, and local labor supply is the research and analysis units of the state employment services. Theirs is the most direct access to the major sources of data on present employment, employer needs, and job opportunities. The employment service research and analysis units also serve as local data gathering arms of the federal Manpower Administration and the Bureau of Labor Statistics and have the most direct access to those bodies of data.

Finally, since some of the research and analysis units have already constructed industry-occupation matrices for their states, sufficient methodologies have been developed for all to follow and use. It is therefore appropriate for the state bureaus of employment security to undertake this responsibility and for governors and mayors involved in the direction of state and local manpower planning to require them to do so.

However, whether or not manpower planners have the responsibility for data collection and projections, they must be aware of the sources, the strengths, and the limitations of the data to make sensible use of them. Essentially, there are three approaches to constructing a continuously updated industry-occupation matrix for a state or for a subdivision thereof. Since projections of the future employment outlook can be made only upon the base of a substantial period of actual employment data, these approaches will underly projections as well as current estimates. The major reason for the reluctance of federal agencies to push for and state employment security agencies to undertake the matrix construction task is the recognition that the matrices will be inevitably rough, faulty, and subject to criticism, at least in their early formulations. Yet the manpower planner does not have the luxury of eschewing data because they may not be accurate. The relevant question is: Is it better than nothing? The planner must plan, and to do so, must rely on whatever is available.

The three approaches depend upon what is available or within reach. Available to every state manpower planner or employment service analyst are the current national industry-occupation matrix and the matrix for his state, constructed from the decennial census. The national matrix has the disadvantage of probability that the industry mix and the occupational mix of each industry may not be representative of the local employment scene. The census matrix suffers from rapid obsolescence. However, by establishing ratios for the census year between the national and state matrices and applying them year by year between censuses to the national matrix, the planner can expect a reasonable estimate of the actual industry-occupation status of the state's labor markets.

However, employment by industry in a particular state or locality may not move in parallel with national developments. Rather than simply assuming that employment by industry in a state or labor market is rising and falling as shown by the national matrix, the planner can find a variety of data sources from which to construct a state or local matrix based on local employment trends. All local employment data can be obtained, where they exist, from the state departments of employment security. For example, the Employment Security Automated Reporting System

(ESARS) compiles state agency operating data. These data are compiled in various ways by various states. For example, generally available are MA 5-62 ("applicants and nonagricultural job openings by occupation, 3-digit classification") and ES 202 ("employment, wages and reporting units by firm size"). The former is limited in detail but has the advantage of frequent availability. The latter is the most detailed but is gathered only annually and sometimes published with a one and a half year lag.

It is also possible, though less likely, that the occupational mix by industry in a state or locality may not follow national patterns. This is most likely if the age or size of local installations or the local wage structure encourages use of a different technology. The only ultimately accurate way of maintaining an updated industry-occupation matrix is to undertake continuing employer surveys, recording actual employment by industry, establishment, and occupation. This ultimate exigency is not likely to be necessary for maintenance of a reasonably accurate matrix, but it can have particular importance for the identification and projection of job openings. It is hoped that soon state industry-occupation matrices will be available. Translation of those data to an SMSA level is farther away and will require estimates and manipulation of state and other data by the manpower planner or local employment service office.

Forecasting Manpower Requirements

Whereas the manpower program administrator is constantly involved in preparing for and filling today's jobs, or those which will be available at the end of a training or other program which prepares for employment, the planner is always concerned, by definition, with future happenings. Measuring today's conditions is only a prerequisite for planning to meet tomorrow's exigencies. National projections have the advantage of prevailing economic policies as a control over total employment opportunities. National economic authorities have tools to influence, if not to control national levels of economic output and employment. Because it is potentially costly to do so, any political administration is not likely to allow unemployment to remain above about 5.5 percent for long. The apparent inflation proneness of the U.S. economy is unlikely to allow those actions necessary to bring the unemployment rate below about 4.5 percent, given the current age-sex mix within the labor force.

Since the total population from which the labor force is to be drawn is known, the major uncertainty is the labor force participation rate — i.e., the proportion of the adult population working or seeking work. The participation rates of youth and women fluctuate considerably, but those of adult men vary little. Thus it is possible to project within rather narrow limits the total size of the labor force and the total employment which will be politically required. This employment figure serves as a control as employment is projected industry by industry.

Nationally, employment projections by industry are made by projecting the likely output by industry, based on whatever variables are most likely to determine that output, and tempering those output projections by expected changes in man-hour productivity. Employment by industry is the dividend of this calculation. If adding all industry employment projections together results in a figure which departs significantly from the employment necessary to keep the total employment projections within the politically acceptable range, the industry projections are restructured and adjusted to accord with expected political realities.

No such convenient control exists for local projections. State and local governments have little short-run influence on employment levels. The labor force may vary significantly by in- and out-migration as well as by labor force participation. Nevertheless, projections of manpower requirements are essential to planning, and reasonably accurate ones can be made.

The first input to such projections is a historical base of employment data by industry and occupation which goes back a sufficient period of time to establish trend lines. Even in a rapidly changing society and economy, the near-term future will be more like than unlike the past. The necessary process is to identify past trends and extend them into the future, then to identify current circumstances which promise to send those trend lines in directions different from those indicated by simple extrapolation.

Returning again to the principle that the demand for labor is a derived demand: The output of many industries is determined by such inexorable demographic factors as birthrates, the age structure, and family formation. Despite evidence of recent failures of foresight, nothing is so easy to project as the demand for elementary school teachers. Other industries will be influenced by such independent variables as the population size and age structure and by economic factors such as personal incomes, interest rates, or tax policies.

Projecting past trends in output and employment by local industry, comparing these trends with national growth projection, and seeking to identify factors which will make the future different from the past will result in an industry output projection transferable into employment projections by estimating likely changes in technology and productivity. Though technological change is endemic and feared, it remains true that virtually no new technology threatening major employment dislocations can pass through the invention, innovation, implementation, and permeation cycle in less than ten years. Local applications of known technology may occur in shorter time periods, but they should be foreseeable by local employers and trade associations. This methodology provides one system of forecasting future employment trends with some degree of accuracy.

For a number of years state departments of employment security have attempted short-term employment projections based on employer surveys. Employers were asked to predict their total employment from two to five years ahead. Few could do so accurately, and the projections fell into disrepute. Few employers have control over their own markets. To ask them to project their future employment is to ask them to guess the future state of the economy and the incomes and tastes of their customers. It is better procedure to project the likely output and total employment by industry and the likely gross impact of those national projections on the local labor market from sources external to the employer. Then the employer can estimate the occupational mix of that employment based upon technological developments. This combination procedure is more likely to lead to accurate and usable projections. Use of employer surveys primarily to foresee major changes in technology and other industry conditions and practices has the additional advantage of not requiring a statistically representative sample. In fact, statistics from local trade associations or a handful of employers may be all that is necessary to foresee major technological change.

There is also limited value in attempting to project employment by industry and occupation at a point in time dependent upon the state of fluctuating levels of economic activity. Programs to prepare people for employment encompass substantial periods of time. It is more useful to project and prepare for trends, even if conditions at a moment in time may find the actuality above or below that trend line. Some waiting periods to place people prepared for jobs promised by foreseeable trends or some temporary shortages are preferable to attempting precision in the projection of fluctuating demands.

For long-term projections of labor market developments by industry and occupation, there is no better tool than an input-output table for the local economy. Any single economic change nationally and locally will have widespread reverberations throughout a local economy. Having documented past economic relationships, the planner can foresee how any particular change impacting at one point in the economic system will echo through every part of the system. Translation of those likely impacts into employment terms is then possible if employment relationships have been a major factor in constructing the input-output system.

As aids to state and local manpower planners, the Labor Department has derived two systems for transferring national manpower projections into a state or local labor market context. The first is built upon projections of industry employment and the latter on direct occupational forecasting. Both systems have their strengths and weaknesses.

The industry approach depends upon relating the Labor Department's projected 1980 industry-occupation matrix to the most recent available data on state or local employment by industry and occupation. Industry employment for the geographical area in question is projected by such indicators as national employment by industry, population change, local consumer income, and any available information about state or area industry trends. With total employment by industry for the area projected to 1980, the planner can then compare both the occupational mix projected for the national matrix and the matrix projected via the local industry-occupation mix from the most recent available census data. The projector's judgment must reconcile any differences between the two. Applying the adjusted occupation ratios to the 1980 area industry projection of employment by industry and adding them across industries result in a projection of occupational demands for the area. Modifying these figures for self-employment,

unpaid family workers, and multiple job holders provides an estimate of the total number who will be employed. The difference
between total present employment and the projected employment
by occupation is an estimate of the net new demand to be expected.
Information on age and sex distributions by occupation, as related
to labor force participation rates, is necessary to estimate replacement needs, which added to net new demand represents the total
of additional persons who can be employed by the target date.

Of course, the projection will still represent a "best guess,"
but an educated one. The finer the occupational detail, the greater
the impact of nonaccuracies in the local forecasting component.
The longer the period of the projections, the greater the likely
departure from the present industry-occupation profile. Firms may
enter or leave the area, technology may change, but the availability
of skills affects technological decisions, the business cycle affects
the ratio of production to nonproduction workers. Nevertheless,
an educated guess is a better planning tool than no guess at all.

Because the long ten years between censuses can allow substantial shifts in the internal occupational composition of industries,
an alternative approach provided by the Labor Department
attempts direct prediction of occupational demand. It differs primarily in requiring the development of a base period matrix for
the target area. Once that is available, the process is a relatively
simple one, consisting of essentially four tasks: (1) projection of
industry employment to the preferred date, (2) transformation of
the base period matrix coefficients to the same projected target
year, using cell-change factors developed by the Bureau of Labor
Statistics, (3) development of occupational employment estimates
by industry through the application of the projected matrix, and
(4) determination of the total target year occupational requirements
by screening the separate industry estimates.

An example of a modification of the latter approach is the
projection of nonagricultural employment made periodically by
the research and analysis unit in the Utah Department of Employment Security. Percentage distributions of employment by occupation and by industry have been developed over several years,
based on establishment mail surveys. A sample of all nonagricultural employers — excluding only self-employed, unpaid family
workers, domestic workers, and agriculture — is stratified by
industry and by employment size for all large firms, with a random

sample of small firms included. Industry employment is projected, based on long-term trends gathered as a byproduct of unemployment insurance administration. This is also supplemented by voluntary reports from federal, state, and local governments, public schools, railroads, and nonprofit institutions. Given the length of time over which the industry-occupation matrix has been developed, changes in the mix are also projected and applied to the industry employment projections. Assuming that no major shifts will occur in the rate and nature of economic growth, that economic and social patterns will continue to change at familiar rates, and that there are no significant shifts in the pace of scientific advancement, the projections have proved reasonably accurate. The projection to 1975, completed in the late 1960s, appears to have suffered only from a modest underestimate of the pace of employment growth. A total of 170 industries and three thousand occupations are involved in the projection, of which Table 6-2 is a one-page sample.

This approach to forecasting the future industrial and occupational mix has some significant advantages. By surveying local employers yearly, the matrix is updated yearly, thus providing a current estimate of employment by occupation. Also, with passage of time, this methodology reflects changing industrial-occupational trends which then can be identified and utilized in forecasting future trends more accurately.

The Utah system, a simple one, is an example of what several states are doing and all could do. The only substantial commitment other than staff effort is the periodic establishment survey. The cost is low and the product useful. Pending completion of efforts of the Bureau of Labor Statistics to produce an integrated national-state industry-occupation matrix, the Utah model demonstrates what a state can do by itself if it has the interest.

Labor Turnover and Job Openings

Future changes in employment by industry and occupation are still only a step toward the data needed by manpower planners. What are the implications for training requirements or for employment opportunities? Jobs become available even in declining labor markets as job incumbents are promoted or transferred or if they quit, retire, or die. A projection of future requirements allows

estimates of the difference between present and future requirements; i.e., the increases promised by economic growth or the
deficits from decline. Total manpower requirements will include
those promised by growth trends (whether positive or negative)
plus replacement needs. To estimate replacement needs by industry
and by occupation will require knowledge of the age and sex
structure of employment, actuarial factors related to age, industry
retirement practices, and the turnover experience of the industry.

Industries and occupations which employ women and youth
will experience higher turnover than those which hire primarily
adult men. With fixed retirement ages, it is possible from the age
structure of a work force to estimate accurately the replacement
needs, tinctured to a minor degree by actuarial experiences and
to a high degree by turnover experiences. Employers in small-scale
industries are unlikely to compile turnover data, whereas larger
firms generally keep good turnover records — but they may not be
willing to release them. It is possible also to construct turnover data
from unemployment insurance. The research and analysis unit of
a state department of employment security would again be the
agency best prepared to provide such total manpower requirement
(growth plus replacement) measures and projections by industry
and occupation for the state and for each SMSA within the state.

For current measurement of job opportunities and projection
of future ones, the most useful statistical tool would be a job
vacancy series. Just as the number and proportion of persons actively seeking work comprise the unemployment statistic, the
number and proportion of jobs for which employers are actively
recruiting employees would provide a job vacancy rate. Fluctuations in the overall rate would serve as an economic indicator,
while specific vacancies by occupation and industry would aid both
the manpower planner and the placement officer. Currently, the
Bureau of Labor Statistics publishes some labor turnover data in
terms of accession and separation rates by state and major SMSAs.
These data are useful but are published only for the manufacturing
and mining industries.

The introduction of Job Banks in the federal and state employment services provides a measure of job openings for those
industries which make frequent use of the employment service for
their kinds of occupations. There is strong evidence that the occupational mix of employment service job orders is representative of

Table 6-2

Occupations of Employees on Utah Nonagricultural Payrolls

Occupa-tional Code	Occupational Title	Employment			
		1960	1967	1971	Pro-jected 1980
20	Steno., typing, filing, and related occupations	17,690	24,330	27,820	37,460
201	Secretaries:	5,090	7,100	8,510	12,060
	Legal secretary	70	100	140	190
	Medical secretary	230	350	450	700
	Secretary	4,790	6,650	7,920	11,160
202	Stenographers:	2,850	3,550	3,920	5,350
	Stenographer	2,820	3,520	3.880	5,300
	Stenotype operator	20	30	30	40
203	Typists:	950	1,160	1,390	1,900
	Telegraphic-typewriter operator	110	110	130	150
	Typist	830	1,040	1,240	1,750
204	Correspondence clerks	90	110	110	150
205	Personnel clerks:	190	230	230	270
	Personnel clerk supervisor	30	30	30	50
	Personnel clerk	130	160	160	170
206	File clerks:	530	690	750	980
	File clerk I	410	530	580	740
	File clerk II	110	140	150	210
207	Duplicating-machine operators:	200	270	300	420
	Duplicating-machine operator, II	20	20	20	20
	Duplicating-machine operator, III	80	130	150	220
	Offset-duplicating-machine oper.	70	90	100	140
	Duplicating-machine operator, I	10	20	20	20
208	Misc. office machine operators:	180	220	230	310
	Transcribing-machine operator	170	200	210	290
209	Stenography, typing, filing, and related occupations (nec*)	7,610	11,000	12,380	16,020
	Steno-pool supervisor	40	60	60	40
	Cancellation clerk	70	70	70	80
	Clerk-typist	4,860	6,500	7,100	9,400
	Mortgage clerk	40	50	50	70

*Not elsewhere classified.

SOURCE: Utah Department of Employment Security, *Occupations of Employees on Utah Non-agricultural Payrolls, 1960–1980* (June 1973).

all labor market transactions and that the employment service is the source of more and better information on what is happening in the labor market than any other single source (Walsh *et al.*, 1974). With that base, planners can establish, by a one-time study, a statistical relationship between job vacancies and employment service job orders. With that accomplished, they can inflate the continuously available job order data into an estimate of job vacancies. Such a device would not help the placement officer but would provide useful data for the manpower planner. However, if employment service placement staff could be satisfied with aiding job seekers to find jobs, regardless of direct employment service participation in the placement, providing information on "who hires what types of workers in this labor market" would assist job seekers in finding their own jobs (Johnson, 1973).

For the manpower planner, labor turnover data, added to other elements of the replacement need formula, provide a measure of present and future job opportunities by industry and occupation. They also indicate occupations in which there will be a "reasonable expectation of employment" for manpower program enrollees and other target group members, but also warn of jobs which may have undesirable attributes, leaving job retention in doubt. However, it is necessary for the planner to read the proper meaning into these indicators in order to make appropriate use of the data. For instance, discovery that a high percentage of workers in an industry or occupation is nearing retirement simultaneously may indicate high past and low present growth. High turnover in an industry of strong employee-employer attachment may signal the availability of job opportunities. High turnover can occur in an industry of more casual employment attachment such as construction, even though a surplus of workers exists in the industry. A high incidence of retirements may occur, correspondent to a change in retirement benefits, without indicating a new continuing higher rate. A low growth rate and a high layoff rate generally accompany a recession, with the opposite occurring in prosperous times. Read properly, however, turnover and vacancy data are vital to good manpower planning.

The foregoing discussion of sources, methodologies, and related labor market indicators is important to manpower planners in their preparation of a current and projected industry-occupation matrix for their states or local areas. It is the first step in identifying accessible job openings for assigned or chosen clientele.

Potential Competition

The manpower planner responsible for programs to improve the employment and income experience of a designated group (e.g., the disadvantaged) may not be concerned with the overall availability of job opportunities in the local labor market. The relevant question is: Can the clients of my program gain access to attractive job opportunities? In this case, both the long-term outlook and the present unfilled demand for labor must be supplemented by data from the supply side as well. What is the local unemployment rate? How many are out of the labor force but waiting for job opportunities? The answers to these questions will indicate the level of present competition for jobs. What is the longer term outlook for labor force growth and for the output of the skills development system? What are the routes through which access is to be found to available jobs?

Enough has been said about the workings of the labor market. It remains but to enumerate some sources of local labor market information, emphasizing the supply of labor; to suggest other approaches for conceptualizing and measuring the output of the skills development system; and to explore the problem of access for disadvantaged workers.

Local Supply of Labor

The gross supply of labor for the long run in a labor market can be foreseen by projecting population trends and labor force participation rates. It is likely that a bureau of economic and business research, a department of employment security, a bank, or some other interested entity will have made long-term population projections for the state, if not for the community. If there is none, a base for projection is readily available in past decennial census reports, which provide almost any level of detail of possible interest. The most tenuous part of any such projection is the possibility of basic shifts not easily recognizable in the most recent data. Is the birthrate slowing or is it accelerating? Are there occurring or portending significant departures from the past in the rates of in- and outmigration?

Since changes in birthrates portend changes in the size of the labor force only after sixteen years have passed, those shifts are not a threat to the labor force projector. Keeping an eye on the school population will be warning enough for projections to ten years ahead. School censuses, building permits, and telephone hookups are examples of information sources concerning in- and outmigration. For most states and SMSAs, reasonably good between-census data on population are available to provide the base and trends for projections. Labor force participation rates are even more stable than population trends, given shifts in migration. The key to projecting labor force size from population trends is disaggregation by age, sex, race, education, and family income. As previously noted, labor force participation rates differ radically, particularly for age and sex. In fact for most purposes, disaggregation by age and sex will be sufficient to project the size of the labor force. The other factors are important, not so much because they influence labor force size, but problems of absorbing new labor force entrants into jobs can be foreseen.

A number of current series available in nearly every SMSA provides short-run information on the supply available to fill emerging and accessible job openings and the potential competition to be faced by manpower clientele. Area unemployment estimates for the 150 largest SMSAs and all states are developed monthly by state employment security agencies. Occupational and labor force characteristics are not available, since the estimates are based on unemployment insurance rates by methodology supplied from the national level. Nevertheless, general information on the relative tightness or looseness of the labor market is useful. There is also available in each state a monthly report of unemployment insurance statistics showing occupational attachment of the insured unemployed for certain selected occupational groups.

State employment security agencies also issue, quarterly, a printout showing the number of persons registered for work by occupational background, cross-classified against other characteristics such as age, sex, and race. All unemployed are not registered at the employment service, but this occupational distribution applied to the estimated number of unemployed is a reasonable representation of reality. The Current Population Survey, the basic source of national labor force and labor market data, provides some useful data for those areas which happen to be covered in the sample.

Some geographical detail (on an annual average basis for labor force, employment, and unemployment, by age, sex, color, and so forth, for nonparticipants in the labor force) has been available for several years for the ten largest states and the twenty largest SMSAs (as well as for fourteen central cities). In addition, quarterly data have been published for various geographical area groupings: (1) all SMSAs, (2) SMSAs of 250,000 population and over, and (3) urban poverty areas in the hundred largest SMSAs. However, a new series of quarterly data will soon be available. This series will include a summary of characteristics from all poverty areas in the nation (based on a new poverty criterion — those areas with 20 percent or more persons with income below the poverty line — instead of the previous five-step method), totals for all metropolitan and for all nonmetropolitan areas, and those SMSAs of a million or more population. In addition, the Current Population Survey sample will be expanded to include thirty SMSAs and sixteen states in the near future. Although these data cover only a limited number of areas and only partially meet the planner's needs, they do add currency to the basic survey data; and an analysis of urban area movements, quarterly or annually, could serve as signals to planners in those areas not covered directly.

Occupational Supply Mix

By crude definition, the existing labor supply consists of all those persons employed in the economy, plus all those actively seeking work in the economy, plus all those who could be drawn into the economy if the appropriate job opportunity existed. This definition could, in part, work in reverse. For example, during periods of high unemployment, the number of unemployed would obviously increase, but the total supply of labor would likely decrease as workers left the labor force in reaction to decreasing job opportunities. This is a pattern particularly true for secondary family workers.

While the estimation of current labor supply in specific terms is an "iffy" subject and one not aggressively pursued by economic researchers, the manpower planner must proceed to establish some estimated measure of labor supply. In this connection, the concept of the matrix can again be used. The beginning foundation for this matrix is the previously discussed matrix of employment by industry

and occupation. To this are added estimates of the unemployed
by industry and occupation. These estimates can be developed by
using local unemployment insurance data, by benching to the most
recent census data, by using national unemployment data (such
as the Current Population Survey), or by any combination of these
sources. It is suggested that attempts to establish the occupational
direction of those persons who could be drawn into the labor force,
if the suitable job were available, be ignored in this matrix calculation — or at least for the estimating of current labor supply. There
are unlikely to be any dramatic shifts in the short run in the propor-
tionate choices of occupation, given availability of jobs. However,
when future labor supply matrix projections are forecast, this question should be dealt with. As suggested earlier, the manpower
planner should request the services of the local employment service
research and analysis units in developing and supplying this
information.

Once this matrix is established, it then can be compared to
an occupational labor supply matrix such as the one illustrated in
Figure 6.2. This ready comparison of the labor demand and
labor supply matrices is the beginning step in identifying those
occupations which have accessibility for client placement. Simply
stated, the manpower planner should identify those occupations

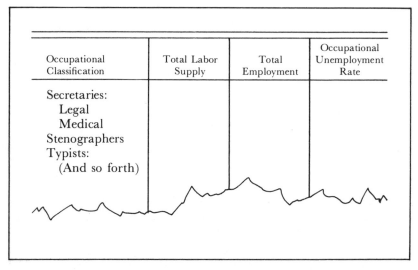

Occupational Classification	Total Labor Supply	Total Employment	Occupational Unemployment Rate
Secretaries:			
Legal			
Medical			
Stenographers			
Typists:			
(And so forth)			

Figure 6.2. Suggested Table for Constructing the
Occupational Labor Supply Matrix

which have the lowest occupational unemployment rate. These occupations should be further studied in order to determine whether they are suitable areas for client training and job placement. Once this list of occupations is developed, the planner should determine their ports of entry, turnover patterns, wage structures, promotion ladders, skill requirements, and so forth.

Rather than totally accepting the conclusions of this matrix comparison, manpower planners can also refer to some other data sources to confirm their observations. One obvious source is appropriate census data; another could be ESARS. Under this system, state employment security agencies should be able to provide data indicating by occupation the number of applicants and job openings processed through their agencies. Such data, including employment data, could be compared and evaluated as shown in Figure 6.3. In this tabular comparison, the planner should identify those occupations which have a low ratio of applicants to job openings, which have a low ratio of applicants to total employment, and which have a high ratio of job openings to employment. The subsequent list of occupations should then be compared with the list prepared from the supply and demand matrices and thoroughly examined in terms of questions of port of entry, turnover patterns, job quality, and so on.

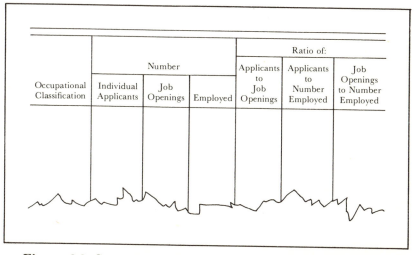

Occupational Classification	Number			Ratio of:		
	Individual Applicants	Job Openings	Employed	Applicants to Job Openings	Applicants to Number Employed	Job Openings to Number Employed

Figure 6.3. Suggested Table for Determining Relationships between Manpower Demand and Supply

The combined list of occupations should give the planner a "best guess" of those occupational areas in which the program's clientele would have the best chance of obtaining stable employment and income opportunities. All that remains is the comparison of these selected occupations to that of the skills-educational output through educational institutions, apprenticeship programs, and employer on-the-job training programs, another important angle of labor supply which will be dealt with separately in the following pages.

The Skills Development System

In addition to the numbers of persons available now and in the future to fill job openings, the manpower planner should be vitally interested in the process by which skills are developed to meet employer needs. The manpower planner is generally involved in planning for an increasingly important part of the skills development system — a remedial system to improve the employability of those facing various disadvantages in the competition for jobs. Unless the competition from other components of the skills development system is known, it is difficult to plan quantitatively and qualitatively for the remedial component.

The manpower planner who would plan for successful working careers for people and for efficient allocation of manpower resources must be as concerned with the process by which skills are acquired as with the process of job creation. Economic reasoning in the past has looked to investment and consumption as the primary energizers of economic activity. Therefore a process has been assumed that began with:

(1) Customers demanding goods and services

(2) Businessmen organizing firms to meet these demands

(3) Engineers designing technology to perform the production

(4) Workers responding by developing skills to meet the production requirements

In fact, the causation moves in every direction among these activities. Firms are organized and products developed in hopes that through advertising, customers will be attracted. New technologies sponsor new products. Rarely have demands been created to provide jobs tailored to the skills of people. However, it has happened, and does happen in employment crises when governments and other organizations (such as sheltered workshops) create jobs to provide earning opportunities to the unemployed. Entrepreneurs, as they estimate the profitability of investment, continually consider the availability and cost of labor; engineers as they design technology make it conform to the labor available. Thus technology developed in the United States, where a high average level of literacy and basic education can be assumed, will differ in sophistication from that designed in other lands with less sophisticated labor forces. The manpower planner, whether assigned to find or develop jobs to fit the needs of a target population or to assure adequate supplies of appropriate skills to support economic development, must understand the skills acquisition process and the sources of skills development.

The Process of Skills Acquisition

The first step in gaining the understanding discussed above is to clarify the nature of the skills to be acquired. Successful employment and productivity usually require the ability to perform whatever tasks are peculiar to a particular job, but they require far more than that. If one reviews the process by which a human infant ultimately becomes, among other things, a successful worker, a variety of necessary attributes will be noted: physical and mental health; a commitment to effort as a source of reward; the acceptance of internally and externally imposed discipline as necessary to the achievement of goals; the general intellectual skills of communication and computation; familiarity with basic science and technology; understanding the nature of labor markets, the alternative opportunities available therein, and the process of seeking and finding jobs; and the skills of decision making. All of these are prerequisites and accompaniments to the skills required to perform specific job tasks. And all are skills which must be acquired for career success.

The listing indicates the complexities of the skills acquirement process. The home, family, neighborhood, community, churches, schools, employing establishments, unions, fellow employees, supervisors, and so forth, are all involved. The primary responsibility, of course, rests with the individual, but no one can achieve career success without help. Each institution has its role to play, but failure of one institution can sometimes be accommodated by remedial input from others. Current evidence indicates that those inputs which came earliest in personal development — the home, family, neighborhood, peer groups, and so on — may be the most influential and the most difficult to compensate for when they fail.

Career Education

It is this recognition of the lifelong nature of the employability development process which underlies current advocacy of what is being called "career education": The assumption is that without interfering with other education goals such as culture, citizenship, or successful family life, individuals can be more effectively prepared for successful working lives through attention to these career development needs (Hoyt *et al.*, 1974).

Career education is perceived as consisting of five components:

(1) The home and family from which the individual develops initial attitudes and concepts

(2) The classroom in which all possible learnings are articulated in terms of career application for both understanding and motivation

(3) Career development programs for exposure to occupational alternatives and for derivation of a work ethic and a set of work values, allowing the individual to visualize himself or herself in various work settings and to make career decisions which appear to promise the preferred life-style

(4) Interaction among training institutions, employing institutions, and labor organizations to provide more fertile learning environments than the schoolroom

(5) The ultimate acquiring of vocational job skills, whether they are learned on the job, in the structured classroom situation, or from general life experiences

These five components interact, in career education, as intervention strategies, beginning no later than kindergarten and continuing through the adult years, to provide positive assistance to persons in their career development. Thus career education, while concerned with the continuing process of making work possible, meaningful, and satisfying to the individual, includes special attention to assisting persons as they move toward vocational maturity — the choice of a primary work role. By stressing a broad career development emphasis, career education seeks to ready youth for acceptance of the probability that each will, in all likelihood, change primary work roles (vocations) during their lifetimes.

Thus we can speak of vocational maturation as an integral part of the total process of career development. As part of the career development process, vocational maturation can be pictured as occurring in growth stages which, in sequential order, includes: (1) awareness of primary work roles played by persons in society, (2) exploration of work roles that an individual might consider as important, possible, and probable for himself or herself, (3) vocational decision making (which may go from a highly tentative to a very specific form), (4) establishment (including preparing for and actually assuming a primary work role), and (5) maintenance (all of the ways in which one gains — or fails to gain — personal meaningfulness and satisfaction from the primary work role he or she has assumed).

Career education theorists generally see the awareness, exploration, and decision-making stages as coincidental and consistent with what tends to be occurring in the broader maturation of youth at the elementary, middle/junior high school, and high school levels of the education system. As one of many devices to aid this sequence, the U.S. Office of Education has designed and promulgated the concept of occupational clusters into which all occupations can be conceptually subsumed. As currently used, these are as follows:

(1) Agribusiness and natural resources

(2) Business and office

(3) Communications and media

(4) Consumer and homemaking education

(5) Construction

(6) Environmental control

(7) Fine arts and humanities

(8) Health

(9) Hospitality and recreation

(10) Manufacturing

(11) Marine science

(12) Marketing and distribution

(13) Personal services

(14) Public services

(15) Transportation

The Office of Education's proposal is that elementary school youth be exposed to all fifteen clusters in developing awareness of the world of work, but that they select fewer occupations for deeper exploration at the junior high school level, ultimately leading them to choose and train in one occupation at the senior high school level or beyond. However, there are many alternative ways to cluster occupations and other effective ways to accomplish the awareness, exploration, and decision-making objectives.

The career education concepts have triple interest to the manpower planner. First, if career education were effectively undertaken in the schools of the community the planner serves, young people would enter the labor market better prepared to function effectively throughout their working careers. Those concerned with the effectiveness of the manpower system should be strong advocates of career education in the local schools and participants in its community component. Second, the single most important lesson to be learned from the career education approach is that job skills are only one of several necessary components of an employability development system. At least equal attention must be given to the development of work values, work habits, and decision-making skills if manpower programs are to be effective for those who enter the labor market without adequate preparation. Third, the career development process is a lifelong one, not merely an experience of youth. Adults must continue to become aware of new and changing opportunities, explore them in terms of their relationship to changing abilities and personal interests, and be able to adjust and adapt as either economic circumstances or personal interests change.

Lack of education has been one of the most serious of labor market disadvantages in the last 25 years of rapidly rising educational attainment, at a time when employers generally had the option of hiring relatively well-educated people and were convinced these were the best employment risks. There is some indication that employers and others are becoming less convinced that a school diploma is the best evidence of competence and stability. Better predicters of employment success are being developed, and employers are more cynical about the quality of education.

Offsetting this tendency is the continuing rise in educational attainment, increasing the competitive disadvantagement of the undereducated. According to the Bureau of Labor Statistics the proportion of the labor force with four years or more of college will rise from 14.6 to 23.8 percent between the early 1970s and 1990. The proportion of high school educated will rise only from 37.5 to 41.2 percent, while the proportion with one to three years of high school will drop from 16.9 to 12.5 percent, and those with eight years of education or less will fall from 19 to 6.1 percent. Four out of five workers will have completed high school by 1990. The number with little education will be few, but their competitive disadvantages will be more seriously aggravated by the fact that most of them will be older workers. On the other hand, with the majority having some post-secondary education and training, those with no more than high school education may be at a disadvantage, unless it prepared them for employment.

There is also a persistently rising trend for adults to return to school or continue part-time activities designed to upgrade their education and employability. In 1972, for instance, 1.5 million adults — about one out of every fifty men and women over 35 years of age — were enrolled in and attending schools, three-fourths of them in the work force and most apparently with career ambitions as their motivation.

All of these proportions and trends differ widely by location. In assessing training needs of the population served, the manpower planner needs to know the educational attainment trends of the community labor force as well as the competitive education situation of the target clientele.

The Education-Output Matrix

The first step in determining the output of the skills development system of a community is to identify each of the institutions providing job skills in a school setting. Public institutions, if not already known, can be identified through state boards of education, of vocational education, and of higher education, and through community college or technical college boards or other governing structures for public education. Private proprietary schools can be identified from chambers of commerce, better business bureaus, or licensing authorities. High schools, area vocational schools, community colleges, technical colleges, technician training activities at universities, and private proprietary schools offer training skills at the less than baccalaureate level. Four-year colleges and universities have a near monopoly on training at the professional level.

Annual reports can provide some data, but it will probably be necessary to contact each institution separately to determine their past, present, and projected output of trainees by occupation. A matrix should be constructed listing all of the institutions on the vertical axis, all of the occupations for which training is given on the horizontal axis, with summarization of numbers of current enrollees and current year graduates at the bottom. A notation should be made in code on each program, whether its completers can be concluded to have attained only exploratory knowledge, entry-level skills, or full competence. The planner should construct such a matrix for each of the past three to five years as well as the current year. He should then work with each of the institutions to project their output for the following three years, updating that matrix annually. Dropouts from such skills training programs constitute a problem for the planner. When will they have attained sufficient skill to be counted as part of the total supply of skills? As a general rule, it is best to count only those noncompleters who are known to have obtained a training-related job upon leaving the school.

The total output of the schools will not be added to the available stock of skills in the labor market. Some will not enter the labor force. They will continue to further schooling, or may undertake homemaking as a full-time career. Some will migrate to other labor markets. The higher the educational level of the credential earned, the more likely the individual is, in general, to move to other areas. Those trained in some skills, e.g., engineering or construction, are more likely to be geographically mobile than others. Some will accept jobs in nontraining-related fields, though their skills are potentially available if the training occupations are available and attractive.

Most schools will have some data on the placements and residences of their graduates. Others can be influenced and aided by the planner to undertake such studies for future classes. From such studies, factors can be developed to deflate completion and graduation statistics to a close estimate of the actual addition to the skills supply of the local labor market.

The Output of Employer Training Programs

It is more difficult to account for and assess the output of training programs within industry. They tend to be of five kinds:

(1) Employers pay the tuition or other costs of employees who attend school-based courses, either in nonwork hours or in excused time for which the employee is paid. The output of such programs can be counted as part of the school output.

(2) Vestibule training is undertaken at the work site (i.e., the training occurs in the employing establishment), often in a simulation of working conditions, but the student is not engaged in production.

(3) Formal on-the-job training is undertaken, including a formal trainee status, a curriculum, and an instructor who is perhaps a supervisor.

(4) Apprenticeship programs involve two or more years of a structured training program in which the apprentice works a specific number of hours before advancing to the next year and ultimately to journeyman, and usually receives related theoretical or classroom instructions. Some of these apprentice programs will be conducted jointly by management and unions and will be registered with the

Labor Department, while others are unilaterally undertaken and controlled by managements.

(5) Informal on-the-job training occurs in which the initiate
is given casual instruction at the job site by another employee or a supervisor.

Types (3) and (5) will often involve job tasks so specialized to the
particular employer that they should not be considered a contribution to the total labor market supply of trained manpower. They
belong in a broader category of experienced operatives without
specific occupational skills. Types (2) and (3) will often involve
skills transferable to at least one other major employer or several
small employers in the labor market. That should be the test for
inclusion in a skills inventory for the community. Apprenticeships
as well as school-based courses will always be, by definition, in
identifiable, transferable occupations.

The planner must understand, in general, the practices of
employers in his labor market. Each employer faces a choice between recruiting persons already having requisite skills or hiring
those without the skills but providing training. The choice may be
dependent upon availability and relative cost, or it may be industry
or company practice. As noted before, it is customary for construction firms, being predominantly of small size, either to participate
jointly in a multi-employer–union-administered apprentice program or to depend upon hiring those who have already acquired
the required skills in some more haphazard fashion. The small
average size of the firms and casual or temporary nature of the
employer-employee relationship mitigate against unilateral training investments. Public utilities have customarily trained their own
nonprofessional employees. These utilities are generally of substantial size, tend to establish permanent employing relationships,
and can pass the costs on to the consumer.

In general large firms with specialized skills do their own
training; smaller firms without the luxury of company personnel
and training departments depend upon the public schools and
"pirating" from other employers. Craft-type skills — i.e., those
which incorporate a wide variety of tasks and skills applied under
varying settings and under limited supervision — are often supplied
from two- to four-year apprenticeships, either jointly union-

management supervised for casual, small-firm industries or unilat-erally company-sponsored in large-scale industry. The alternative is for the employee to gradually pick up the skills of the craft through extensive but haphazard employment experience or to attend vocational and technical schools; but these ordinarily offer only entry-level skills, leaving continued need for apprenticeship and on-the-job training. Those jobs of substantial but relatively narrow skills can be taught either institutionally or in formal company-sponsored on-the-job training programs. Semiskilled operatives and unskilled laborers learn on the job in a less formal manner.

Also as a generalization, employers will be willing to support their own training programs where the skills are specialized to their operations or where they can be reasonably assured that the em-ployee, once trained, will remain with them long enough to return the investment. Most will shift the training costs to public institu-tions or to other employers whenever they can. But they will be very reluctant to train where the skills have application to a wide variety of industries and employers or where there is high turnover among the employees.

Manpower planners should be reluctant to plan institutional training programs for those occupations for which on-the-job training or no training at all is the customary practice. It may be necessary in order to bring a disadvantaged worker to equal com-petitiveness with others already available to the employer. However, subsidized on-the-job training to gain entry for the disadvantaged is probably a better choice. On the other hand, on-the-job training and work experience programs are unlikely to be effective in occupations where the employer is accustomed to receiving trained personnel from the schools or to the breadth of skills provided through apprentice programs. Institutional training should be undertaken in manpower programs wherever it is cus-tomary for the labor market at large, and should be of sufficient length and quality to bring the manpower program completer to equality with those to whom the employer has access. Where apprenticeship is the recognized pattern, preapprentice programs linked to the management-union structure in control of labor market entry can bring to the disadvantaged access already avail-able to the nondisadvantaged. Whatever the situation, it is impor-tant that manpower planners be aware of customary labor market practice and either take advantage of it or be sure their artillery is adequate if they choose to confront it.

Probably no labor market now has data or methodology for accumulating data on the output of employer-sponsored on-the-job training activity. However, this does not mean the data are not needed or cannot be obtained. One of the advantages of employer and union representation on planning councils is the establishment of credibility with the employing community for obtaining such data. Always suspicious of federally sponsored research into their internal labor market practices, employers may be more willing to cooperate with a local planning process in which their peers are involved. Either by sampling or by interviewing all employers in the labor market, the manpower planner can obtain data on the number of people trained, by occupation, over an appropriate time period and the content of that training. Probably the nearest to the ideal system are the occupational training information systems developed by some state departments of education, notably those in Oklahoma and Missouri, which record the output of technically qualified workers for the entire state by source of training. Table 6-3 is a page from the Missouri report for 1972–73.

Matching Training Needs with Training Output

Surveying major employers and adding their output and turnover to the education-output matrix will provide information on the flows of new skills additions to be added to the current employment shown by the industry-occupation matrix advocated earlier in this chapter. Knowledge of job growth and turnover, compared with the output of the skills development system, can identify discrepancies.

It is not enough simply to assume that job vacancies or unemployed workers do not accumulate. Employers will generally "make do" by accepting undertrained workers when they are needed to meet customer demand and better trained or more experienced workers are not available. Workers will similarly downgrade themselves to available jobs when more attractive jobs are not available. The costs may be low productivity, high prices, shoddy workmanship, or underemployment. Yet the planner's tools for bringing equality between supply and demand are stronger when observed job vacancies and unemployment are present.

If the responsibility of the planner were the overall condition of the labor market, it would be appropriate to do or see done an analysis of the reasons for inadequate investment in training where it appears to be the case. Individual employers may not have recognized that, though one can "pirate," all cannot. Encouragement and assistance in organizing an industry-wide or multi-employer training program for that particular labor market may be the answer. Technical assistance in starting an on-the-job or coupled institutional–on-the-job training program may be another. Training schools, public and proprietary, may need to be alerted to the needs and possibilities in appropriate occupations. It is a rare employer who has any notion of the costs of his training efforts or of the costs to him of not training. Difficult as it is, such costs can be calculated and may be useful in motivating appropriate investment. Needed in particular are numerous studies of the relative *real* costs and benefits—social and private—of institutional and on-the-job training and informal learning for particular occupations.

Locational patterns of training, employment, and migration are needed. Some institutions train for regional and national as well as local labor markets. Since each labor market is a beneficiary as well as a contributor to such flows, balkanization may hurt more than help. Interesting differences between supply and demand relationships can be observed. In high educational investment communities, incumbents of certain jobs may be college graduates, while these same jobs are filled by those with a high school education only in areas of low education investment.

Entry requirements of training institutions as well as employer hiring criteria may be unrealistic, blocking access for persons with adequate skills potential. Identifying these situations and encouraging the required changes in practices may be a necessary task of transforming plans into results.

Since labor markets are never static, projections of training output must be kept up for sufficient future time periods to allow response. Employers are generally aware of the job requirements of emerging employment opportunities. On-the-job training has built-in correspondence between job content and training practices. Educational institutions too often teach only what the instructor knows and what the training equipment and materials are designed for rather than what the labor market demands. Considerable

Table 6-3
Training Sources of Technically Qualified Workers
(Statewide data)

U.S. Office of Education Code (17)	Instructional Program	Vocational Education, Student Accounting Components, 1973 Completions			MDTA and Related Programs				On-the-Job Training				Apprenticeship			
		Public		Private	1971		1972		1971		1972		1971		1972	
		Preparatory	Suppl. and Appr.		En-rolled	Com-pleted	En-rolled	Com-pleted	En-rolled	Com-pleted	En-rolled	Com-pleted	En-rolled	Com-pleted	En-rolled	Com-pleted
.100301	Maintenance – heavy equipment															
.100302	Operation – heavy equipment	21	1		46	37	50									
.1004	Masonry	50	15		24	24							85	20		
.1005	Painting, decorating															
.1006	Plastering															
.1007	Plumbing and pipefitting	41	48						49	8	61	7	374	48	388	63
.1008	Dry wall installation															
.1009	Glazing	1	1													
.1010	Roofing															
.1099	Other construction, maintenance training	124	71	3					36	10					11	
.1100	Custodial services	45		1												
.1200	Diesel mechanics	31	3													
.1300	Drafting	244		12												
.1400	Electrical occupations	103	100													

.1401	Industrial electrician										
.1402	Electrical lineman	4	18								5
.1403	Motor repairman										
.1499	Electrical occupations, other	1									
.1500	Electronics occupations	133	19	8							
.1501	Communications	8		1							
.1502	Electronics	143	12	153							
.1503	Radio and TV repair	95	27	94							
.1599	Electronic occupations, other										
.1600	Laundry and drycleaning	15	4		3						
.1601	Drycleaning	1									
.1602	Laundering										
.1699	Fabric maintenance services, other	1									
.1700	Foreman, supervisor — management division	28	21								
.1800	General continuation										
.1900	Graphics arts occupations	136	2			18	12	185	20	183	22	132	28	99	19
.1901	Compositor, makeup, typesetter	5									
.1902	Printing	76									
.1903	Lithographer, photographer, platemaker	1									
.1904	Photoengraver										

SOURCE: Division of Career and Adult Education, Missouri Department of Education, *Missouri Occupational Training Information System: 1972–1973 School Year Report* (Jefferson City: Research Coordinating Unit, Missouri Department of Education, 1973), pp. 84–85.

prodding may be necessary to match educational output to occupational requirements.

However, for the planner of manpower programs on behalf of the unemployed, underemployed, and disadvantaged, unfilled demand is an opportunity rather than a problem. It opens the challenge to find a route of access to those jobs for the people the planner is assigned to serve.

Channels of Recruitment

Given the growth and replacement needs of occupations, the problem emerges of ascertaining access to jobs for those for whom it is the planner's objective to plan. The problem has essentially three dimensions: (1) getting information to the job seeker, (2) bringing the job seeker and the potential employer into contact, and (3) achieving agreement between potential employer and employee on the requirements of the worker and the job and the conditions under which hiring will occur. Performing these tasks is not the responsibility of the planner, but understanding their realities and the likelihood of closure is.

It is a trusim of labor market studies that most job information is spread informally by word-of-mouth, and most matching of available people and available jobs takes place informally as information is spread by family and friends and by incumbent employees. Numerous intermediaries exist in the labor market: company personnel offices, union hiring halls, professional and trade associations, public and private employment services, community action agencies, and the like. Discrimination by employers on the grounds of age, sex, racial and ethnic origin, education, and so on, is a reality of the labor market and must be accommodated, circumvented, or confronted. Workers and potential workers have their own convictions about the kinds of jobs they are willing to accept and stick with once obtained, depending upon alternatives and their own economic circumstances. Planning must include incorporation of and response to these realities. Knowledge of legal requirements, employer and union practices, available tools for gaining information and access, and the relative competence of the various public intermediaries is a planning capability.

It is the planner's job to determine what job opportunities are and will become available for whatever target group the plan encompasses, to determine which would be available to individuals in that target group under what conditions, and to advise program administrators about routes to these jobs and probabilities of success. As the most generally available source of placement assistance, an early liaison should be established with local offices of the state employment service to take advantage of and at the same time encourage improvement in the effectiveness of that resource. Nevertheless, the planner's first loyalty is to the labor market and to the chosen target groups. Every route to job access for them should be expected.

References

Hoyt, Kenneth B.; *et al. Career Education: What It Is and How to Do It.* Second edition. Salt Lake City: Olympus Publishing Company. 1974.

Johnson, Miriam. *Counter Point: The Changing Employment Service.* Salt Lake City: Olympus Publishing Company. 1973.

Office of Management and Budget. *Standard Industrial Classification Manual.* Washington, D.C.: U.S. Government Printing Office. Various years.

U.S. Department of Commerce, Bureau of the Census. *General and Social Economic Characteristics.* Washington, D.C.: U.S. Government Printing Office. Various years.

U.S. Department of Labor. *Dictionary of Occupational Titles.* Washington, D.C.: U.S. Government Printing Office. Various years.

——————, Bureau of Labor Statistics. *Tomorrow's Manpower Needs.* Volume IV, revised. Washington, D.C.: U.S. Government Printing Office. 1971.

Walsh, John; *et al. Classified Help Wanted Ads: How Much Help?* (working title). To be published by the U.S. Department of Labor, Manpower Administration, Washington, D.C. 1974.

7
Development of a Local Manpower Policy

Having successfully assessed the population account and the accessible jobs account of the local labor market, the manpower planner must now devise a manpower strategy and mix of services which have the greatest promise of becoming a bridge between the target groups and the target job opportunities. No single task is more central to the planning process than the development of this local manpower policy. At the core of this task is careful allocation, among a set of activities, of scarce resources determined by the planner to be optimal, given what the planner has learned, or assumed, about the sociopolitical constraints of the planned-for area, the demographics of the local population, the dynamics of the local labor market, and the capabilities of local delivery systems. Since the task is crucial to the success of such planning, it is ironic that no aspect of manpower planning is less developed in the quality of its analytical tools.

This chapter begins with a discussion of the linkages between national economic policy and local manpower policy, the hierarchy of goals, and the limitations of direct translation to local labor market levels. It then turns to the presentation of a model for the development of a local manpower policy as an integrating focus for the products of the planner's studies of the labor market and the UON. The model is really a "model of models" in that it provides a framework for the development of labor market-wide manpower policies and the allocation of resources to the implementation of these policies. The chapter ends with a discussion of an approach to fitting client-group–job-opportunity segments with general service prescriptions that in turn provide the basis for chapter 8, which deals with the mix and staging of manpower services in the local labor market.

Linkage between National and Local Policy Goals

The setting of manpower goals in the local labor market is inextricably intertwined with the historical development of American manpower policy. Throughout, manpower programs have been expected to achieve goals beyond their capability. During the 1960s they were expected to serve first as a substitute for, and later as a complement to, broader economic policies. Despite criticisms of manpower achievements, recent years have been even more oriented toward panaceas. Manpower policies allegedly could shift the Phillips curve, correct the structural imbalance between the characteristics of the demand side and the characteristics of the emerging supply, reverse productivity declines and geographic disparities, and serve as countercyclical tools. Aside from questions of the realism of these perceptions of the potentialities of manpower policies, the historical debates have left a legacy which confuses the formulation of the shape, scope, and substance of *local* manpower policy. Policy formulation in the local manpower arena is not a scientific undertaking; it is best characterized as an art. While the data base might give one the impression that there is some available underlying, cold, analytical approach, nothing could be farther from the truth. In reality, the quantitative data must be turned into information. This translation process is necessarily subjective, intuitive, and creative.

There is a basic discontinuity in the structure and measurement of the goals of U.S. manpower policy. This problem results from the differences in the impact of fiscal and monetary policy, the two principal tools of modern economic policy, and the impact of manpower policies. Manpower policies are disaggregative, "particularistic," and selective; they operate primarily on the supply side of the market and function in the local labor market context. In contrast, fiscal and monetary policies operate on aggregate demand, are broad-gauge and diffused in their impact, and operate in the context of the national economy. While manpower, fiscal, and monetary policies are all directed at full employment, economic growth, and price stability goals, the impacts of local manpower policies cannot be measured by the direct indicators of these goals. This is due in part to the relatively small size of manpower programs. More important is the fact that adequate labor market theory for accounting for displacement effects on nonparticipants is not yet available.

Manpower programs have been defended politically upon their supposed impact on broad aggregates such as unemployment, poverty, and the gross national product, but their reality has been services to individuals without measure of aggregate impact. Still, sufficient evidence exists to support the development of local manpower policies linked to broad macro-economic goals, and therefore local policies should reflect these ties. However, rational planning at the local level requires that goals be formulated which are measurable to an extent that is reasonable and consistent with good sense. Therein lies the discontinuity.

In a seminal work (Scanlon *et al.*, 1971), a team of researchers came to the following conclusion:

> To be able to speak of effectiveness in meeting a goal requires that the goal and the intervention designed to achieve it be related in some common system of measurement. . . . [G]iven the present state of knowledge, the most appropriate framework for this measurement at present is not the national economy or the target groups in the labor market, but the success of the applicant in the labor market (p. IV-10).

The planner necessarily had to develop local goals based upon assumptions about linkages between observed dysfunction in the labor market and programmatic interventions involving persons affected by the dysfunction. For example, if an objective was to reduce unemployment for a specific population group, the planner might assume that increasing the probability that individual members of the groups would find and keep employment decreased the group's average unemployment. The planner might then prescribe a set of manpower and skills training services and enroll individuals from the group into the training. While it is clear that the prescription of service was developed from the goal to reduce unemployment among the target group, the measurement of that goal directly is a much more difficult step. Simple data gaps, the relatively small size of the programs, unsolved problems concerning displacement effects, and the impossibility of controlling for other variables confound direct measurement of the impact of the services rendered in reducing unemployment of the target group. In contrast, the planner can measure the impact of the intervention on the employment and income of the individual enrollee, and as a result, the assumptions relating to the prescription of service to individuals in the target groups can be validated or invalidated. More definitive validation of the assumed impacts of specific interventions upon aggregate economic conditions and upon the economic and social conditions of specific target groups awaits more sophisticated theory and measurement.

What does all this mean in the context of local manpower policy development? Simply this: While the planner must necessarily be concerned with economic conditions and how specific groups fare in the labor market in order to make wise selections among target groups and to suggest appropriate interventions, goals developed round these conditions and groups generally cannot be measured directly from the conditions and groups themselves. Theory and measurement are simply not yet up to the task. The local planner should develop local manpower policy, and the goals of that policy, round the changes desired in the labor market success of individual enrollees or changes desired in specific institutions. This is the approach of this chapter in presentation of a model for the shaping of a local manpower policy.

Model for the Development of Local Manpower Policy

A model substitutes a simpler system to represent and make understandable the essential characteristics of a more complex system. The purpose of the model of local manpower policy development that follows is to provide an integrative framework for use by manpower planners. It is offered as a "model for models"; in short, an organizing framework for the development of local models more precisely calibrated to the particular environments of each manpower planning authority.

There are ten basic elements in the planning model. They begin with a description of problem areas and end with an output of planning elements used in operational planning. They are:

(1) Identify the manpower problems of the local labor market.

(2) Identify, by age, sex, race, and income, the specific population groups directly affected by the problem and estimate the numbers in each group for each of the planning periods.

(3) Classify each of the groups into the following employability preparedness categories and estimate the numbers in each subgroup:

  (a) High mobility.

  (b) Job capable.

  (c) Moderate barriers.

  (d) Severe barriers.

(4) Generate alternative approaches for meeting the manpower problems of each of the subgroups along the following lines:

  (a) Alternatives which improve the basic employability of individual enrollees.

  (b) Alternatives which remove institutional or systemic obstacles that impede access to available jobs.

  (c) Alternatives which create new jobs for specific groups of individuals.

  (d) Alternatives whose primary thrust is to transfer payments to target populations, although the approach might include some work activity short of a recognizable job.

(5) Evaluate the alternatives and choose appropriate alternatives for each subgroup.

(6) Prioritize the preferred subgroup-alternative sets within each problem area.

(7) Make a tentative allocation of available resources against the problem areas.

(8) State the goals of the manpower planning authority in terms of the problems addressed, the resources allocated, the groups and institutions affected, the general approaches to be taken, and the measures that will have impact.

(9) Fit available job opportunities (or jobs to be generated) to each subgroup-alternative set.

(10) Prescribe the service strategy to be used to move the sub-group into the identified job opportunity.

The following pages describe these elements in greater detail and present some of the available methods for accomplishing the work involved. Figure 7.1 illustrates in simplified form the sequence of elements. The descriptions of the elements are keyed to the circled numbers.

1. Identify the Problem Areas

The process of policy formation begins with a review of the findings developed from the planner's analysis of the local labor market, the accessible jobs account, and the population account. The planner's review is directed at the identification of labor market-related pathologies: the size and nature of unemployment, underemployment, labor force participation, and poverty; the supply of labor; the demand for labor; the market institutions; and the labor market intermediaries. It also surveys the structure of employment: What are the growth industries? What are the growth occupations? Which industries and occupations are in decline? What are the significant market intermediaries? How significant are they? What are the jobs to which they control access?

The planner needs to develop a feeling for differences and commonalities about the local labor market, and this can best be done by a comparative approach. The information for this review is readily at hand in the Bureau of Labor Statistics' monthly *Employment and Earnings*, in its wage series, and other widely distributed data series. The planner compares the measured portions of a general image of the local labor market with similar measures for other comparable areas. The objective of course is to gain perspective — feeling, if you will, for the structure and size of the local labor market. This suggestion is easily carried out by planners in most of the SMSAs. Planners should develop a perspective on participation, labor force size, industrial composition, wages, hours, vacancies, turnover, employment, and unemployment. They should pursue a similar perspective in relation to the size and structure of the planning area population and should develop a feeling for how

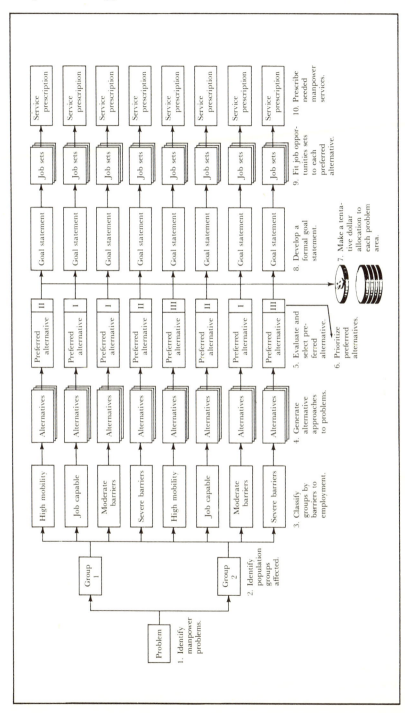

Figure 7.1. Local Manpower Policy Planning Model: Single Problem Example

the area compares and contrasts with other areas of similar size and close proximity: How does the local population differ in age structure? In ethnic composition? In education levels? In income levels?

Perspective is also needed on the social and political climate of the labor market — all those factors which relate to the social and political power (or lack of it) of identifiable population groups, of relevant bureaucracies, and of significant elective and appointive decision makers: What groups are organized to articulate their particular interests? What are the "manpower politics" of the area? Who are the relevant "hell raisers"? Which issues have been the focus of significant controversy in the past? What influence do the community action agencies carry? Which manpower issues have racial implications? Which have been involved in local electoral politics? In short, planners should develop some intuitive grasp of where both the skeletons and the land mines are. While a preoccupation with these issues is to be avoided, they should develop a healthy appreciation for the social and political power structure of the planned-for area.

From these three perspectives, the manpower planner develops a list of significant manpower problems. The problems should represent the important disparities, gaps, inequities, and deficiencies in the operation of the local labor market.

2. Identify the Specific Population Groups Directly Affected by the Problems

The next step is to develop an understanding of who is directly affected by the significant pathologies of the local labor market. The planner is looking here for differential impacts and draws on the population account analysis to determine the population groups which experience a disproportionate share of the given problem. If the problem involves an institutional or systemic failure, the planner seeks to find out who is directly affected by the failure. If the problem involves unemployment, poverty, underemployment, or labor force participation, again the planner looks for groups which experience a disproportionate share of the given problem. He or she then identifies these groups by age, sex, race, and income characteristics and estimates the number of individuals in each group. These population groups form the basis for all further planning.

3. Classify the Population Groups by Their Preparedness for Employment

To this point, the planner has identified the significant manpower problems of the local labor market and estimated the numbers of persons affected in the groups identified, according to their age, sex, race, and income characteristics. Before alternative approaches to the problems can be developed, the planner must possess a more detailed estimate of the extent and severity of the barriers faced by these populations in the labor market. In addition to assisting in the development of alternative approaches, the planner must also have knowledge of the extent and severity of the barriers, for these will also govern the ultimate costs of the needed interventions, as well as the prospects of success.

A useful approach to classifying potential manpower client groups was first developed by the Manpower Administration as part of the early preparation for implementation of the manpower provisions for the Administration's now defunct welfare reform proposal. This method employs a set of criteria designed to indicate preparedness for employability. The criteria used to classify potential clients suggested in the welfare reform working papers were as follows:

(1) Work experience as an indicator of readiness for employment and as a function of length of time in an occupation; stability of participation in the work force and occupational skill levels achieved

(2) Education — both achievement (meaning the measured level of the client's functional ability to perform) and attainment (meaning the grade level completed)

(3) Health, including both mental and physical dimensions

To this minimal set the planner might add an attitudinal-behavioral dimension (if reliable and useful classification could be developed) as well as locational and racial dimensions and sex, age, and various other criteria, if these criteria were determined to be useful for matching target groups with job opportunities. The planner should be cautioned, however, that while these factors are useful for defining barriers and identifying persons, their use in the matching process may lead to narrow stereotyping. The criteria are used to classify persons into one of the following four employment preparedness categories:

(1) *High mobility:* Enrollees who are the best prepared to hold self-support jobs. The following standards could be used to identify the high-mobility registrants:

   (a) Work experience — has held a transitional or self-support job, or . . . .

   (b) Education — has a high school diploma.

   (c) Health — has no health barriers requiring more than remedial attention.

(2) *Job capable:* Enrollees could be expected to compete successfully for transitional or stable low income, but not self-support jobs. Illustrating the standards for this classification are:

   (a) Work experience — has held a stable low-income job, or . . . .

   (b) Education — ninth to eleventh functional grade range.

   (c) Health — no health barriers requiring more than remedial attention.

(3) *Moderate barriers:* These enrollees bring with them little in the way of positive indicators of future job success, yet have none of the barriers defined in (4) below as "severe." Standards for this group could be:

   (a) Work experience — may have no stable work experience, or . . . .

   (b) Education — eighth grade or less functional level.

   (c) Health — no health barriers requiring more than remedial attention.

(4) *Severe barriers:* These enrollees have one or more of the following barriers:

   (a) Education — functional education below third grade.

   (b) Health — requires extensive rehabilitation.

   (c) Work attitudes — severely dysfunctional.

Estimates of the size of the employability preparedness categories are made from a fairly creative analysis of the barriers data. The key to developing these estimates is the ability of the planner to construct a cross-tabulated table of estimates of the incidence of the specific criteria defining each employability preparedness category. The choice of classifying criteria will depend both on the availability of estimates and on the preferences of the planner. In the example in Figure 7.2, the planner chose work experience, education, and health factors for ranking the population sub-groups. The table in the figure shows a completed analysis and indicates the cells which yield estimates for the employment preparedness categories.

There are three primary methods for developing the cross-tabulated estimates. The first method would start with estimates of the distribution of each criterion within the parent population and assume a proportional distribution. For example, if those with a high school educational level constituted 40 percent of the parent population, this group would be allocated 40 percent of those with health problems, self-support work experiences, and so forth. This method is probably the least satisfactory.

A second method for constructing the cross-tabulated estimates would be to conduct a sample survey of the population and to apply the relationships found in the sample population to the population under study. A well-designed and -executed sample survey would probably yield the most reliable estimates of the cross-tabulated classifying criteria. However, cost and time factors are likely to preclude this approach. It is strongly recommended that the planner considering a survey approach consult one of the many handbooks on social surveys before proceeding too far.*

A third approach to the construction of the cross-tabulated estimates would be to derive the estimated relationships from a sample of individual client administrative records on persons from the parent population who have been served by manpower service agencies. The techniques for the sampling and analysis of administrative records are widely available to local manpower

---

*An excellent introduction to manpower surveys is Morton, 1972. Complete publishing information is given in the references at the end of this chapter.

planners and probably offer the most cost/effective approach to these types of analyses.*

While it is clear that considerable experimentation is needed in developing methods for translating data on barriers into useful criteria for classifying potential manpower service target populations, it is even clearer that present classification methods are not well adapted to the planner's needs. For example, the most widely used system, that of the employment service, employs a three-way classification under which most of the present clients of manpower programs would be lumped into a single classification ("employability development"). Although we deal at much greater length with this problem in the related context of service strategy prescription, it is clear that the methodology for measuring or predicting the existence of significant barriers to program success and employability is far less developed than is currently needed. Consequently, the estimation of the proportions of the target populations must, at this point, be a fairly creative exercise. Nonetheless, it is essential that the planner make these estimates.

4. Generate Alternative Approaches

Following the classification of the population groups by their preparedness for employment, the planner turns to the task of generating alternative approaches to each of the problems. Alternatives are developed along the four primary interventions open to local manpower planners:

(1) Those which improve the basic employability of individual clients

(2) Those which remove institutional or systemic obstacles which impede access to available jobs

(3) Those which create new jobs for specific groups of target clients

(4) Those whose primary thrust is to transfer payments to target populations, although the approach might include some work activity short of a recognizable job

---

*An excellent practical approach to the use of administrative records for planning purposes is a May 1974 draft by the Manpower Administration, *Data Options for Prime Sponsors*. See references for publishing data.

Functional Health Criteria	Functional Education Criteria	Work Experience Criteria				Summary Estimates
		Has Held Good Self-Support Job	Has Held Stable Low-Wage Income Job	May Have No Work Experience	Total	
No health problems	High school	273	270	125	668	
	Ninth to eleventh grade	165	210	90	465	High mobility group 708
	Third to eighth grade	110	205	145	460	(165, 273, 270)
	Below third grade	30	87	140	257	
Health problems	High school	7	10	15	32	
	Ninth to eleventh grade	10	15	10	35	Job capable group 445
	Third to eighth grade	15	20	5	40	(110, 210, 125)
	Below third grade	15	18	10	43	Moderate barriers group 440 (205, 90, 145)
TOTAL	High school	280	280	140	700	
	Ninth to eleventh grade	175	225	100	500	Severe barrier group 407 (257, 32, 35, 40, 43)
	Third to eighth grade	125	225	150	500	
	Below third grade	45	105	150	300	TOTAL 2,000
	TOTAL	625	835	540	2,000	

Figure 7.2. Employment Preparedness Categories by Classifying Criteria

Each alternative should additionally specify the particular group of persons, systems, or institutions central to the intervention, as well as the degree of intervention implied by the approach. The alternatives should also pay explicit attention to time. Planning is, at its heart, a future-oriented activity. The planner needs to make a determination as to the future implications of the problems-alternatives sets. Which sets are short term? Which sets are long term? What are the time implications of each alternative approach? Have all the alternative approaches been spelled out? Are there any long- or short-term approaches which have been missed?

5. Evaluate Alternative Approaches and Choose a Preferred Approach

After developing alternative approaches to meet the problems faced by the identified population groups, the planner proceeds to evaluate the alternatives and select preferred approaches. A useful technique for integrating subjective and quantitative inputs, as well as time considerations, into the development of alternatives is scenario writing. Scenario writing is a method of developing alternative futures by starting at the present and systematically and sequentially considering a complete range of alternative choices or events that will carry the narrative into the future (Chadwick, 1971, p. 380). The planner who uses the scenario technique for evaluating alternatives simply takes all the information currently available, both perceptive and quantitative, and develops a "story" based on "best guesses" as to how each alternative might work out. Missing quantitative indicators are invented; changing social and economic environmental factors are considered. The completed scenario might be a group project which is "talked out" by the planning staff, in which case the more sophisticated designation of "Delphi" method might be appended to the process. A more formal description of the Delphi method would include the requirements that the persons participating be recognized experts and the expression of their views be structured in a formalized question framework.

Scenario writing is used as a device for narrowing the range of alternative interventions. The local planner should discard alternatives which are obviously impractical or whose perceived probability of success are very low. He or she should exercise

caution, however, against discarding alternatives whose only negative aspect is their unfamiliarity on the local scene. In the broadest
professional sense, the planner has the obligation to bring to the
planner–decision-maker relationship a wider range of alternatives
than the decision maker would have had at his disposal without
the planner. Alternatives beyond the obvious, the planner's analytical skills, the planner's systematic approach, and an orientation
toward the future, are the stock-in-trade of the planning profession.
Bringing these tools to the planner–decision-maker relationship is
at the core of the planners' professional responsibilities.

With the evaluative scenarios in hand, as well as any other
relevant evaluative materials, the planner selects one or more
preferred alternative approaches to the manpower problem of the
population-subgroup–employment-preparedness sets. These choices
are then presented for final approval by the decision-making
authority, with appropriate narrative justifications.

6. Prioritize Alternatives within Each Problem Area

After selecting preferred approaches for subgroups in each
problem area, the planner turns to the task of prioritizing the
subgroup-alternative sets. The planner should structure an explicit
priority-setting exercise to narrow the range and number of alternatives to an appropriate size and to structure the subgroup-
alternative sets within each problem area for later steps in the
planning process. Although there is no single best way to approach
priority setting, it is clear that the problems identified and the
alternatives generated will differ in importance, immediateness,
likelihood of success, and so forth. The objective of priority setting
is to determine the preferred *order* in which subgroup-alternative
sets will be addressed. It may be appropriate to designate which year
in a multi-year plan a particular alternative will be addressed.
The planner should also distinguish which of these sets represents
causes and which represents effects, drawing on the perceptions
developed earlier of the labor market, the population, and the
sociopolitical environments. In short, the planner should bring all
of the information available to the prioritization of the sets and
yet realize that priority setting at this point in the planning process
is essentially subjective.

7. Make a Tentative Allocation of Resources to Each Problem Area

With priorities assigned to each of the subgroup-alternative sets, the planner can turn to the setting of broad-gauge allocations to the problem areas. The purpose of allocation at this point is twofold: First, the planner needs to begin to integrate the information and decisions made to this point which indicate local priorities. The process of evaluating the alternatives and of selecting and prioritizing the preferred approaches has served to winnow down the list of all possible alternatives. The planner also has some notion of the relative importance of the groups and alternatives. Attaching money figures to the alternatives at this point is a logical next step. Second, the planner needs to begin to get some idea of the ultimate size and shape of the population to be served and of the service mix. Attaching tentative dollar figures to each of the problem areas

Table 7-1
Measurements of Goal Achievements for the Service Approaches

Service Approach	Measurement Frames	
	Direct or In-Program Impacts on Participants	Overall or Out-of-Program Impacts on Participants
Improve basic employability	Changes in: education, behavior, appearances, skills, location	Changes in: labor market participation, wages, incomes, job stability, job satisfaction
Remove institutional and systemic obstacles or barriers	Changes in: job discrimination, mobility, career patterns, availability of service, effectiveness of service	Changes in: labor market participation, wages, incomes, job stability, job satisfaction
Create jobs	Numbers of enrollments, dollars transferred, changes in work habits	Changes in: labor market participation, wages, incomes, job stability, job satisfaction, useful work performed
Transfer payments or work experience	Numbers of enrollments, dollars transferred, changes in work habits	Changes in: dollars transferred (including from in-program to post-program), wages, incomes, job stability

serves to place a working limit on what ultimately can be done in the shorter term about the problem.

The technique for allocating available resources to the problem areas is essentially judgmental. The role of the planner is to structure allocation options, to lay out the implications of these options, and then to present the options to the manpower planning decision-making authority. The planner should take this task very seriously because it represents the core of local manpower policy development. Whereas there are readily applicable allocation formulas which integrate efficiency and distributional considerations to be used at later stages in the planning process for allocation among groups and service strategies, allocation to the problem areas is not handled so simply. The planner looks at the problems, at the groups experiencing the problem, and at the distribution of the groups among the employment preparedness categories and examines the alternatives and their likelihood of success. Given this information, and perceptions of future changes in the market, the planner makes a tentative gross allocation of the available resources on the basis of professional judgment: so much to counter unemployment, so much to increase labor force participation, so much to change the characteristics of the supply, and so forth.

8. State and Local Manpower Goals

With the completion of the allocation to problem areas, the planner is ready to draw up goal statements. The goal statements developed at this point will serve as the basis for the later development of specific objectives, as well as a keystone in outcome and impact evaluation. The goals are stated in group-specific terms and make use of the basic information on: (1) the general service approach, (2) the groups to be served, (3) the priorities among the groups, (4) the problems being addressed, and (5) the changes expected in enrollees. By stating the general approach to be taken, the planner also lays the foundation for measurement of the goal, which includes both in-program and overall or out-of-program changes. The basic measurements of goal achievements for the service approaches are shown in Table 7-1. A suggested approach for structuring goal statements for the problem area is as follows:

Unemployment: In fiscal year 1976, the *X Y Z* Manpower Planning Authority will allocate 37 percent of its resources to countering unemployment. The specific goals of this effort will be the following:

(1) Improve the wages, incomes, and job stability of 21- to 34-year-old, poor, male minorities, with moderate barriers to employment, through service approaches designed to improve the basic employability of program enrollees.

(2) Provide needed public services and increase the wages, labor market participation, incomes, and job stability of unemployed 21- to 34-year-old, poor, Caucasian, and minority females, with no major barriers to employment ("job capables") by creating teacher-aide jobs in the local school system.

(3) Increase the labor market participation, wages, incomes, and job stability of 44-year-old (or older), poor, female minorities with moderate barriers to employment by removing systemic obstacles to their hire into clerical positions covered under the municipal civil service system.

The next task is to create more specific objectives for each one of the prioritized groups within the framework of: (1) the goal statements pertaining to each group, (2) the service approach pertaining to each group, and (3) the specific measured targets to be achieved. Objective statements are structured for each group and consist of the following three elements for goals that deal with the flow of individuals.

(1) Group identifiers

(2) Target jobs

(3) Service strategy — specific services designed to move identified groups into target jobs

Objective statements for goals which deal with changes in institutions or systems, but which do not deal directly with individuals on a client basis, might be developed as follows (although the above form is preferred):

(1) System or institution problems

(2) Desired conditions

(3) Specific methods of change

We will not deal extensively with this second set of objective statements. The establishment of objective statements for goals which deal with individuals is accomplished in two stages. The first fits a job set to the identified group, consistent with its appropriate service approach frame. The second takes the match of group and jobs and fits a service strategy to the match (designed to move persons in the group into the identified jobs).

9. Matching the Group to the Jobs*

The crucial component of a workable schema for matching groups of target clients with groups of job opportunities is the development of a common language for classifying jobs and clients. The common language should permit the synthesis of information on client group characteristics, individual and institutional barriers, and job requirements. This section outlines a suggested approach to such matching through a set of organizing categories.

When the manpower planner gets to the point of matching the group with the jobs, he or she will already have expended considerable effort on labor market and population analyses. It is important that the planner develop tools for organizing and classifying this mass of qualitative and quantitative information. The most crucial step in organizing this information is the specification of criteria by which the target group and job data can be classified. The development of client group and job classifications should rest on the perception that the allocations of manpower service resources represent an investment in human resources. This investment will entail costs which are expected to result in benefits. Even though formal cost/benefit analysis is an evaluative, rather than a design concept, the basic relationship should underly the service design. Costs in this sense are a function of the investments required to move people into the job opportunities; and benefits in this context are a function of the wages and other changes brought about by the positioning of the person on the job. Consequently, the criteria used to classify clients and jobs will reflect the general perceptions of the costs and benefits in the classifying schema employed.

---

*This section draws from unpublished materials developed by the staff of the Manpower Administration in preparation for the welfare reform proposal.

With this idea of perceived benefits, the criteria for classifying jobs would at minimum include the following:

(1) *Wages:* These include not only the amount of income the client can expect at the outset, but also the range of wages for certain types of jobs, the median wage paid for certain jobs, and the mode of payment by the firm.

(2) *Employment duration:* Significant to the client, together with wage expectation, is length of time he or she can expect to be employed in the job. This also serves as an indicator of anticipated income.

(3) *Upgrading potential:* If the job provides upward mobility, the likelihood of long-term stability and income gains resulting from such employment will appeal to prospective recipients of the planning.

And the idea of perceived costs would suggest the following now-familiar criteria as a minimal set for classifying the target groups:

(1) *Work experience:* This is generally an indicator of readiness for employment and is a function of the length of time a client has already spent in an occupation, his or her stability of participation in the work force, and the occupational skill levels he or she has achieved.

(2) *Education:* Determining educational levels is a necessary part of the total planning picture. "Functional education" is the achieved and measured level of a client's ability to perform; "actual education" is the grade level completed by the client.

(3) *Health:* This component includes both mental and physical dimensions.

As discussed previously, the target group classification criteria are used to estimate the numbers of the target population in employment preparedness categories.

In the welfare reform working papers, income above "break even" was used as the basis for the development of job categories. "Break even" was defined as "cash benefits plus market value of services received," which would terminate for the welfare recipient upon placement. They also defined five job categories according to the estimated benefits they were expected to provide:

(1) *Cycle breaking:* Annual income, 25 percent above the self-support threshold level for 80 percent of the client population. Self-support income levels to vary with family size.

(2) *Self-support threshold:* Break even or above for 80 percent of the population.

(3) *Transitional:* Clear evidence that the job leads to the self-support threshold or above. The wage is from the federal minimum to the self-support threshold.

(4) *Stable low income:* Little potential for advancement, but of long duration. The wage is from the federal minimum to the self-support threshold.

(5) *Marginal:* Temporary, seasonal, or at low pay ($1.60 or less).

When calibrating the job categories for local use, the manpower planner might use the poverty level as a self-support threshold. An alternative method for categorizing jobs for planning purposes is known as the Occupational Opportunities Rating System (OORS). First used operationally by the Baltimore City Planning Authority, the OORS has recently been given wider notice in the technical assistance guides prepared for use under CETA (U.S. Department of Labor, March 1974, pp. III-22 and -23).

With the jobs assigned to categories according to income and upgrading potential, the planner develops information profiles on each job. The occupational profiles describe the jobs in terms of:

(1) Number of anticipated openings
(2) Location
(3) Discriminatory hiring practices
(4) Educational requirements
(5) Skills and experience requirements
(6) Wages and wage potential
(7) Advancement potential
(8) Health requirements
(9) Seasonality
(10) Unionization

The analysis of accessible jobs described earlier is the primary source of this information. Jobs are then grouped within each job category by occupational cluster. The planner then proceeds to match the job groups with the target population subgroups. After

finishing step (8), the planner will have a set of planning elements
in the following form:

> *Moderate Barrier Subgroup III:* Five hundred 19- to 21-year-old unem-
> ployed, poor, male minorities, with moderate barriers to employ-
> ment. (No stable work experience, ninth to eleventh functional
> grade range, no major health barriers.)

Job opportunity descriptions will take the following form:

> *Cycle-breaking job number 5:*

Mechanical assemblers	190 openings
$3.50 to $4.20 per hour wages	Good advancement potential
Equal opportunity employer	Non-unionized employers
Six months' related experience required or "appropriate" training	High school diploma or general education diploma required

The planner will now match the target population subgroups with
the job groups by using a predetermined sorting algorithm. The
following list is one sequential process for matching:

(1) Sort all subgroups and job opportunities by major trans-
    portation zones.

(2) Within transportation zones, assign all cycle-breaking job
    opportunities to the high-mobility group until the number
    of jobs or the number of clients in the group is exhausted.
    Then assign the remaining cycle-breaking job sets to the
    job-capable groups, or if high-mobility groups remain,
    assign self-support threshold jobs to the high-mobility
    group until that number is exhausted. Continue in this
    manner until all job opportunities or population sub-
    groups have been matched so far as possible.

(3) For each population subgroup, sort jobs assigned thus far
    into "work experience required" and "no work experience
    required" categories. Sort population subgroups into
    "work experienced" and "nonwork experienced" cate-
    gories. Pair the "nonexperienced" and "no experience
    required" categories together, and then do the same with
    the "experienced" and "experienced required" categories.

(4) Within each of the experience sortings, re-sort all on the
    basis of education required and education possessed.

Match groups to minimize gaps between subgroup education and education required for the job.

(5) Within the above sortings, correlate other common denominators to reduce to minimums the gaps between the job profile and the characteristics of the potential enrollee group.

Note that the algorithm outlined above is based on a maximum-impact strategy in that the jobs with the best prospects are allocated to the groups with the best prospects first, and those population subgroups with the severest barriers get what is left. This is a straightforward "skimming" strategy designed to move the largest number of target group members into employment as quickly as possible. Alternative approaches might set some formula for allocating a larger portion of the better job opportunities to population subgroups with more severe barriers to employment. The result of course would have cost implications insofar as the gaps between the relevant characteristics of the potential enrollees and the requirements of the jobs would be greater. Presumably the cost of the needed interventions would also rise.

As a practical matter, few local manpower planning authorities presently have the capability to implement the subgroup and job-matching process in the detail outlined above. It is more likely that for the near future local planners will assign known job opportunity blocks to population subgroups on a trial-and-error basis and assign the remaining subgroups to "safe" occupational training areas derived from historical program experience. Consequently, we are likely to continue to see large amounts of training resources assigned to welding, auto mechanics, and practical nurse's training, which have proved to be areas of persistent job openings, even when they are not the highest priority. It is important, however, that the local planner begin to develop more appropriate methods for the selection of occupational emphases for target groups.

10. Prescribe the Service Strategy

After assigning job opportunities to each of the subgroups, the planner turns to the task of prescribing a service strategy to be used to move the subgroup into the identified job opportunity. In addition to the subgroup-job matches the planner will have information on the characteristics and barriers to employment of each subgroup, as well as information on the characteristics and requirements of each set of job opportunities. The planner will also have the goal statements developed for each subgroup, defining the desired outcomes and the preferred approach to be taken.

The basic approach for determining the services needed to move subgroup members into the assigned job opportunities is to contrast the requirements of the job with the characteristics and barriers to employment of the population subgroups. From this comparison, the planner develops one or more sets of services designed to result in the desired outcome. Table 7-2 illustrates this process for a subgroup of forty to fifty poor, male chicanos, 21 to 34 years of age, with moderate barriers to employment. The job opportunity match consists of 35 to forty anticipated job openings for precision grinders. The preferred service approach is to bring about basic employability improvements.

Similar comparisons are drawn for each of the subgroup-job sets and one or more service prescriptions created. The result of the process is a set of tentative service prescriptions which can be used to design the basic components of the local service delivery system.

Program and Service Mix

Nomenclature in the manpower business is constantly changing. The newness of the field, the continuing changes in what is classified as "manpower" and what is not, and the fact that a great deal of experimentation has been encouraged account for the fact that there is considerable confusion over the appropriate taxonomy for classifying what manpower programs offer clients. When is an activity called a "program"? How does a program differ from a service? How does a service differ from a component? Lack of common definitions can cause considerable confusion both for novice planners and for lay people. Some standardization is needed before we can proceed very far in the discussion of the program and service mix.

The current use of the term "program" has come about from the historical evolution of U.S. manpower policy. Recent manpower debate has focused on abolishing what had come to be the "categorical programs." Categorical programs were prepackaged sets of activities which developed from the Manpower Development and Training Act and the Economic Opportunity Act. Specific models were developed under each authority and were more or less

Table 7-2

Deriving the Service Prescription

Dimension	Known and Unknown Characteristics of Subgroup	Requirements of the Job Opportunity	Barriers	Services Needed
Work experience	Unknown — estimated as minimal	Six months required — job related	Lack required experience	Six months of on-the-job training
Skills	Unknown	Employer specific: a. Use of precision templates b. Specific manipulative skills acquired on the job	Assume that subgroup lacks required skills	Six months of on-the-job training
Education	Average eleventh grade (language problems not severe)	High school: a. Diploma desired b. Solid basic math required	Lack average of one year of education	Six months of general education diploma preparation, stipends, and training (math emphasis)
Health	No major barriers	Good	None	None
Unionization	Unknown	Not unionized	None	None
Equal opportunity qualifications	Chicano males, 21 to 34 years of age	Equal opportunity employer, but supervisors have posed problems in the past	Supervisors' acceptance of enrollees	On-site supervisory orientation sessions
Transportation	45 percent have cars	Plant is located 10 miles from town, but on public bus line	None	No expected problem

uniformly set in place across the country. Thus we think of all of the programs — each called a category — which were created: MDTA institutional and on-the-job training and residential institutional training for "hardcore" youth (Job Corps). Other categorical programs included the Work Incentive Program, the Neighborhood Youth Corps, the Concentrated Employment Program, Operation Mainstream, Public Service Careers, New Careers, National Alliance of Businessmen–Job Opportunities in the Business Sector, and various others. The Public Employment Program was the last categorical program created, and all such programs have often been called the "alphabet soup" because of the widespread use of acronyms to identify them.

Historically, programs have consisted of set combinations of services directed to more or less specific target groups and designed round a particular set of assumptions relating the causes and effects of the groups' perceived problems in the labor market. For example, MDTA institutional training assumes that the primary problem is a lack of skills or basic educational competencies. Consequently, the primary services offered are an intake process designed to identify persons with low skill levels, a counseling process designed to determine vocational interests, a classroom training service designed to impart necessary job performance skills, a stipend service designed to provide financial support while the person is being trained, and a placement service designed to match the trained client with job openings.

Thus programs are a more or less set package and sequence of services designed to serve a specific target group thought to be experiencing a particular problem. A more useful concept is the service strategy typology. Two definitions are central to this concept:

(1) *Component:* A well-defined portion of a service delivery program (i.e., a skills training program, a general education diploma program, a work experience program).

(2) *Service strategy:* The entire path to be followed by a type or group of applicants from intake to placement to follow-up. The service strategy includes all the major and minor components to be used and the sequence (order) in which they are used.

The familiar service components, some with long histories and others developed within the last decade, are shown in Figure 7.3.* This extended list can be categorized in a variety of ways. Most Labor Department issuances involving CETA use a five-way classification which relates to the content of the components:

(1) Basic manpower services

(2) Classroom education and training

(3) Subsidized public and private employment

(4) Work experience training

(5) Supportive services

For purposes of this book, it seems more useful to rely on a categorization that is more concerned with the objective of the various service components. This approach involves four primary or direct service groupings and two secondary or indirect ones:

(a) Primary components:

    (1) Employability improvement — those which improve the basic employability of individuals

    (2) Job access — those which remove obstacles that impede access to available jobs

    (3) Job creation — those which create jobs for the target individuals

    (4) Income maintenance — those which provide income through transfer payment, often attached to some work activity short of a recognizable job.

(b) Secondary components:

    (5) Entry services — those which recruit and enroll manpower clients and assess their needs

    (6) Supportive services — nonmanpower services which facilitate participation in manpower programs or jobs

---

*The reader who is interested in more information on specific service components is referred to the excellent bibliography in U.S. Department of Labor, Manpower Administration, *Program Activities and Service Guide* (March 1974), and the National League of Cities-Conference of Mayors, *Focus on Manpower Planning* (December 1973). Complete publishing information is given in the references at the end of this chapter.

1. Entry services
   a. Outreach and recruitment
   b. Intake
   c. Assessment (including testing)
   d. Orientation
   e. Counseling

2. Employability improvement
   a. Academic education (includes high school diploma, general education diploma, and degree preparation)
   b. General education (including remedial education and basic education, as well as English as a second language)
   c. Skills training (or vocational education; conducted in single occupation groups, in broad occupational clusters, or purchased singly for an individual)

3. Job creation
   a. Subsidized employment (including transitional subsidized employment and work experience with either private or public employers)
   b. On-the-job training (including job upgrading for in-service personnel and apprenticeship)*

4. Job access
   a. Job development (including job solicitation and redesign)
   b. Job placement
   c. Job retention counseling
   d. Removal of artificial barriers to job access (including elimination of discriminatory or meaningless hiring qualifications and practices and rigid attitudes of supervisors)
   e. Equal employment opportunity measures
   f. Job restructuring
   g. Personnel and merit system reform

5. Income maintenance
   a. Stipends and living allowances
   b. Work experience training

6. Supportive services
   a. Coaching
   b. Transportation support
   c. Relocation support
   d. Health services
   e. Child care
   f. Homemaking and consumer counseling
   g. Emergency aid
   h. Residential support

---

*Categorization is sometimes arbitrary, and different observers may read different purposes into various components. On-the-job training can be interpreted as employability improvement or as subsidized employment, depending upon the employer's intent and performance. Work experience programs such as the Neighborhood Youth Corps, funded under the Economic Opportunity Act, were sometimes interpreted as employability improvements, sometimes as job creation, but more often as a device to give income to youth from poor families. How prime sponsors treat these functions remains to be seen.

Figure 7.3. Manpower Service Components

A crucial task of the manpower planner is adjusting the mix of services to changing labor market conditions. Changes in local economic conditions have two basic impacts on the mix of services. First, changes can alter the UON. For example, the characteristics of the unemployed change as the unemployment rate changes. A rising unemployment rate will generally increase the proportion of whites, raise the average educational level, and generally decrease the proportion but not the numbers of the unemployed with serious barriers to employment. The second major impact of rising unemployment on the appropriateness of the service mix is the obvious decrease in accessible jobs. Not only does the absolute number of job openings decrease, but the selection criteria of employers are likely to rise. Competition for available jobs increases, and workers are generally willing to settle for lower wages than their skills and education would warrant at other times. Placement rates out of skills training programs fall off. On-the-job contracts are harder to write. Referrals tend to come less and less from the disadvantaged population. Job creation begins to look more attractive. The program operator and the planner begin to question the appropriateness of the current service strategies.

The perceptive planner should remain constantly aware of the need to adjust the composition of service strategies to changing labor market conditions. One of the most frequent sources of failure in past manpower program decision making, and one of the most controversial areas in the manpower planning profession, is the appropriate method of skills acquirement to use for any particular occupation. Costs vary widely for different skills acquirement methods. To train by a more expensive method for skills acquirable by a cheaper approach is a waste of scarce funds. At times the handicaps and disadvantages of a particular individual may require a more expensive method, while a cheaper method would be successful for most applicants. The training method is often more than simply an approach to skills acquirement; it is also an access route to the job. To train for a job by a training method which is in conflict with the "ports of entry" into that job is both expensive and frustrating.

There has been need throughout the manpower experience for a set of criteria to determine which skills acquirement method is most effective and efficient for which people, for which jobs, under what conditions. While such criteria are being developed,

reliable estimates of the relative incidence of specific barriers to
stable employability within the subgroups included in the UON
are lacking in most local manpower plans at present. These barriers, once identified, can become the basis for service prescription.

The problem, of course, is that current methods for predicting
the existence of barriers within population subgroups are inadequate for the purposes of prescription, particularly in regard to
attitudinal factors. This problem was addressed in chapter 5. Until
techniques are available for identifying the barriers faced by individuals and estimating the incidence of barriers within specific
subpopulations, manpower planners and practitioners will be left
with only the most general notions of barriers and how they relate
to particular occupations and service strategies. Nevertheless,
decisions must be made, and the planner should do so on the best
information and judgment currently available.

References

Chadwick, George. *A Systems View of Planning*. Oxford, England:
    Pergamon Press. 1971.

Morton, J. E. *Handbook for Community Manpower Surveys*. Kalamazoo,
    Michigan: W. E. Upjohn Institute for Employment Research.
    October 1972.

National League of Cities–United States Conference of Mayors.
    Focus on Manpower Planning: Planning Process. Vol. I. Washington,
    D.C.: National League of Cities–United States Conference of
    Mayors. December 1973.

Scanlon, John; *et al. An Evaluation System to Support Planning, Alloca-
    tion and Control in a Decentralized, Comprehensive Manpower Program*.
    Washington, D.C.: The Urban Institute. March 1971.

U.S. Department of Labor, Manpower Administration. *An Approach
    to Strategic Manpower Planning*. Washington, D.C.: U.S. Depart-
    ment of Labor. May 1972. Unpublished materials in preparation
    for the implementation of the welfare reform proposal.

——————. *Data Options for Prime Sponsors*. Census Use Study, Man-
    power Series No. 3. Washington, D.C.: U.S. Department of
    Labor. Draft of May 1974.

——————. *Program Activities and Service Guide: Training Draft*.
    Washington, D.C.: U.S. Department of Labor. March 1974.

8

The Mix and Staging of Manpower Services

The manpower planner not only must make priority choices for allocating limited funds among a variety of eligible persons and target groups and among a range of possible services to be supplied to them, but he or she must also be aware of which service agencies are available to deliver these services. The mix of services in part determines the service deliverers, *but only* in part. A variety of relationships is also possible between the planning body and the service agencies. The prime sponsor may choose to hire staff and organize its own service delivery system — though this is generally a second choice. It may choose to assign overall delivery responsibility to one agency, either to provide all services or to act as a prime contractor, subcontracting various functional specialties to other agencies. The planning body may itself act as a prime or general contractor, subcontracting all delivery services to a variety of agencies. Whatever the choice, the planning body has the responsibility to design the delivery system with effectiveness, efficiency, and relative cost as the criteria.

Choice among delivery agents should be based upon some concept of service strategy: What is to be delivered, to whom, when, where, and how takes precedence over choice of who is to provide the service(s). The first part of this chapter is concerned with the allocation of resources among alternative target groups and service functions, the second part deals with choice among service delivery agencies, and the final part focuses on strategic planning.

213

Allocation among Groups and Services

The allocation process advocated in this book is a "step" approach: Funds are first allocated to problem areas, then to population groups affected by each problem area, and finally among service strategies designed for each employment preparedness category within each group. This process is illustrated in Figure 8.1. In chapter 7 it was suggested that total resources be allocated among the problem areas after alternative service approaches had been chosen and prioritized. Early in chapter 7 the process of specifying the group affected by each problem was also described.

The next task of the planner is to establish a set of tentative allocations of funds to these groups and to develop a working estimate of the numbers of clients the delivery system can be designed to handle. An alternative approach would be to design the system as if it were to serve all of the target groups and to scale down at a later stage to levels within budget constraints. This latter alternative is generally more suited to machine models than it is to human planning systems. The approach we suggest is basically heuristic. A tentative allocation of resources to potential clients is made, and a rough estimate is derived of the outputs which the resources will buy. The planner uses the estimates as targets for establishing the basic scale, sequencing, and scheduling patterns of the system. The inputs and the system capacity are then adjusted to reflect optimal use of design capacity. The result is that at the last step of the planning process, the planner has a usable operational plan and does not have to recycle through the planning process several times before a usable plan is generated.

Allocation to Target Groups

Allocation to the target groups can be approached in several ways. A widely used device is the weighted multifactor model. Factors are chosen which reflect the relative need for manpower services by the group. Weights are given to the factors which indicate a judgment as to the importance of a particular factor. The planner will also need to determine the appropriate mix of equity or distributional considerations as related to efficiency considerations for the jurisdiction. Distributional factors are chosen which indicate the relative need for manpower services by members of the

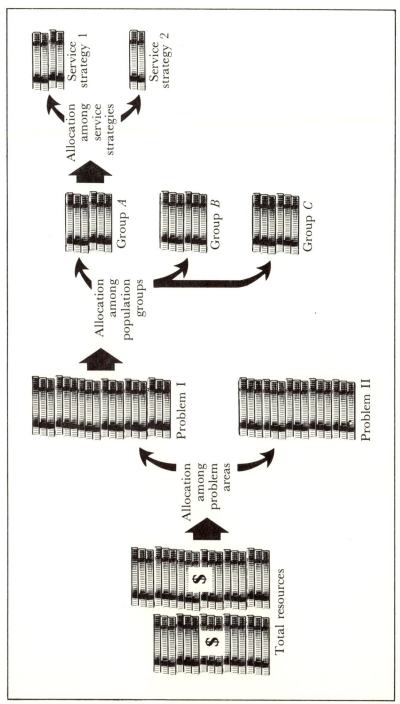

Figure 8.1. Allocation Approach

group. Examples of measures of need include group-specific unemployment rates, labor force participation rates, income levels, educational levels, and so on. Efficiency factors relate to the effectiveness of manpower programs in meeting the needs of each group and the costs at which they are met. It should be noted, however, that group-specific relative effectiveness data are not common at the state and local levels. Consequently, allocation to groups will most likely employ proxy measures of social and economic well-being as indicators of the need for manpower services.

Information on the selected factors is standardized by calculating the total quantity of need represented by the factor and then calculating the percentage of the total factor found in each group. The percentage of need factors is then multiplied by an assigned weight, reflecting the importance that state and local decision makers place on the particular factor. The sum of each group's need factors is then divided by the total weighting to yield a set of figures that represent the percentage of the appropriations which should be allocated to each group. In Figure 8.2, we have assumed that a total of $4 million was appropriated and that the decision makers chose the relative size of the groups, the income levels, and the education levels as the factors which best reflect the needs of each group. Income was given a double weight because in their judgment the decision makers thought it should receive twice as much consideration in allocating resources as education and group size. In determining the weighting of need factors and in choosing the factors themselves, the planner should bring to bear as much empirical support as possible. The basic fact remains, however, that the weighting given to allocation factors will always be more or less arbitrary. To facilitate understanding and a full discussion of the implications of particular weightings, the planner has the responsibility of making the weighting as explicit as possible.

High impact allocation is another approach to dividing monies among target groups. A high impact approach would select target groups from the group and job sets on the basis of a desired geographic or demographic concentration. For example, the manpower strategy of the local area might be closely tied to an intensive redevelopment effort in the central city area; the overall redevelopment plan might call for a concentrated employment and training effort to support the redevelopment effort. Consequently, the

Allocation Factors	Group			Total
	A	*B*	*C*	
Size of group	3,000	2,000	1,500	6,500
Percentage of all potential clients	46.15%	30.77%	23.08%	100%
Weight = 1	46.15%	30.77%	23.08%	100%
Those with below-poverty incomes	1,500	1,500	500	3,500
Percentage of all with income below poverty level	42.86%	42.86%	14.28%	100%
Weight = 2	85.72%	85.72%	28.56%	200%
Those with less than twelfth grade education	1,500	1,800	600	3,900
Percentage of all with less than twelfth grade education	38.46%	46.15%	15.39%	100%
Weight = 1	38.46%	46.15%	15.39%	100%
Total weight	170.33	162.64	67.03	400
Average percentage of value (total weight divided by 4)	42.58%	40.66%	16.76%	100%
Allocation (average percentage of value multiplied by total appropriation)	$1,703,200	$1,626,400	$670,400	$4,000,000

Figure 8.2. Example of Use of Multifactor Allocation Models

planner would choose appropriate target groups in accordance with characteristics of the redevelopment area population.

Whatever the priority system for allocating resources among groups, it is important to look beyond the mechanics and concentrate on the objectives of the allocation. The technique chosen should result in an allocation of resources among groups which focuses on the goals defined in the local manpower strategy.

Allocation among Service Strategies

The selection of alternative service strategies follows the allocation of resources among groups. The objective of the selection is to develop a tentative systemic capacity for use in the design of the client flow. This activity can be approached in several ways. The curriculum priority matrix and linear programming are described in this chapter as two useful methods for evaluating alternative service strategies. The relative cost/effectiveness approach, described at length in chapter 9 as an evaluation tool, is equally useful for choosing among alternative strategies: Those strategies with the highest payoff would be pursued first, recognizing that diminishing marginal returns would reduce the relative cost/benefit ratio of each, making the next most promising strategy more attractive at some point. Common to all approaches is the need to account for as many of the relevant constraints as possible.

Curriculum Priority Matrix

The curriculum priority matrix was developed at the Center for Vocational and Technical Education at Ohio State University. This method was designed as a practical tool for integrating a variety of considerations into decisions involving the choice and allocation of resources among vocational curricula. The curriculum priority matrix employs a ranking system for scoring individual service alternatives on priority criteria. Table 8-1 illustrates a curriculum priority matrix slightly modified for use in comparing alternative manpower service strategies for a particular target group. In the example the analyst has listed nine criteria for choosing among alternative service strategies. For purposes of this example, the policy emphasis of the planning authority favors serving the disadvantaged, and therefore this criterion has received double weighting in the matrix. Each strategy is then evaluated by assigning a ranking value to each matrix cell. Prior to assigning the criteria rankings, the analyst will have defined each value. For example, for the entry wage criterion shown in the table, the rankings go from 0 to 3.

When the service strategies have been ranked on each criterion, the analyst completes the matrix by adding the values across each strategy and ordering these values as indicated in the far

Table 8-1
Curriculum Priority Matrix for Comparing Alternative Manpower Service Strategies for a Particular Target Group

Service Strategy	Net Openings (0 to 1)	Student Interest (0 to 1)	Academic Performance (0 to 3)	Entry Wages (0 to 3)	Seniority Wages (0 to 3)	Job Satisfaction (0 to 3)	Entry Requirements (0 to 3)	Strategy Cost (0 to 3)	Serving Disadvantaged (Weight = 2) (0 to 3)	Service Strategy Priority Index*	Rank Priority Order
				Priority Criteria							
Licensed practical nurse (institutional)	1	1	2	2	1	2	3	2	2×2=4	18	4
Nurse's aide (on-the-job training)	1	0	1	1	0	0	0	3	1×2=2	(8)	**
Typist (institutional)	1	1	2	2	1	2	3	3	2×2=4	19	3
Machinist (institutional)	1	1	3	2	3	2	2	0	3×2=6	(20)	**
Machinist (on-the-job training)	1	1	3	2	3	2	2	3	3×2=6	23	1
Carpenter (on-the-job training)	0	1	2	3	3	2	1	1	2×2=4	(17)	**
Computer operator (institutional)	1	1	3	3	3	3	1	1	3×2=6	22	2

General ranking of cell scores:

0 = inappropriate for manpower training
1 = low priority score
2 = moderate priority score
3 = high priority score

General ranking scheme as applied to the "entry wages" column:

0 = entry wages below federal minimum wage
1 = low but acceptable entry wages
2 = moderate entry wages
3 = very good entry wages

*Parentheses indicate that according to one criterion or more, the program is inappropriate for manpower training.

**Scored inappropriate for manpower training under one or more criteria.

Source: Adapted from Robert C. Young, William V. Clive, and Benton E. Miles, *Vocational Education Planning: Manpower, Priorities, and Dollars* (Columbus: Center for Vocational and Technical Education, Ohio State University, 1972), p. 132.

right-hand column. With the strategies ranked, the analyst then proceeds to allocate available resources among the strategies. Just as the policy emphases of the planning authority can be reflected by the choice and weighting of criteria on the matrix, the allocation procedure can be structured to reflect local values and perceptions. Young *et al.* (1972) offer four alternative approaches as follows:

(1) A training-related placement emphasis

(2) A labor market success emphasis

    (a) A low-cost, maximum coverage option

    (b) A moderate cost, moderate coverage option

Common to each allocation approach is the need to calculate a rough estimate of the per-student cost for each strategy. With the per-student cost estimated for each service strategy, the analyst chooses the allocation approach and procedures. For example, if the analyst chooses the training-related placement emphasis, the allocation procedure would go as follows:

(1) The analyst estimates the net annual related job openings accessible for each service strategy.

(2) The analyst then estimates the number of enrollees who need to be entered into each strategy so that the completers available for placement will equal the numbers of annual related openings for each strategy.

(3) The analyst then estimates the average annual number of enrollees who would normally prefer each service strategy.

(4) Starting with the highest ranking service from the matrix, the analyst allocates the available resources by multiplying the per-student cost by the *lesser* of (2) (completers needed to equal job-related openings) or (3) (the number preferring the strategy).

Funds are allocated to the strategies in order of their matrix ranking until resources are exhausted. This approach to allocation results in a distribution of resources which ensures that student preferences are followed until they exceed what the labor market is likely to absorb.

The second allocation approach emphasizes labor market success defined by the likelihood of job satisfaction and good income. The analyst choosing this approach would initially structure the criteria rankings to reflect a heavy emphasis on the job satisfaction and income criterion. As a result, strategies which produced high incomes and satisfaction would rank high on the matrix. The analyst would then allocate funds to the strategies by multiplying the per-student cost by the estimated number of interested students, starting with the highest ranking strategy and moving down the rankings until available resources are exhausted.

The low-cost, maximum coverage, labor market success emphasis places a high priority on low-cost programs. This approach requires that the planner complete'the matrix with the cost criterion omitted. Then the service strategies are grouped by cost and strategies, with very low labor market success rankings eliminated, after which the available funds are allocated according to the formula used in the labor market success emphasis. The planner funds the lowest cost strategies first in order of their decreasing priority matrix ranking until funds are exhausted.

The moderate cost, moderate coverage emphasis eliminates programs costing over a certain level and then funds programs according to their ranking on the client interest criteria.

Linear Programming

Linear programming enables the planner to handle a number of constraints simultaneously while optimizing some particular objective function. Its application to the problem of allocating limited resources among service strategies designed to serve a particular group is highly appropriate. The use of linear programming in this context is best seen by illustration; therefore an example is given below in a highly simplified manner to focus attention on the principles involved, rather than on the mechanics.

The planner's task is to decide how to allocate $2,400,000 assigned to a particular target group between two alternative service strategies proposed in the mix-of-service design. Strategy *X* is designed to move members of the target group into appliance repair occupations, while strategy *Y* is designed to move members of the target group into metal assembler/fabricator positions.

Criteria

The planner wishes to allocate money between the two alternative service strategies in such a way that placement and incomes above poverty level are maximized; i.e., the allocation which maximizes the value of

$$X\left(P_X\frac{I_X}{I_P}\right) + Y\left(P_Y\frac{I_Y}{I_P}\right) =$$

where

X = number trained for appliance repair jobs

Y = number trained in metal assembler/fabricator jobs

P_X = placement rate for strategy X decimal form

P_Y = placement rate for strategy Y in decimal form

I_X = estimated income from appliance repair jobs

I_Y = estimated income from metal assembler/fabricator jobs

I_P = poverty level income

Constraints

The planner determines that the relevant constraints which must be dealt with at this point are: (1) cost, (2) job opportunities, and (3) training capacity. These three constraints are handled in the following manner.

Cost

Costs are one of the most common considerations in choosing between service strategies. In this example, the planner estimates that training for appliance repair will take an average of six months, while training for metal assembly/fabrication will take an average of nine months. Estimated total costs per man-month of training services for the planning year are $571.43. Therefore, the planner estimates that the allocation of $2,400,000 will purchase no more than 4,200 man-months of training, regardless of what mix of the two service strategies is chosen. Combining these data the planner can write the cost constraint equation as

$$6X + 9Y \leq 4,200$$

Job Opportunities

The labor market analysis has resulted in estimates of the availability of employment opportunities for the graduates of each service strategy. The planner conservatively estimates that no more than 400 appliance repair jobs and no more than 500 metal assembler/-

fabricator jobs can be accessible to the program. Consequently, the job opportunities constraints are written as

$$0 \leq X \leq 500$$
$$0 \leq Y \leq 400$$

Training Capacity

Limitations on existing physical capacity of service delivery agents are another common constraint on the local manpower planner. Training facilities represent large investments, and while some short-term modification and substitution are possible, expansion requires considerably more time. In this example the planner has met with the probable delivery agent and they have decided that the maximum number of enrollees which can be handled by the local Skills Center in either or any combination of these occupational training areas is 600 for the planning year. Consequently, the short-term training capacity constraint can be written as

$$X + Y \leq 600$$

The constraint equations are plotted in the graph of Figure 8.3. A fundamental theorem of linear programming states that the optimal solution will occur at one of the vertices of the line enclosing the solution space.

Having determined feasible solutions to the problem, the planner must take the next step of determining which of the feasible solutions maximizes the objective function. To do so requires that the values of the objective function terms be estimated. Historical program performance records are useful in estimating placement rates. Income levels are a function of wages and duration of employment. Consequently, to estimate income the planner needs to obtain an estimate of entry wages and expected duration of employment for the targeted training areas. In the example the planner's estimates are as follows:

Job	*Estimated Placement Rate*	*Estimated Income Levels*
Appliance repair workers	78%	$7,000
Metal assembler/ fabricator	85%	$7,500

Inserting these figures and a poverty-level income of $3,500 in the objective function equation results in

$$X\left(P_X\frac{I_X}{I_P}\right) + Y\left(P_Y\frac{I_Y}{I_P}\right) =$$

$$X\left[0.78\left(\frac{7,000}{3,500}\right)\right] + Y\left[0.85\left(\frac{7,500}{3,500}\right)\right] =$$

$$X[0.78(2.0000)] + Y[0.85(2.1429)] =$$

$$X(1.5600) + Y(1.8214) =$$

The objective is used to evaluate each one of the vertices of the solution line.

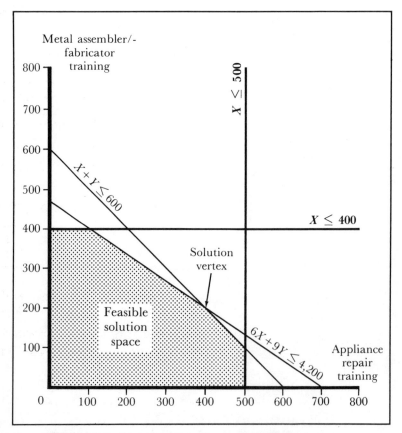

Figure 8.3. Plotting the Constraint Equations

The values are determined in Table 8-2. The evaluation of each of the vertices indicates that the value of the objective function will be greatest when 400 appliance repair workers and 200 metal assembler/fabricators are trained. At no other point in the solution space is the objective function higher.

Table 8-2
Evaluation of the Vertices of the Solution Line

Number	Vertex X	Vertex Y	Total Trained	Evaluation of $X(1.5600) + Y(1.8214) =$
1	0	0	0	0.00
2	0	400	400	728.56
3	100	400	500	884.56
4	400	200	600	988.26
5	500	100	600	962.14
6	500	0	500	780.00

A more sophisticated approach would involve the estimation of benefit/cost ratios for each service strategy and the formulation of an objective function incorporating the ratios. This type of objective function would enable the planner to more easily evaluate the cost of the various constraints in comparable terms. For example, the planner could remove the training capacity or the accessible job openings constraints and evaluate the new solution vertices. The added benefits of the new optimal solution could be compared to the costs of removing the constraint. This type of analysis would tell the planner the real cost of limited training capacity or inadequate job development.*

Although this problem has been limited to a small number of constraints and only two service strategy alternatives, the method, theoretically, is not limited in the number of variables it can handle. Computer programming exists for treating far more complex problems. The chief difficulty in applying the tools of mathematical programming to manpower planning problems lies in the reluctance of planners to use other than "perfect" data. The result:

---

*For an excellent introduction to linear programming, see Hughes and Grawiog, 1972. Complete publishing information is in the references at the end of the chapter.

"Nothing ventured, nothing gained." In fact, linear programming was developed for use in business, and planners in business generally seem much more willing to use the best data they have and guess the rest. The data are never perfect, and measures of benefit/-cost ratios in the public sector will always be subject to debate. However, the manpower planner, while trying to improve the data, should begin to exploit the available data with the best methods he or she can bring to bear for the decision-making information it does contain.*

Sequencing

Having first made a tentative allocation of resources among target groups and then having allocated the resources among the service strategy alternatives, the planner should now develop a design for the flow of clients into a delivery mechanism among its service components and out of the mechanism into the employment opportunities which were the original objectives. The process of determining this flow is called "sequencing" (U.S. Department of Labor, March 1974, pp. III-31–45; and Scanlon *et al.*, 1971, chapter V). Very simply, the purpose of sequencing is to decide the chronology of events — or "what goes after what."

Sequencing is accomplished by "stepping through" the service strategies and ordering their components in such a way as to create a sequence of service that is designed to accomplish the objectives intended. The planner should go through this process for each of the service strategies selected during the previous step. Sequencing involves: (1) describing the components which make up the service strategy, and (2) developing a flow diagram of the desired sequence.

The service strategy is defined as the total sequence of services through which an enrollee will pass in the program. Each service is a component of the service strategy. The planner begins the sequencing process by describing all of the components which make up a service strategy.

Having listed the component services of the strategy, the planner then develops a sequence for each service strategy. Table 8-3 illustrates the sequencing of the service components of

---

*For an interesting broad-gauge application of linear programming in the manpower context see Thelwell, 1972. Publication data are in the references.

three service strategies. The choices at this point are more imagined than real. Intake, assessment, and other activities designed to bring a person into the system *must precede* everything else. Job development, placement, and follow-up activities *must follow* everything else. Services designed to change skill and education levels should be ordered so that basic skills needed to comprehend more advanced skills have been learned before they are needed. Provision for supportive services should be made so that the client can attain "access" throughout the program. When a tentative sequencing has been completed the planner should review this work with a competent training specialist.

Table 8-3
Sequencing the Service Components

Order of Service Components	Service Strategy for:		
	Mechanical Repair	Assembly Occupations	Machine Operator
Intake	x	x	x
Assessment	x	x	x
Basic education	x (two months)	x (three months)	x (three months)
Mechanical repair (skills training)	x (three months)		
Machine operator (skills training)			x (one month)
Assembly occupations (on the job)		x (two months)	
Machine operator (on the job)			x (two months)
Placement	x	x	x
Objective — number placed after training	500	200	150

Next, the planner converts the ordered sequence of service components into a flow chart such as in Figure 8.4. The chart will enable the planner to graphically test the logic of the ordering of the component services of each service strategy. When the flow charts for each service strategy are combined, the planner has a graphic map of the tentative manpower service delivery system.

Loading the System: Determining the Capacity

After the proper sequence of service components has been determined, the planner estimates how many persons must flow through the system to achieve the final desired output. Everyone who enters a program does not go through the entire sequence of services available. Some enrollees drop out. Others are placed directly after assessment. Others need only limited services before placement. The planner needs to estimate the flows through the system in order to determine the needed capacity of each service component. The loading diagram is a graphic tool for estimating needed capacity.

In developing the loading diagram, the planner first draws a diagram which will show the possible flows out of each service component and the destination of these flows. For example, what are the possible flows out of an assessment component? Figure 8.5 illustrates a portion of the needed diagram. The planner develops a complete diagram of all of the components in proper sequence and the destination of flows out of each component. He or she then estimates the proportion of the flow from each component going to each destination. For example, what percentage of those who go to assessment will drop out? What percentage will go to direct placement? What percentage will move to the next component in the service strategy sequence? The planner would develop a table of estimated flow percentages for each service strategy similar to that in Table 8-4. The percentage estimates of flows from components to destination are used to develop estimates of the actual number of persons moving through the system. This is illustrated for the three service strategies in Figure 8.6.

Scheduling the Flows

The next task in developing the design of the delivery system is to convert the capacity estimates generated in the construction

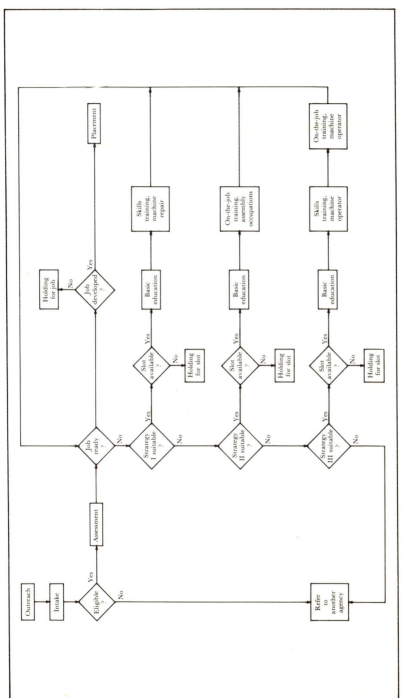

Figure 8.4. Sample Flow Chart of Three Service Strategies

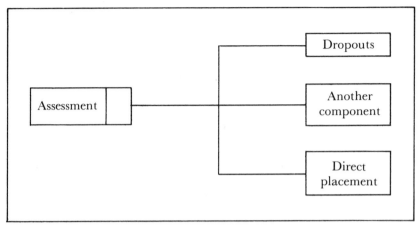

Figure 8.5. Portion of Loading Diagram

of the loading diagrams into a time-phased flow of persons. The time-phased flow is a plan for the month-to-month inputs, activities, and outputs of the delivery system. Because the basic unit of planning is the individual group-specific service strategy, the time-phased flow must be developed service strategy by service strategy and then aggregated into a program-wide time-phased flow.

Three constraints dominate the scheduling of a time-phased flow: client availability, job availability, and service capacity. The reasons for this are not difficult to understand. There are significant seasonal differences in the availability of potential enrollees, for example. Although there is a great deal of regional variation, demands for manpower services seem to increase dramatically during the months of September and October and again in late January and February. In contrast, the holiday period and the months of July and August typically see a substantial falling off of persons seeking services. (School-age youth seeking summer employment are notable exceptions to this last statement.) Consequently, the planner must consider the seasonal differences in the extent to which persons from the planned target groups will make themselves available for enrollment.

Seasonal differences in the availability of targeted jobs are also a constraint on the scheduling process. A service strategy which "dumps" enrollees on the labor market in December, when the job opportunities they were to fill were open and filled in October, must be considered something of a failure.

Capacity constraints are more amenable to modification and adjustment, but nonetheless must be considered. A basic dichotomy exists between those service strategies which can best be described as "batch" flows, and those that represent continuous flows. For batch flows, the planner should determine the minimal economic size of each batch for later use in the scheduling process. Similarly, the planner should develop an early understanding of capacity constraints which are likely to be imposed by physical limitations. For example, suppose the intent is to train eighty numerical-controlled milling machine operators; there is enough equipment to train twenty at a time, and the average training time is three months. If we assume that no additional equipment can be purchased, there is only one schedule that would meet the objective. A time-phased flow that called for training forty at one time would be disastrous.

It is essential that the planner keep these constraints in mind during the scheduling process. The planner begins the scheduling process by identifying seasonal job availability and critical capacity constraints for each service strategy planned. These constraints become the controlling variables for those service strategies for which the constraints are judged to be substantial and not subject practicably to modification. The planner then projects the seasonal variation in potential enrollee availability for each target group. Having identified the relevant scheduling constraints on the avail-

Table 8-4
Estimated Flows through Components

Origin	Intake	Assessment	Basic Education	Skills Training	Completion of Service Strategy	Placement	Dropouts
					Destination		
Outreach	80%						20%
Intake		80%					20
Assessment			80%			10%	10
Basic education				85%			15
Skills training					95%		5
Completion						90	10

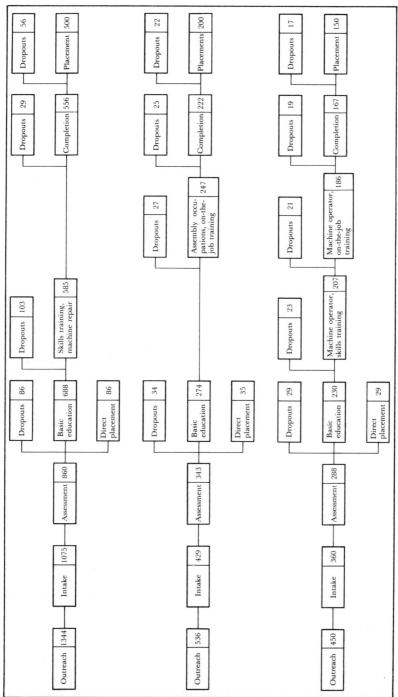

Figure 8.6. Samples of Loading Diagrams

ability of each target group and the service strategies designed to serve the target group, the planner can begin to schedule the individual service strategies.

The conventional technique for developing the time-phased flow is to work up the flow, service strategy by service strategy. This is accomplished by projecting input and output objectives service component by service component for each service strategy. Figure 8.7 provides a suggested format for this process. Month-to-month flows are projected and adjusted for each major service component.

The basic scheduling process is a trial and error simulation of the flows through the service strategies. The adaptation of more sophisticated mathematical programming techniques such as the job-shop problem, network analysis and queing theory to the problem of scheduling faced by manpower planners should be a priority research and development area for the future. While mathematical programming would appear to offer a substantial improvement over present techniques, few applications have been worked out.

A mathematical model with great potential in scheduling work is the Markov process. A Markov-type model uses a matrix of transition probabilities to project the flows of persons through a service delivery system over time. The transition matrix is used to show the probability of movement from one state (service component) to another over a discrete time period. This is essentially a probability model for a time series, with the desired time series in this case being the flow of persons into, through, and out of a manpower service delivery system.

The model is potentially useful for scheduling service strategies which are basically continuous flows. For example, let us suppose that we have a set of service strategies that include two or more of the following components: intake, basic education, skills training in mechanical repair occupation (SK_1), skills training in clerical occupations (SK_2), and job placement. Each of the components, plus two absorbing states — dropouts and successful placements — represents all of the states an enrollee can be in at a given point in time. From historical records and service strategy design specifications, the planner would develop a set of estimates showing the probability of a client's moving from one state to another over a specific time frame. These probabilities would be updated with

Manpower Planning for Local Labor Markets

feedback from actual operations periodically. The estimates are arrayed in matrix form and the probabilities are read from left to right.*

Figure 8.8 is a sample transition matrix. It shows the estimated probability of client movement from each state to another during a month. For example, there is a 0.450 probability that a client in intake will move on to basic education over the course of a month, and so forth. With this matrix of transition probabilities, the planner can simulate the effect of various intake schedules and estimate the capacity needed in the components at different times, as well as simulate the effects of unusual occurrences such as a large increase in intake.

The planner can use the transition matrix to simulate the resultant loading, month to month, of the various components for a given pattern of intake. For example, let us assume that the plan calls for a total intake of fifteen hundred persons in the service strategies covered by the matrix. Furthermore, the planner wishes to estimate the effect of a heavy intake of two hundred persons per month for the first three months and another hundred per month for the remaining nine months. The initial step would be to create a table of flows for each component, showing entries, exits, and carryovers for each component (state). Then the planner would apply the matrix to each group of entries and transfers, resulting from previous applications of the matrix, to obtain the estimated flows for each time period.

In Figure 8.9, we have plotted several of the resulting time series. The heavy line shows the intake per month, and the broken line the required placements. The fine lines show the number on board (an estimate of needed capacity) for the basic education and skills training components as labeled. The planner could also examine flows in and out of each service component. In this example, we chose to focus on estimates of capacity. The curves represent the simulated effect of the chosen intake pattern and the estimated transition probabilities. From the plotting, it can be seen that equilibrium capacity in the basic education component will be about 120 enrollees and that the impact of the heavy early intake pattern will require an early expansion of capacity up to

---

*For a reasonably readable introduction to matrix methods, see Rogers, 1971. Full publishing details are in the references at the end of the chapter.

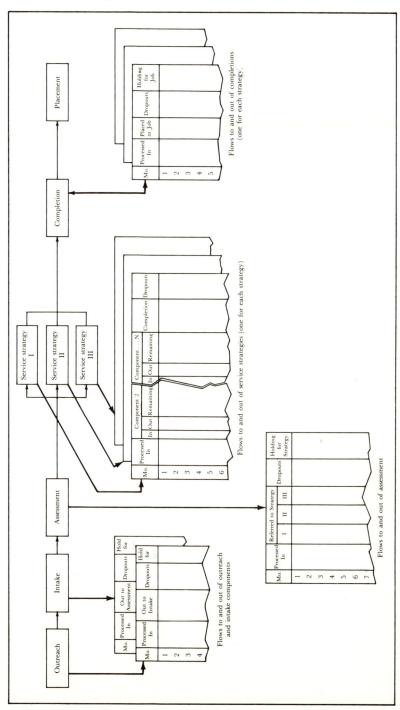

Figure 8.7. Scheduling Process Formats

about 150 enrollees (or about three to four additional classroom units, depending on class size) and a subsequent contraction. Similarly, the planner can use the curve plots to estimate the capacity requirements of the other components month to month. For example, the plot of SK_2 capacity requirements indicates that for the given pattern of intake and transitions, equilibrium in this component should not be expected to occur during the twelve months of operations shown in the figure. In contrast, a near equilibrium level in SK_1 capacity requirements can be expected to occur less than four months from startup.

Actual application of Markov models to state and local manpower planning are not known to the authors, although there is sizable literature reporting on applications to internal manpower planning environments. Pioneers of this and other more sophisticated techniques can certainly expect some difficulties; however, we are convinced that the next few years will see widespread adaptation and application of numerous planning methods not now in the local manpower planner's tool kit. Although the planner interested in the application of quantitative methods to local manpower planning environments will not find too much help in the planning literature, one source, Catanese (1972), is useful in gaining an overview of the possibilities.

Initial State (from . . .)	Intake	Basic Education	SK_1	SK_2	Placement Component	Dropouts	Successful Placements
			Succeeding State (to . . .)				
Intake		0.450	0.135	0.135	0.180	0.100	
Basic education		0.725	0.075	0.100	0.100		
SK_1			0.650		0.350		
SK_2				0.813	0.187		
Placement component					0.200	0.100	0.700
Dropouts						1.00	
Successful placement							1.00

Figure 8.8. Sample Matrix of Transition Probabilities

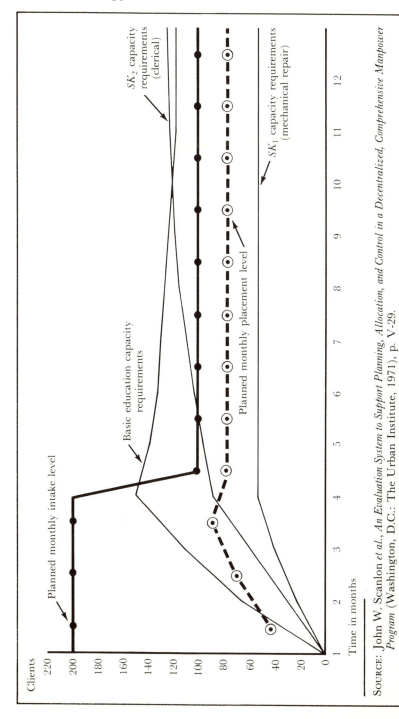

Clients

Planned monthly intake level

SK_2 capacity requirements (clerical)

Basic education capacity requirements

Planned monthly placement level

SK_1 capacity requirements (mechanical repair)

Time in months

Figure 8.9. Schedule of Capacity Requirements Simulated as a Markov Process

SOURCE: John W. Scanlon *et al.*, *An Evaluation System to Support Planning, Allocation, and Control in a Decentralized, Comprehensive Manpower Program* (Washington, D.C.: The Urban Institute, 1971), p. V-29.

Adjustment for Constraints

Adjustments for seasonal variations in client availability can be made in several ways. One such method is to vary the intensity of the outreach effort: Outreach would be intensified during lows in client availability and decreased at peaks in client availability. Holding patterns are another method which might be designed into the system to smooth the flow of clients. Figure 8.10 illustrates this situation. The planner may also deem it necessary to build in adjustment mechanisms to account for projected variations in job openings. Again, the use of a holding status is the most common adjustment. Figure 8.11 illustrates the application of holding to smooth the flow of clients out of a service strategy.

Conventional Scheduling Process

Current scheduling practices involve a basic trial and error exercise. The following process summarizes the core of current scheduling practice.

Step 1

Identify the batch flow service strategies. Establish a required batch size in accordance with (a) significant fixed capacity constraints, or (b) flexible capacity needed throughout the planned period. Tentatively distribute the requisite number of batch flows uniformly over the period. For example, if there are a hundred planned starts for a batch flow (and each strategy lasts for three months) and the required batch size is 25, start a batch every three months to get the tentative flow.

Step 2

Identify the continuous flow service strategies. Tentatively distribute continuous flows uniformly over the period. For example, if there are 120 starts planned, distribute them ten to a month to get the tentative flow.

Step 3

Identify significant job availability constraints. Determine the changes needed in the tentative flow required to meet these constraints. Determine how much of the needed change can be absorbed by a holding mechanism. Adjust the flow in accordance with the holding mechanism. Adjust the flow in accordance with the remaining change needed to compensate for the variations in job availability.

Step 4

Project client availability month by month for each target group. Determine the difference between the intake resulting from projected client availability and the intake needed to support the tentative flow. Determine the extent to which differential outreach effort intensity and holding mechanisms can be used to absorb this difference. Reschedule according to the outreach and holding adjustments as follows:

(a) Reschedule blocks of longer batch flow service strategies to start and end at peaks in client availability projections as needed to smooth the flow of clients within the system.

(b) Reschedule smaller sized portions of shorter batch flow service strategies to start at the troughs and end at the peaks in client availability as needed to smooth the flow of clients within the system.

Figure 8.12 illustrates this recommendation.

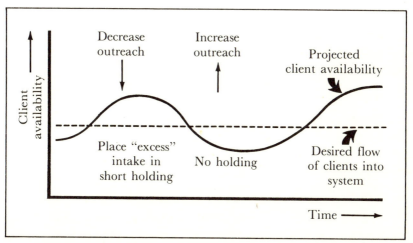

Figure 8.10. Planned Adjustments for Variations in Client Availability

Step 5

After adjustments have been made according to steps 1 through 4, reexamine the resulting time-phased flows and recycle through steps 1 through 4 if further adjustments are needed.

Assigning Roles among Service Agencies

At the completion of sequencing, loading, and scheduling the target group service strategies, the planner possesses a time-phased plan for the flow of clients through a system. Sequentially, the next step in the planning process is the assignment of responsibility for carrying out the work implied by the time-phased plan. It is obvious that the assignment of roles will have already been given either implicit or explicit consideration at earlier stages in plan development. From selection of service strategies to identification of capacity constraints, the planner will have already made a great many preliminary judgments about role assignments. However, with the completion of the time-phased plan, these role considerations must be firmed up in a form for use in plan presentation and for purposes of negotiation.

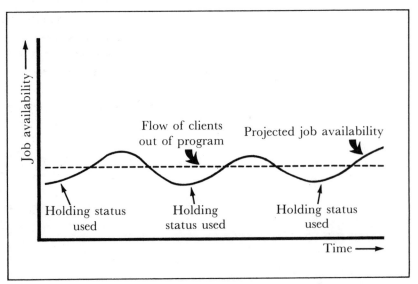

Figure 8.11. Planned Adjustments for Variations in Job Availability

Few labor markets are devoid of existing manpower service delivery mechanisms. An early task of the manpower planner is to make an assessment of the existing service providers. The purpose of this assessment is to determine the extent to which the various service providers, taken as a whole, constitute an integrated and efficient *system* for the delivery of manpower services in the local labor market.

Few words have been used more often with less specific meaning than "delivery system." Yet every community has agencies and organizations providing manpower services; and collectively, they do constitute a delivery system. As a general rule, the characteristics of the existing delivery system can be described with an aside which denotes that there are a few exceptions to most generalizations. The principal public agencies are: the employment service, vocational and technical schools, junior colleges, community colleges, four-year universities, welfare agencies, community action agencies, Model Cities demonstration agencies, municipal youth agencies, government personnel agencies, municipal government social services, aging service agencies, vocational rehabilitation agencies, and public day-care agencies. The principal private agencies are: minority group organizations, employer and business or trade associations, unions, private training institutions, private employment agencies, consulting firms, and various fraternal orders and special interest organizations. While the roles of each actor in the delivery system can be approximately identified in terms of present and past practices, there is no general or specific agreement on the long-term roles, functions, or powers of the actors in the delivery system. Probably the most significant characteristic to understand is that the actors in the present manpower delivery system are not accountable to any common authority in the normal course of affairs. Each marches to the tune of a different drummer. Essential to sound manpower planning is the ability to predict and influence, if not control, the roles, functions, and powers of all actors in the local delivery system.

There are four key questions which can guide the planner in organizing his approach to the assignment of roles:

(1) Who will facilitate access of persons to the proposed service mix?

(2) Who will guide and control the movement of individual clients from one service component to the next?

(3) Who will deliver specific services to individual clients?

(4) Who will be responsible for moving the client into employment?

It is essential that the planner focus his or her attention on the answers to these questions in the context of the local situation. Generalization as to the efficiency of particular classes of existing service providers or of a unified single operation over a coordinated system of semi-independent operators is unwise. Consequently, the following discussion focuses on basic considerations which must be given operational clarity at the local level.

"Who will facilitate access of persons to the proposed service mix?" Any delivery system for manpower services must provide some method for matching the characteristics of persons outside the system with the characteristics used to define the planned target groups, and enrolling these persons in the program. The most obvious choice is between established agencies which have a ready-made flow of persons coming to the agency for manpower or related services and the alternative of creating a new agency which will seek to establish the flow.

Most labor markets possess several established institutions which might be possible contenders for the access-intake role, such as the employment service, the vocational rehabilitation service, the school system, community action agencies, and welfare departments. Each of these institutions is characterized by its established flows of potential manpower service clients. Criteria for choosing among the established institutions or for assessing the feasibility of a new mechanism will vary considerably from community to community but will usually include some of the following considerations:

(1) The visiblity or attractiveness to the population of potential clients as an access point for manpower services

(2) The past or potential success of each alternative agency in serving persons similar to the planned target groups

(3) The actual or potential capability of each alternative for sustaining the required flows of enrollees into the system from the planned target group

(4) The potential access of each alternative to the necessary physical capacity

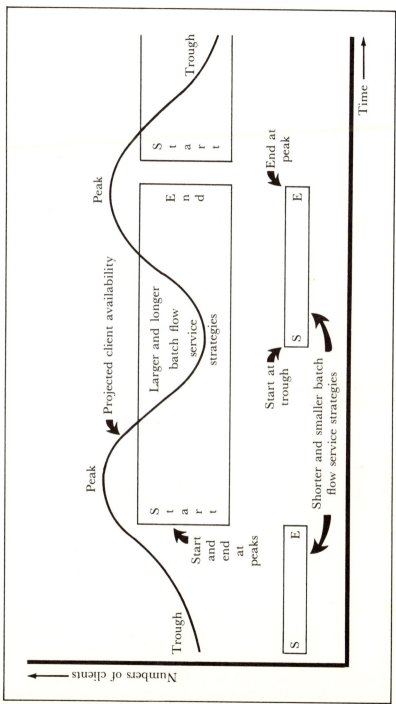

Figure 8.12. Adjustment of Batch Flows to Variations in Client Availability

(5) The availability to each alternative of experienced access-intake services staff

(6) The prospects of each alternative for establishing effective working linkages between the access-intake function and other significant portions of the planned community manpower service delivery system

(7) The quality and responsiveness of management available to each alternative and its willingness to meet planned performance levels, maintain prescribed service and cost records, and place a high priority on this function within its total workload

"Who will guide and control the movement of individual clients from one service component to the next?" The manpower service delivery system must provide some method for guiding the movement of individual clients from one service to the next. Assuming that the person has gained access to the system, who will control access to specific services? This function is the basic case management role, which is a core element in most social service delivery systems. It may be better understood by comparing it with its major alternative, a situation where clients hold vouchers. In classic outline, the voucher system operates in a fashion similar to the open academic scholarship. The person first establishes his legitimate claim to the voucher, perhaps by an income or some other form of economic or social means test. The supporting agency then issues a voucher, good only for some general purpose such as purchasing a set quantity of educational services valued at a set dollar figure. The person then takes his voucher to the education agency of his or her choice and purchases the educational services desired. In the voucher alternative, in other words, the client would manage his own "case."

The voucher system presupposes that the client's only real problem is one of income. The client assesses his own alternatives and prescribes his own "service mix." Provided with the necessary monetary resources, the client then purchases the desired service. The voucher approach has generally been deemed inappropriate for meeting the needs of traditional manpower program clientele because, it has been assumed, the clients are not that familiar with their needs. The preferred delivery method for the poor has been to provide a limited amount of heavily budgeted cash assistance, supported by liberal doses of in-kind medical, nutritional, child-care, and other supportive services, laced with doses of mandatory social work. For manpower programs, it has been to provide a fixed service or mix of services that are predestined for the enrollee upon entering that particular program.

The planner has the basic option of creating a new mechanism or of assigning the case management role to an established agency that provides similar services. The planner in most communities will find several existing agencies with case management mechanisms. The most common of these agencies would include the employment service, the Work Incentive Program teams, the vocational rehabilitation service, the casework components of the local welfare agency, Concentrated Employment Programs, Opportunities Industrialization Centers, and SER organizations, and some community action agencies. Again, the criteria for choosing among the existing agencies and assessing the feasibility of a new mechanism are probably different for each community. Nonetheless, the following considerations possess enough commonality to be useful in many situations. The planner should assess the following:

(1) The capacity of each alternative for serving the numbers and kinds of persons planned to be enrolled in the manpower system

(2) The past or potential success of each alternative for serving the kinds of persons planned to be enrolled in the manpower system

(3) The availability to each alternative of staff experienced in case management

(4) The prospects of each alternative for establishing effective working linkages between the case management function and other functional service areas in the total community manpower service delivery system

(5) The relative quality and responsiveness of management available to each alternative and its willingness to meet planned performance levels, to maintain prescribed service and cost records, and to place a high priority on this function with its total workload

"Who will deliver specific services to individual clients?" There are two basic relationships the case manager can have with

the service providers. The first approach is the vocational rehabilitation model, often called the "blank checkbook" approach.
The vocational rehabilitation counselor works out a planned set
of needed services with his client. The counselor then purchases
each of the services for the individual client as needed — from a
wide range of service deliverers. For example, the counselor might
arrange for the client's medical services with a specific private
practitioner, needed education services from an appropriate educational institution, and so on. The key element is the development
of a more or less unique service delivery pattern around the needs
of each client.

Obviously the rehabilitation agency and individual counselor
might develop shortcuts, based on historical experience, and arrange for blocks of services. For example, a block of specialized
medical services might be arranged on one occasion. The rehabilitation agency might also find it more efficient to establish and
operate a specific specialized service such as a work evaluation–work
adjustment unit for the exclusive use of its clients. However, on the
whole, the central mode of operation is to purchase and package
services on an individual client basis.

The second approach is for the case manager to draw against
more or less fixed amounts of prepurchased services from a limited
number of service operators who provide services tailored almost
specifically to the needs of the planned target groups. In this approach the manpower dollars are used to prefund service capacity
or to gain access to service capacity funded from other sources. The
case manager's choices are generally more limited than they would
be in the vocational rehabilitation model.

Both approaches have positive and negative aspects. The
rehabilitation model is obviously the more flexible of the two and
can offer the *client* a wider range of services and sources, but presupposes great flexibility and a high ceiling on per-client expenditures. The prepurchasing model has the benefit of establishing
new and specialized service delivery capacity where none existed
before, and is potentially the least costly approach. In determining
which approach is appropriate to the local situation, the planner
should consider the capacity and range of existing services available
on a "buy-in" basis and the specialized needs of the planned
enrollee groups. Availability of funds related to the numbers to
be serviced will be an important constraint. The most appropriate

approach for a particular community might be a combination of the two approaches, with some services purchased on an as-needed basis and other specialized or tailored services purchased on a pre-funded block basis. Only local conditions can determine what the specific approach should be.

"Who will be responsible for moving individual clients into employment?" Service strategies which provide for the movement of clients into unsubsidized employment require that a mechanism be established for facilitating a match between a jobless client and an appropriate job vacancy. Again, the basic choice of the planner is to establish a new mechanism or to rely on an existing one. The principal criteria for making the choice are as follows:

(1) The probable access of each alternative to a wide variety of job openings appropriate to the needs of manpower clients on a continuous basis

(2) The capacity of each alternative for placing manpower clients in job openings which are appropriate to their abilites and training and which provide relatively stable employment prospects at a wage level which will result in above-poverty income levels

(3) The past or potential for success of each alternative for placing the clients of manpower programs

(4) The availability (present or potential to each alternative) of staff experienced and competent in the placement function

(5) The prospects of each alternative for establishing effective working linkages between the job development and place-ment function and other manpower service areas

(6) The quality and responsiveness of management available to each alternative and its willingness to meet planned performance levels, maintain prescribed service and cost records, and place a high priority on this function with its total workload

Focus on Strategic Planning

As previously stated, the manpower planner should not be-come overly involved in detailed operational planning of specific programs. The core of the manpower planner's work should be the exercising of broad-gauge, strategic planning skills. Program area specialists, whether operating as a part of the manpower planning staff or with a program subcontractor, should be utilized for detailed operational planning. At the core of the manpower planner's skills are the following:

(1) The ability to assess the local labor market and identify the existence, importance, and magnitude of dysfunctions relative to the local manpower council's goals

(2) The ability to assess and choose an appropriate strategy for attacking the problems identified earlier from a range of alternative strategic approaches

(3) The ability to recommend an appropriate allocation of resources among a set of proposed or ongoing activities directed at implementing the preferred strategic approach

(4) The ability to identify and quantify with appropriate precision persons or institutions to be served or acted upon by the recommended program mix

(5) The ability to identify appropriate delivery mechanisms for implementing the recommended program mix

(6) The ability to assess the effectiveness of the prescribed program mix in effecting the preferred strategy and in achieving the stated manpower objectives

(7) The ability to articulate the planner's analytical findings and to effectively communicate his or her recommended course of action

One of the most widespread misconceptions of novice planners is that a major use of their technical skills should be in precise program design and execution. Curriculum design, the details of intake processes, fine distinctions between counseling methodology, contract monitoring, Management Information System maintenance, and so forth, are needed and valuable functions. The planner should arrange for the provision of these services by appropriate specialists and periodically assure himself or herself that this work is progressing. However, the prime task is broad-gauge, strategic planning. The planner should concentrate on determining what should be done and who should do it — the details and responsibility for execution are the province of the functional specialists. The manpower planner continually immersed in operational concerns may be neglecting his or her real function.

At this point in the planning process, the planner should have a time-phased plan for the flow of persons into, through, and out of the proposed delivery system. These flows are based on total service strategy objectives and tentative costs developed earlier in the process. The planner will also have a tentative set of role assignments for each service component. At this stage, five basic tasks remain to be performed:

(1) Negotiation of specific role assignment, details, workloads, costs, and performance standards with potential contractors

(2) Development of specific organization and staffing arrangements for the provision of services

(3) Adjusting the delivery system design and resource allocations as necessary after final operational arrangements have been made

(4) Installation of needed management and support systems necessary to maintain the system, such as fiscal disbursements and accounting systems, management information, and reporting systems

(5) Installation of appropriate evaluative reporting systems if these cannot be derived from the Management Information System

Essentially these tasks should be performed by the various functional area specialists whose work should be closely monitored by the planner. The planner should make use of specialists in contracts, training, accounting, and information. Guidance can also be drawn from the current program planning and technical assistance of federal funding agencies. The planner and the functional area specialists will find the series of technical assistance publications developed in support of the fiscal year 1975 CETA planning cycle particularly helpful in the performance of the various implementation tasks. Monitoring and evaluating this service delivery is the subject of the next chapter.

References

Catanese, Anthony J. *Scientific Methods of Urban Analysis.* Urbana: University of Illinois Press. 1972.

Hughes, Ann J.; and Grawiog, Dennis E. *Linear Programming: An Emphasis on Decision Making.* Reading, Massachusetts: Addison-Wesley Publishing Company. 1973.

Rogers, Andrei. *Matrix Methods in Urban and Regional Analysis.* San Francisco: Holden-Day Publishing Company. 1971.

Scanlon, John W.; *et al. An Evaluation System to Support Planning, Allocation and Control in a Decentralized, Comprehensive Manpower Program.* Washington, D.C.: The Urban Institute. 1971.

Thelwell, Raphael. "Linear Programming Applied to Federal Manpower Programs with Multiple Objectives over Several Years." Paper presented to the Joint National Meeting of the Operations Research Society of America, the Institute for Management Science, and the American Institute for Industrial Engineers at Atlantic City, New Jersey, on November 9, 1972. The paper also appears as an Office of Management and Budget staff paper under the same title.

U.S. Department of Labor, Manpower Administration. *Manpower Program Planning Guide.* Washington, D.C.: U.S. Department of Labor. March 1974.

Young, Robert C.; Clive, William V.; and Miles, Benton E. *Vocational Education Planning: Manpower, Priorities, and Dollars.* Columbus: Ohio State University, Center for Vocational and Technical Education. 1972.

9
Evaluation of Local Programs

Evaluation is a hallmark of American manpower planning. Despite the shortcomings of evaluation techniques, no set of public programs has ever been more thoroughly evaluated. From their beginnings, the programs have been viewed with suspicion, and there was demand that they prove their worth. As a new generation of American manpower programs begins with CETA, it is unlikely that this concern with evaluation will diminish, but there will be a fundamental change in focus. Until now, the emphasis has been national: "Did the program as a whole produce sufficiently favorable results to justify its continuance?" Under CETA, that concern will continue at the national level, but the new focus at the local level will be the improvement in service mix and service delivery within the program.

Emphases in Manpower Evaluation

Three principal foci have characterized evaluation in the manpower field. The first has been concern with the manpower responses of the organization — evaluation of internal manpower programming. The second focus of evaluation has been the national programs' evaluations, directed at the development of workable program models, and the determination of the effectiveness of a centrally designed mix of programs to meet the expections of national policy makers. A third focus encompasses the limited body of methodological and analytical work concerning the evaluation of manpower programs at the service delivery level. Each will be reviewed before devoting this chapter to the third focus.

Internal Manpower Program Evaluation

Internal manpower programming evaluation has grown from the need of manpower planners to determine the effectiveness of their prescriptions for solving the manpower problems of the organization. Manpower planning within the business firm or the public agency has generally developed as an outgrowth of the older, more limited personnel function, while manpower planning at the national and at the state and local levels has grown from the policy and program responses of the federal government to do something about the persistent demographic and geographic pockets of unemployment and underemployment. There is a distinct difference in the professional orientation of manpower planners working for organizations and those working for federal, state, and local manpower authorities. The hand of the economist can be seen in all arenas. However, methods and language of the micro-manpower planner — the planner concerned with the internal manpower needs of the organization — dip heavily into the personnel and industrial engineering professions, while the federal, state, and local public manpower planners seem heavily influenced by the teaching, counseling, and social work professions.

Much of the evaluation work coming out of the internal organization context has concerned the effectivenss of efforts to ensure adequate supplies of managerial or technical personnel to the organization; the effectivenss of the organization in training or retraining disadvantaged or minority employees is a more recent theme. Another major direction consists of the efforts to evaluate the effectiveness of policy alternatives for meeting the manpower needs of the military. But in all, the emphasis is internal — How well is the organization doing vis-à-vis its manpower needs? — rather than the provisions of external manpower services.*

*For a good introduction to the tools and current concern in the internal manpower planning field, see Burack and Walker, 1972.

National Manpower Program Evaluation

By far the largest and best known body of analytical evaluation work consists of the numerous manpower program evaluations contracted by federal departments and private foundations. The federal sponsors of manpower program evaluation have been the Manpower Administration of the Labor Department, various units in HEW, the OEO, and the community development units of HUD. Although these agencies have conducted a considerable number of in-house evaluations, most of the federal evaluation resources have been allocated to contract studies. Private profit and nonprofit research organizations, public and private institutions of higher education, and to a much lesser extent manpower program operators and units of state and local governments have been the most frequent recipients of federal evaluation and research contracts. As a result, the evaluation of federally supported manpower efforts has resulted in the creation of a relatively large research and development community.

The choice of the federal agencies over the years to rely heavily on "outside" evaluation has had both positive and negative results. On the positive side the reliance on outside evaluation has resulted in a more objective body of work than would probably have been the case if operating agencies had done the work themselves. No other federal programmatic efforts in either the domestic or military areas have been subjected to the scrutiny of open evaluation by "outsiders" as frequently or in-depth as have federally supported manpower programs.

Another positive result of the federal approach to manpower program evaluation has been the development of a wide variety of evaluation methodology. While it is difficult to determine the extent to which national manpower policy has been affected, this approach has resulted in a substantially improved understanding of the relative costs and benefits of alternative programmatic approaches to the delivery of manpower services. The application of the findings of programmatic evaluation work can be seen in most of the significant program redesign efforts preliminary to the implementation of CETA.

The reliance on outside evaluation has also had some negative characteristics. Because the evaluations were designed to support national purposes, the evaluation methodologies which were developed have generally not been directly translated or translatable for the use of manpower planners or policy makers at the state and local levels. Even where data were gathered which would have been helpful to these units of government, they have not been fed back to these units in usable form. This failing had little real impact until the advent of decentralized and decategorized planning under the comprehensive manpower pilot programs and their legislated successor, CETA. As implementation of CETA proceeds, the needs of state and local manpower policy makers and planners for workable evaluation methods will become more crucial.

Evaluation at the State and Local Levels

The overriding purpose of the evaluation of manpower programs at the service delivery level is optimization. The state or local manpower planner develops a description of the problem, identifies alternative prescriptions for solving the problem, makes a choice among these alternatives, and develops appropriate programming to implement the preferred alternative. Another unit of state or local government or a private organization usually is assigned to deliver the manpower services designated within the program, while the planner retains responsibility for evaluating the results of his or her programming and then reprograms as need is indicated by the evaluation. However, the program operator or service deliverer retains an internal evaluation responsibility to determine how effectively his or her organization is fulfilling its assignment. The intent may be to improve or defend that performance. The planner assesses both the appropriateness of the mix of services provided and the efficiency and effectiveness of the service deliverer, since he or she may recommend change in either.

The state or local manpower planner is generally limited to reprogramming within a limited range of services that can be provided from available resources and by alternative deliverers of those services. In contrast, evaluation in support of national policy development must always implicitly or explicitly provide measures which allow comparison of both the alternative manpower uses and the nonmanpower uses of the available resources. Consequently, from the perspective of the state or local manpower planner, the national evaluators have been overly preoccupied with more absolute measures of impact translated into dollar terms (such as cost/benefit ratios) which might support the consideration of all alternative uses of resources but which offer little assistance in improving program effectiveness. State and local planners have a greater need for evaluation techniques that assess the efficiency of current operations; measure the short, intermediate, and longer term effectivenss of alternative manpower approaches in behalf of various target groups; and feed information back, suggesting improvements. They rarely have reason to consider nonmanpower uses of the available resources.

Each of these evaluative viewpoints is appropriate and necessary. If the federal budgetary process is to result in rational allocation of limited resources among alternative national priorities, work must continue on evaluative methods which result in measures of benefit that are comparable across functional areas. The Executive branch of government has an obligation to the Legislative branch which directs the overall allocation of resources (and to the taxpayers who provide the funds) to assess the relative contribution to the national good of alternative uses of resources and allocate and reallocate in pursuit of the general welfare. Any analytical effort which results in a more accurate assessment of the relative contributions of alternative uses of limited resources should be supported. However, all too often data reporting systems of federal manpower programs have bypassed operating levels in the computation, analysis, and dissemination of useful management information.

National program evaluations could have done more as a byproduct to offer insights to local program operators that would be useful in improving their performance. With the advent of state and local discretion in the choice of target groups, the design of functional services, and the choice of service delivery systems, the emphasis must shift. First priority must be directed to the development of evaluation methodologies geared to the needs of state and local manpower planners and administrators, without neglecting the national need for assessment of the overall effectiveness of the decentralized manpower approach and of the social returns of this particular use of scarce resources.

Recognizing this need for decentralized evaluative tools, the Manpower Administration has issued a simplified evaluative approach as a technical assistance guide for the use of state and local CETA grantees. That approach is well designed to meet the immediate needs in the early stages of decentralization, but it is recognized not to be adequate for the longer run. As local manpower programs will reflect the particular needs of their local labor markets and populations, so will evaluation techniques need to be sufficiently flexible to adapt to local need. Since CETA represents only a portion of the manpower action in any labor market, these evaluative techniques must feed information back concerning the end results of other programs, in order to optimize the effectiveness of the entire manpower system. The remainder of this chapter attempts a modest contribution to filling this void.

Typology of State and Local Manpower Evaluations

Evaluation approaches can be categorized according to a variety of dimensions. One approach would be to distinguish between process and product. Process evaluation would focus on activities, whereas product evaluation would focus on the results of activities. Another approach would be to classify evaluations by their methodologies; for example, empirical evaluation and participant observer evaluation. Time might also be used as a classifying device: current, short-term, and long-term approaches to evaluation. The choice of evaluator can be a classifying device; e.g., self-evaluation, as opposed to outside and independent evaluation. This book uses a three-way classification scheme which seems to reflect an emerging pattern. In substance, if not in emphasis, it is similar to a classification scheme first offered by Borus and Tash (1970).

Three basic forms of evaluation are of prime importance to manpower planners at the state and local levels:

(1) *Operational control and assessment:* This includes the monitoring of current operations for compliance with a pre-established model of efficiency and general principles of prudent management; and the regular and systematic review of current operations against quantitative and qualitative program performance targets, generally expressed in a time-phased operational plan.

(2) *Alternatives effectiveness assessment:* This includes the periodic assessment of the success and costs of achieving specific plan, program, and program component outcomes in the

intermediate time frame. The focus of alternatives effectiveness assessment is the comparison of the relative effectiveness of alternative strategies for achieving intermediate measures of success.

(3) *Outcomes assessment:* This measures the extent to which a particular plan is achieving its objectives and goals; e.g., improving the employment stability and incomes of the target group to which manpower services are being provided.

A fourth evaluation form — impact assessment — would include those analytical activities designed to measure the long-term changes attributable to the program which impinge upon participants, the labor market, and the community. Impact assessments seek to assess the extent to which long-term objectives are being met and should answer the question: In what way would this community be different from what it is if the manpower program had never existed? However, that would require knowledge of such indirect impacts as the negative displacement effect on nonparticipants who might have held jobs obtained by participants if the program had not existed. Present evaluation methodology is not yet up to this task. Consequently, the manpower planner and program operator must generally content themselves with the knowledge that they were assigned to better the lot of a prescribed group and satisfy themselves with that achievement. It is an acceptable and appropriate social decision to redistribute opportunity in favor of those suffering handicaps and disadvantages relative to society as a whole. But that choice is a policy decision which then provides some of the parameters within which the planner plans. Only the first three evaluation forms are relevant to present purposes.

The principal types of evaluation measures relate to input, process, and output. Input measures define the inputs of resources into a prescribed process designed to achieve a specific set of outcomes. Examples of input measures are staff salaries, equipment costs, supplies, foregone earnings of enrollees, overhead cost, and so forth.

Process measures seek to characterize the process employed to produce specified outcomes. They track flows of persons through a series of services, utilization of system capacity, and movement out of and between components of a system. Examples of process measures include average daily attendance, enrollments, component completions, rates of aptitude or attitudinal change, numbers of termination by reason, and student/teacher ratios.

Output measures describe the result of the process on persons moving through it. Output measures for manpower evaluations are designed to measure the change in enrollee characteristics which best relate to each person's employability in the labor market. Examples of output measures include placement rates, proportion of training-related placements, changes in wage and income levels; changes in skill and educational attainments, and attitudinal changes.

A program can be evaluated only against the purpose for which it is intended. The choice of evaluation measures requires a clear definition of program service or strategy norms. The choice of goals and objectives defines, in turn, the manpower development strategy of the state or local manpower planning authority. Although hard and fast prescriptions are few in this area, experience has shown that the general form and specificity of goals and objectives required for each of the major types of evaluation differ. For example, operational control and assessment requires a set of norms in the form of a time-phased operational plan. Actual levels are compared to planned levels (the objectives in this case) relating to costs, enrollments, services provided, and immediate outcomes. In contrast, outcomes assessment requires a more general statement or broad manpower strategy which delineates the change desired in a specific subpopulation or labor market institution. The choice of manpower development goals reflects the manpower planning authority's analysis of the local labor market and population. This general approach is outlined in Table 9-1. The table shows that the specification of norms for use in evaluation moves from the broad specification of target group and desired changes necessary for outcome evaluation to a specification of services and job types designed to achieve the desired goals necessary for alternatives effectiveness assessment, to a detailed specification of periodic enrollment, cost, service, and immediate outcomes necessary for operational control and assessment.

The objectives of service strategies are likely to differ considerably. Different objectives might be set for different groups receiving the same service. For example, immediate job placement after an institutional skills training sequence might be the established goal of the manpower planning authority for one group, while satisfactory completion might be set as the prime objective for another group. Service components are likely to have multiple goals and objectives of varying importance. Consequently, it is essential that these goals and objectives be carefully developed, stated, and prioritized before establishing an information system and attempting to evaluate.

The state or local manpower planner is faced with an enormous number of possible evaluation measures. Limitations imposed by costs, as well as rigorous delineation of local manpower goals and objectives, will help the planner reduce the options and then choose among them. In choosing evaluation measures, the planner should give consideration to the following suggestions:

(1) Measures should be keyed to specific goals, objectives, and operational indicators.

Table 9-1
Analysis of the Local Labor Market and Population

Evaluation Type	Form of Goal and Objective Statement	Example
Outcomes assessment	Goal statement	1. Improve the employability and incomes of group X.
Alternatives effectiveness	Objective statement	2. Provide group X with services A, B, and C, and place in jobs of types 1, 2, and 3.
Operational control and assessment	Time-phased operational plan	3. In period 1, z number of group X persons should be enrolled in service component C; y number should be completed and placed in jobs of type 1.

(2) Simple measures should be favored over more complex measures.

(3) Measures which can meet both local and federal needs and also the needs of planners and operators are preferred over measures which meet only one type of need.

(4) The costs of obtaining the information should be less than the costs of not getting it.

(5) Objective quantitative measures are to be preferred to subjective judgments wherever and whenever available.

Many of the values and contributions of manpower services can never be quantified, and there is always the problem that straightforward comparisons of the dollar returns to investments in the employability of alternative target groups may argue for service to the "haves" rather than the "have nots." However, subjective judgments are vulnerable to personnel biases and can justify whatever one wishes to justify. Subjective approaches to evaluation tend to be exposés of what's wrong administratively, rather than answers to "What are the results and how can the outcomes be improved?" The best solution to the dilemma is to stick as closely as possible to a quantitative approach, weighing calculations in preferred directions and ultimately making policy decisions by melding quantitative results with good judgment.

Operational Control and Assessment

Operational control and assessment evaluations are designed to manage the state and local manpower plans. The two most common forms of these evaluations are the plan vs performance analysis and the garden-variety program monitoring.

Plan vs Performance Analysis

This type of analysis is concerned with providing the program operator, the policy maker, and the manpower planner with reasonably current information on the extent to which the program components are achieving the approved plan. In fact, this analysis is best characterized as a tool for managing the plan. It is typically structured by the conventions and definitions of a management information system, which should be built on a flow-process concept, using service centers or key delivery institutions as its basic measuring points. Planned levels of enrollments, cost, services received, and indicators of immediate outcomes are compared with actual levels experienced to determine the extent to which the plan is being followed. The difference between planned and actual levels is used as a basis for allocating intensive on-site monitoring time and as an indicator of the need for reprogramming.

Monitoring

Program monitoring is a process of reviewing the activities of manpower service deliverers against a specific model which describes how a particular service should be delivered. In the context of state and local manpower program management there are two primary purposes of program monitoring. The first is custodial. Custodial monitoring seeks to assure management that contract requirements, fiscal responsibilities, and administrative guidelines are being satisfied. The custodial monitoring system also determines whether the program operator is serving the prescribed clients and providing the mix of services specified by the model. Custodial monitoring is generally established on a regular, periodic basis.

The second general form is best called managerial monitoring. The operative principle of managerial monitoring is "management by exception." The purpose of managerial monitoring is to determine the causes of variance in program performance from planned levels and to identify appropriate remedial actions for management consideration.

Information Requirements

Operational control and assessment analysis relies heavily on the grantee reporting system required of the agency assigned responsibility for delivering a prescribed set of services. The records of the reporting system essential to the support of all three general types of evaluation fall into the following categories:

(1) Records of the characteristics of the persons served

(2) Records of the nature and extent of services provided

(3) Records of the outcomes and results of services provided

(4) Records of the costs of services

These records are generated around two loci: the individual client and the service unit. Minimum records for the individual client would include an entry record, some form of an employability plan or plans for service, status change records to record movement among services, and an exit record to record movement out of the program. Minimum records focused on the service unit would include an activity record that would account for the quantities of services rendered, measured in some standard unit, and a cost record that would assign all direct costs and a portion of administrative costs to the service unit.

With access to these minimal records, the state or local manpower planner can construct a manpower program performance information system to support operational control and assessment evaluation. Several design criteria are essential in the development of an effective performance information system:

(1) The system should be supportable entirely with client and service unit records.

(2) It should provide information in five essential areas: movement of persons, characteristics of persons, services provided, immediate outcomes achieved, and costs of services.

(3) It should reflect the status of the operation as currently as is practicable, with a capability of being updated at least monthly.

(4) It should enable the planner to conceptualize the sum total of manpower activity.

(5) It should facilitate comparison among services, service units, and client groups.

(6) Most importantly, it should facilitate comparison of actual operations with planned operations.

Many of these design criteria can easily be met if the information system is designed as a continuous-process model, resembling a pipeline through an oil refinery. Materials enter the system continuously, move through a series of ongoing modification processes, and then leave the system in various states for a variety of destinations.

The continuous-process model contrasts with the job lot, the batch, or the project models in which a discrete unit of material is modified as a unit and leaves the process as a unit, at which point another discrete unit can be acted upon. Although it is obvious that each client is a discrete unit, the system generally handles thousands of persons at a time. For activities such as open-entry/-open-exit institutional training, which allow individuals to start and stop at any time, the appropriateness of the continuous-process model in manpower service information systems is enhanced (Figure 9.1). The adoption of the continuous-process model allows the planner to structure a set of common data elements round the major points of the model: Clients enter, are in the program, and leave the program.

By slightly expanding this concept and adding a common time unit, the planner can design a common data element set. A minimum set would consist of data elements defined as follows:

(1) *In process:* The number of persons who are already enrolled in the program at the beginning of the month

(2) *Entries:* The number of persons who are enrolled into the program during the month

(3) *Exits:* The number of persons who ceased to be enrolled in the program during the month for any reason, including:

    (a) *Early termination* — persons who did not complete the program and left during the month

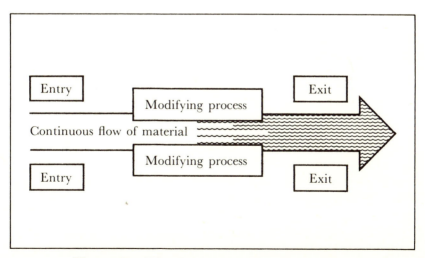

Figure 9.1. The Continuous-Process Concept

(b) *Transfers to other manpower programs* — persons who completed the program and went into another program as a part of a planned service sequence during the month

(c) *Initial placements* — persons who completed the program during the month and were placed in a job during the month

(d) *Completers in holding* — persons who completed the program during the month and are waiting for an appropriate job opening

(4) *Placements:* Persons who complete an initial placement period during the month and remain on the job

(5) *Job leavers:* Persons who fail to complete an initial placement period during the month and leave the job in which they were placed

In addition to the enrollee flow measurements, a tentative set of standard enrollee characteristics data elements, financial measures, and "client days of service provided" should be defined. Some examples of enrollee characteristics measurements tied to points on the flow process model are as follows:

(1) *Disadvantaged:* The number of clients at entry who are disadvantaged according to Labor Department guidelines

(2) *Minorities:* The number of clients at entry who are members of racial or cultural minorities

(3) *Veterans:* The number of clients at entry who are veterans of military service

(4) *Public assistance recipients:* The number of clients at entry who are receiving public welfare

Some examples of financial measures are as follows:

(1) *Expenditures:* The total of accrued expenses incurred during the month by the program

(2) *Cash transfers:* The portion of expenditures transferred directly to program clients in cash, by check, or by money order during the month

In addition, each service unit should provide a monthly tally of "client days of services provided" during the month.

Care should be taken to specify definitions that match points in the continuous-process model. The set of common elements should reflect the key indicators used in the time-phased operational plan and be maintained for each of the components of the plan. For example, if the plan consists of an intake component, a remedial education component, an on-the-job training component, and a skills training component, the information system should track the common data elements for each component. Figure 9.2 shows how an information system might track an intake component.

The common data elements should be supplemented with additional indicators where the essential information is not accounted for by the common data elements. Manpower services are a prime example of this situation. Counseling, testing, and assessment do not lend themselves readily to the continuous-process model, although it would be possible to track them in this form.

Intake	J	A	S	O	N	D	Year to Date	Planned Level	Actual Level
In process									
Entries:									
Disadvantaged									
Veterans									
Minorities									
Exits:									
Early terminations									
Transfers to other components									
Initial employment, period placements:									
Completers									
Noncompleters									
Expenditures:									
Transfer payments									

Figure 9.2. Sample Information System Display of Data Elements Tracking Performance of an Intake Unit

A more efficient approach would be to account for a common unit of service. Consequently, the planner might add the number of counseling sessions and the number of assessments and tests given during the month to the common data elements used to measure flows through the intake unit. If these services were provided by a special unit that has no other services assignment, the common data element might be limited to client characteristics or expenditures, or both. In a similar fashion, special work unit data elements might be established and tracked by the information system for other activities which do not deal with enrollees, or do not deal with them over a significant length of time.

The program performance information system is supported by a system of monthly service unit reports. The service units develop monthly reports from their client record files and from their service activity and service cost records. The service unit report employs the common data element set, supplemented by any work unit measure peculiar to that unit. The service unit also reports the client days of service provided during the month from its service unit activity record. The information specialist posts the service unit report to a master sheet monthly. The master sheet might be used for only one service unit or for all program components. The most practicable approach is to use individual service unit master sheets and then repost to some form of program control board that shows the entire flow of activities. The control board is a device for visually portraying the total manpower program activity operating in a planning jurisdiction. It is also used to highlight the comparison of actual with planned performance. Figure 9.3 shows a simplified control board. (Its sections 1, 2, and 3 correspond to the numbered narrative paragraphs in the discussion below.)

The Program Performance Information
System in Use

The program performance information system is designed to meet the desired requirements specified earlier. It provides the state or local manpower planner with an overview of manpower activity in the planning jurisdiction and with comparable measures of program performance against planned objectives. It also gives the planner a useful tool for conducting operational control and assessment evaluations. To illustrate how a performance information system might operate, a highly simplified example is described, using a limited set of common data elements in a theoretical planning area.

The process begins with a regular review of the planning board by the planner. (Figure 9.3 illustrates this process.)

1. During the review, the planner notes that the cumulative placement rate for institutional training programs has dropped consistently during the months of September, October, and November far below planned levels and below the acceptable range of 15 percent variation from 75 percent planned placement.

2. The figures indicate a significant problem: The drastic fall in the monthly rate has caused the cumulative placement rate to drop 18.4 percentage points (80.9 to 62.5 percent) or 12.5 percent below planned placement levels. An examination of the control board shows that exits for September increased substantially, while placements increased only slightly. This could have been caused by a drastic change in labor market demand or, more likely, by the failure of placement staff to prepare for the completion of training by a class group in September. Further analysis shows that exits returned to normal levels in October and November, while placements continued their radical decline. At this point, the planner might conclude that a major problem was developing in the placement function.

3. To pin down the problem, the planner would examine the common data element tables of the component programs. In the case of "total institutional training," the component programs might be: the metal trades, service occupations, health occupations, and data processing clusters and the water quality technician project and individual referrals. The planner examines component program tables and discovers that the problem appears to be located in the metal trades cluster. A low placement rate from this cluster is identified as the prime source of the problem first noted in the "total institutional training" tables. At this point, the planner would probably initiate an on-site managerial monitoring review of the metal trades cluster to ascertain the cause of the problem.

In this example, the use of the program performance information system as both an operational control and an evaluation aid was demonstrated. The principle at work is management by exception. Any irregular pattern of performance noted in a program table immediately suggests a problem area. Performance is measured against planned objectives. Uniform measurement provides

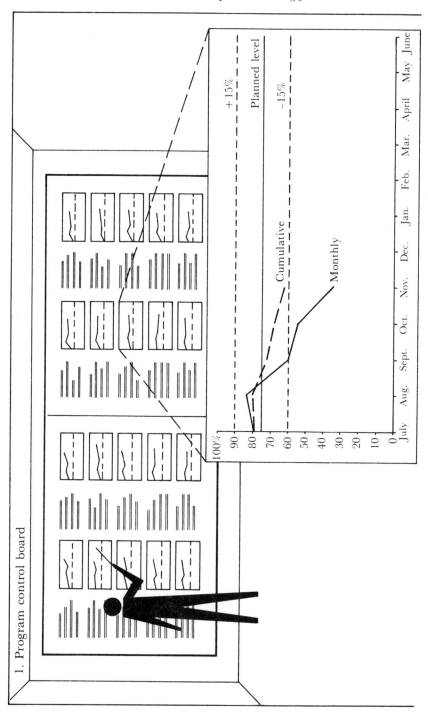

1. Program control board

2. Total institutional training

Common Data Item	July	Aug.	Sept.	Oct.	Nov.	Dec.	Plan to Date	Actual to Date
In process beginning month	490	497	516	527	530	563	550.0 av.	520.5 av.
Entries during month	91	92	119	89	111		85.0 av.	100.4 av.
Exits during month	84	73	108	86	78		85.0 av.	85.8 av.
Placements during month	67	60	65	48	28		63.8 av.	53.6 av.
Placement rate monthly (%)	79.8	82.2	60.2	55.8	35.9		75.0	62.8 av.
Placement rate cumulative (%)	79.8	80.9	72.5	68.4	62.5		75.0	62.5 cum.

3. Metal trades cluster

Common Data Item	July	Aug.	Sept.	Oct.	Nov.
In process beginning month	192	183	160	161	173
Entries during month	20	19	74	34	31
Exits during month	29	42	73	22	21
Placements during month	29	32	34	4	6
Placement rate monthly (%)	100.0	76.2	46.6	18.2	28.6
Placement rate cumulative (%)	100.0	85.9	66.0	59.6	56.1

Figure 9.3. Example of a Simplified Control Board in Use

a comparable frame of reference for problem solving and decision making. On-site monitoring activity is conserved, and attention is focused on real problems.

As we have seen, operational control and assessment evaluation depend heavily upon a sound information system. With this system in place, regular monthly evaluations can easily be conducted. These evaluations should systematically consider the following:

(1) *Capacity utilization:* Comparison of planned with actual component capacity (measured in "client days of service provided" or other unique service unit measurements). The planner would analyze variance from plan, answering some of the following questions:

   (a) Is the variance from plan caused by longer (or shorter) stays in the component than planned?

   (b) Is the variance caused by overestimation (or underestimation) of needed capacity?

   (c) Is the variance caused by more (or less) entries than planned?

   (d) Is the variance caused by more (or fewer) exits than planned?

(2) *Early termination:* Comparison of planned with actual early termination rates. The planner would analyze variance from plan by asking the following kinds of questions:

   (a) Is the variance from plan caused by longer (or shorter) stays in the component than planned?

   (b) What are the reasons for early termination? What proportion of them is "positive" (e.g., military service)? Is a separate measurement needed for positive early terminations?

   (c) What reasons do the early terminees give?

   (d) Are they terminating because one particular service is not being adequately provided?

(3) *Completions in holding:* Comparison of planned with actual number of persons in holding after they have completed

the program. The planner would ask the following kinds of questions:

(a) Is the variance from plan caused by an ineffective job development effort?

(b) Is there an oversupply of persons (who are in this training occupation) in the labor market already?

(c) Are the completers undertained (or overtrained) for the available job vacancies?

(d) Has too much (or too little) capacity been provided in the occupational training area?

(4) *Placements:* Comparison of planned with actual placements (generally defined as "persons who have exited the program as initial placements, have completed a specified initial employment period, and have remained on the job"). The planner would ask the following kinds of questions:

(a) Is the variance from plan caused by overtraining (or undertraining)? Are the clients' skills sufficient for retention?

(b) What reasons do initial employment period dropouts give for losing their initial placement jobs?

(c) What additional services might improve the retention rate?

(5) *Component completions* (transfers and initial employment period placements): Comparison of planned with actual component completion rates. The planner would ask the following kinds of questions:

(a) Does comparison identify the particular component responsible for the deficiency?

(b) Is the variance from plan sufficient to affect capacity utilization of other components?

(6) *Expenditures:* Comparison of planned with actual expenditures. The planner would ask the following kinds of questions:

(a) Is the variance caused by underutilization (or overutilization) of the component?

(b) Is the variance caused by understaffing (or over-staffing)?

(c) Is more (or less) service being given than planned?

(d) How has expenditure per "client days of service provided" been affected?

(e) Have unit costs increased (or decreased)?

(f) Were the planned levels underestimated (or overestimated)? What is the source of the mis-estimation?

(7) *Transfer payments:* Comparison of planned with actual proportion of transfer payments to total expenditures. The planner would ask the following kinds of questions:

(a) Is the variance caused by underenrollments (or over-enrollments)?

(b) Is overstaffing (or understaffing) of the component causing the variance from plan?

(c) Are clients aware of nonstipend transfers available, such as transportation allowances and so forth?

(8) *Client characteristics:* Comparison of planned with actual numbers of clients with specific characteristics entering the program or component. The planner would ask the following kinds of questions:

(a) Are the intake workers aware of the planned levels?

(b) Is more intensive outreach required?

(c) Do the planned levels overestimate (or underestimate) the needs of the population groups with the specified characteristics?

Alternatives Effectiveness Assessment

Alternatives effectiveness assessment is the principal evaluation tool in state and local manpower planning. This type of evaluation involves a systematic analysis of the relative effectiveness and costs of alternative programs, services, and strategies for the purposes of determining the most efficient approach to a given manpower objective. The key operative principle at work in alternatives effectiveness assessment is optimization. Its focus is tactical: Given a specific objective, what is the most efficient way to get there?

Alternatives effectiveness assessment takes three basic forms. The first form — effectiveness analysis — seeks to determine how well a particular service strategy or component is performing, in terms of program objectives and in relation to other service strategies or components without regard to the related costs. The second — costs analysis — seeks to determine the specific costs of serving a specific target group or of providing a specific service. The third form combines effectiveness analysis and cost analysis. Relative cost/effectiveness analysis attempts to estimate the relationship between outcome measures and cost measures of alternative services and service strategies. The results of the analysis are usually expressed as a cost/effectiveness index.

Effectiveness Analysis

Effectiveness analysis is a basic comparative approach whose purpose is to determine the relative effectiveness of alternative approaches to meeting a given objective. The objective might be defined as serving a particular client group, training for a particular job, or maximizing the effectiveness of a specific serious component.

There are two general classes of measures used in effectiveness analysis. The first set examines the outcome experience *within* the program as clients move through a particular component or service throughout. A second set examines the immediate outcomes of the program. Key measures of immediate outcomes include: (1) the movement of clients into unsubsidized employment, (2) the experience of clients in completing initial placement periods and intermediate term retention periods, (3) the movement of clients into training-related jobs or into preplanned, upgraded positions, and (4) changes in welfare status, entry wage experience of former clients, and so on.

Cost Analysis

The manpower planner's analysis of costs should be designed to determine the costs of serving a specific target group or of providing a specific service. An economist's view of costs would subsume the range of direct and opportunity costs associated with a particular program design. Opportunity costs can be defined as the value of the benefits of foregone program alternatives. The calculation of these costs would include the full range of benefits which might have been received if the program resources had been directed into other uses. Opportunity costs would also include lost wages to the client and lost tax payments to the government while an individual is enrolled in a manpower program. The theoretical economist would also be interested in a third type of cost; i.e., marginal costs. Marginal analysis would examine the cost change results derived from adding or subtracting numbers of participants or units of service. Optimization would require that further clients or units of service be added until the additional benefits from that addition equal the added costs.

The planner of the state and local manpower authority generally will not be in a position to mount a serious effort to calculate actual opportunity and marginal costs. Generally neither the state-of-the-art nor the priority needs for basic evaluation would support the allocation of much of the planner's efforts in this direction. It is important, however, that the planner keep in mind the concepts of opportunity and marginal costs and, in an informal way, attempt to consider these costs in planning and implementing manpower services.

The key to effective cost analysis is the ability to identify expenditures with a particular activity and to establish an appropriate measuring unit for that activity. Two data bases are essential to this task. These are the "service unit activity record" and the "service unit cost record." The former is a continuous record of "services provided," maintained for each discrete program activity and, if possible, client. The latter is a continuous record of expenditures maintained for each discrete program activity.

The service unit is analogous to the "cost center" concept employed in many cost accounting systems. The choice of service centers defines the level of precision with which future analyses can attribute specific outcomes and changes to distinctly different service patterns. For example, if the service unit chosen is "total institutional training," cost and effectiveness analyses of various institutional training approaches will not be easily accomplished. Although the level of detail desired for evaluative purposes will vary from area to area, it is important to remember that reconstruction of needed records at a later date is many times more expensive than keeping records at one more level of detail than is currently deemed necessary. The following considerations are useful in determining the level at which separate service unit records should be maintained (still using institutional training as the example):

(1) Costs of training in each occupational area should be separately retrievable.

(2) Costs of each distinct approach to training for a single occupation should be separately retrievable.

(3) Costs of each distinct supportive service should also be retrievable.

(4) Costs of providing the same service from different geographical locations should be retrievable.

(5) Costs of services distinct enough to be given a unique name should generally be separately retrievable.

(6) Costs of services delivered by an administrative unit large enough to require a "nonworking" supervisor should be separately retrievable.

The crucial measure next employed in cost analysis is the cost per unit of service. This cost is determined by dividing the total dollar expenditures for an activity by the number of units of service provided. The cost of strategies is determined by totaling the costs of the units of service that constitute a given service strategy.

Information for conducting cost analysis is derived from two primary data sources. Costs of serving particular client groups are computed from information on services recorded in the individual client records of former enrollees and from unit cost estimates prepared by taking historical service unit activity and cost records and developing an appropriate historical service unit cost figure. Costs of a particular service strategy are developed in a similar fashion. From the file of former enrollees, all the records of persons participating in the strategy are removed. These files are then used to tabulate the average amounts of all services received by participants in a particular strategy. Standard historical unit costs are then applied to the average service mix to develop an average enrollee cost estimate.

Relative Cost/Effectiveness Analysis

Relative cost/effectiveness analysis is a method for integrating effectiveness analysis and cost analysis findings. The objective of relative cost/effectiveness analysis is to determine what results different service strategies achieve for the funds expended on them. The final measure employed in cost/effectiveness analysis is generally a ratio of effectiveness measures over costs. This ratio is usually expressed as a cost/effectiveness index.

Alternatives Effectiveness Assessment in Use

The essential characteristic of alternatives effectiveness assessment is its comparative approach. Comparisons are drawn among alternatives relative to their effectiveness and costs. Simple comparative measures are constructed which are used to compare one alternative to another on a specific dimension of effectiveness, costs, or both costs and effectiveness simultaneously.

To illustrate this process, we have provided an extended sample of a simplified alternatives effectiveness assessment which includes a limited effectiveness analysis, a cost analysis, and a relative cost/effectiveness analysis. This example presents an alternatives effectiveness analysis as it might be applied to a common local manpower planning problem — namely, gauging the relative cost effectiveness of alternative service strategies in placing a particular client group in unsubsidized employment.

Let us assume that the 1975 (fiscal year) manpower plan of "Metroville" has identified as a priority target group unemployed black males, aged eighteen to 21, with less than a high school (completion) education but more than eight years of education. While the plan does not identify specific service sequences for each priority group, enrollment targets were set for the total manpower program for each group. Individuals were assigned to particular services as openings became available and as personal preferences seemed to suggest. The specific service sequences offered (with their identifying numbers for this example) are:

1. Mechanical repair occupations

   Remedial education   Six man-weeks

   Mechanic skills training   Fourteen man-weeks

2. Assembly occupations

   Remedial education   Twelve man-weeks

   On-the-job training   Eight man-weeks

3. Machine operators

    Remedial education   Eight man-weeks

    Metal cluster skills   Six man-weeks
    training

    On-the-job training   Eight man-weeks

4. Various occupations

    Remedial education   Fourteen man-weeks

    Work experience   Four man-weeks

5. Sales occupations

    Remedial education   Four man-weeks

    Sales training cluster   Four man-weeks

    On-the-job training   Ten man-weeks

6. Health occupations

    Remedial education   Twelve man-weeks

    Health service cluster   Twelve man-weeks
    skills training

7. Clerical occupations

    Remedial education   Eight man-weeks

    Clerical cluster skills   Twelve man-weeks
    training

The programs have been operating for nine months, and the planners are now interested in determining which service mixes are most effective in serving specific priority groups so that reallocations can be made in next year's plan. The planners collect the individual records of terminated enrollees and sort them according to priority group and service strategy. An examination of the termination records shows that no male, eighteen- to 21-year-old blacks, with the identified preenrollment education levels, were enrolled in the clerical cluster. With the termination records sorted into the remaining six service strategies, the analysis begins.

The first concern of the analyst is the effectiveness of the different strategies in producing placements. Consequently, a placement rate is computed for each service strategy by dividing the total placements made from each strategy by the total number of terminated enrollees in each strategy. Table 9-2 shows the results of the comparison of the effectiveness of each strategy for placing male blacks (eighteen to 21 years of age, with more than eight but less than twelve years of education).

Table 9-2

Comparison of Service Sequence Placement Rates

Number	Service Sequence	Total Terminees	Total Placements	Placement Rate	Effectiveness Ranking
1	Mechanical repair occupations; skills training emphasis	75	50	0.6667	6
2	Assembly occupations; remedial education, on-the-job training	50	37	0.7400	4
3	Machine operators; remedial education, on-the-job training	67	55	0.8209	2
4	Various occupations; remedial education emphasis	63	45	0.7143	5
5	Sales occupations; on-the-job training emphasis	45	40	0.8888	1
6	Health occupations; skills training, remedial education emphasis	25	20	0.8000	3

The analyst ranks the placement rates and develops an initial impression of strategy effectiveness. However, placements vary in quality. One dimension of the quality of placements is the entry wage received. To get a better idea of the effect of the strategies in moving clients nearer the general labor force, the analyst might compare the entry wages received with the average nonagricultural wage of all persons in the local labor market. This adjustment is made by dividing the average nonagricultural wage into the average placement wage for each service strategy. The resultant figure is a percentage measurement (Table 9-3). The average placement wage as a percentage of the average nonagricultural wage can be used to adjust the placement rate for each strategy for differences in the quality of the placement. The results of these calculations are illustrated in the table. Note that the adjustment of placement rates for difference in wages changes the effectiveness rankings of the service strategies to a considerable extent in several cases.

The planner might now shift his or her attention to a consideration of the costs for the alternatives strategies. This analysis would

Table 9-3

Adjusting Effectiveness Rankings for Differences in Placement Wages

Number	Service Sequence	Average Wage		(a) As a Ratio of (b) (c)	Placement Ratio (d)	Effectiveness Measure* (e)	Ranking of Effectiveness Measure (f)
		Placement (a)	Nonagricultural (b)				
1	Mechanical repair occupations; skills training emphasis	$3.10	$3.15	0.9841	0.6667	65.61	(3)
2	Assembly occupations; remedial education, on-the-job training	2.65	3.15	0.8413	0.7400	62.26	(4)
3	Machine operators; remedial education, on-the-job training	2.90	3.15	0.9206	0.8209	75.57	(1)
4	Various occupations; remedial education emphasis	2.35	3.15	0.7460	0.7143	53.29	(6)
5	Sales occupations; on-the-job training emphasis	2.15	3.15	0.6825	0.8888	60.66	(5)
6	Health occupations; skills training, remedial education emphasis	2.60	3.15	0.8254	0.8000	66.03	(2)

*100(cd) = e

Table 9-4
Illustration of Cost per Enrollee Calculation
(Machine operator)

Service Needed	Average Service Units		Standard "per Unit" Cost		Cost per Enrollee
Remedial eduation (man-weeks)	8	@	$70.31	=	$ 562.48
Metals cluster skills training (man-weeks)	6	@	50.00	=	300.00
On-the-job training (man-weeks)	8	@	83.33	=	666.64
Work experience	None		None		None
Manpower services (intake, counseling, or assessment incident)	4	@	12.50	=	50.00
Health services (incidents)	0.5	@	10.00	=	5.00
Transportation services (incidents)	15	@	1.25	=	18.75
TOTAL (average)					$1,602.87

begin with the calculation of average service units received. The average service units would be multiplied by standard unit costs to arrive at a per enrollee cost figure. Table 9-4 illustrates the calculation of estimated costs per enrollee. The per enrollee cost figures are calculated for all of the strategies and compared. Table 9-5 compares the per enrollee costs for each strategy.

Table 9-5
Comparison of "per Enrollee" Costs for Each Strategy

Number	Strategy	Cost per Enrollee	Ranking Lowest to Highest
1	Mechanical repair occupations	$1,267.06	2
2	Assembly occupations	1,343.07	4
3	Machine operators	1,602.87	5
4	Various occupations	1,301.84	3
5	Sales occupations	1,067.79	1
6	Health occupations	1,621.18	6

With the cost estimates complete, a relative cost/effectiveness index can be computed, using the following equation:

$$\frac{\text{Placement rate} \times \left(\begin{array}{l}\text{Average placement}\\ \text{wage as a percentage}\\ \text{of average}\\ \text{nonagricultural wage}\end{array}\right) \times 100}{\text{Average cost per enrollee}} \times 1{,}000 = \begin{array}{l}\text{Unadjusted}\\ \text{cost/effect-}\\ \text{iveness}\\ \text{ratio}\end{array}$$

The unadjusted cost/effectiveness ratio is put in the form of an index by calculating each service strategy cost/effectiveness ratio as a percentage of the sum of all unadjusted cost/effectiveness ratios. The result is an index figure useful for comparisons with other service strategy indices. Differences between cost/effectiveness indices can be read as so many percentage points more (or less) effective than . . . . Table 9-6 shows the cost/effectiveness indices for the six alternative strategies.

Table 9-6
Cost/Effectiveness Indices for Alternative Strategies

Number	Strategy	Cost/Effectiveness Index
1	Mechanical repair occupations	109.49
2	Assembly occupations	98.02
3	Machine operators	99.69
4	Various occupations	86.56
5	Sales occupations	120.12
6	Health occupations	86.12

Impact Assessment

The realm of impact assessment includes all of those analytical activities designed to measure long-term changes attributable to the program on participants, the labor market, and the community. Impact assessment seeks to assess the extent to which long-term goals are being met, whereas operational control and assessment and alternatives effectiveness assessment measure operational plan and objectives achievement. Borus and Tash (1970) identify beneficiaries of manpower programs as society, participants in the programs, employers, and government. The goals of society for manpower programs focus on such aggregates as gross national product, the distribution of income, the distribution of employment opportunity, and the reduction of the unemployment rate. The goals of the individual participant focus on those benefits which directly accrue to him or her, such as increases in earnings and income and increases in satisfaction. The goals of the employer also tend to focus on those benefits which directly accrue to him, such as increases in productivity. The goals of governments for manpower programs include the goals of society, the participant, and the employer, and in addition include the improvement of the government budgetary position.

Impact assessment in its broadest sense would include efforts to measure the extent to which all of the goals of the various beneficiaries are met. Impact assessment in the context of state and local manpower planning is more limited. The state and local planner will generally not consider nonmanpower alternative uses of the available manpower allocation. The focus of state and local evaluation is on the comparative advantages of alternative approaches in making changes in the distribution of employment, underemployment, involuntary nonparticipation in the labor market, and other local labor market pathologies amenable to state and local manpower solutions.

Central to impact assessment at the labor market level is the comparison of detailed preenrollment and post-program information for a sample group of enrollees, with detailed information on a control group of similar persons who did not receive manpower services. The operational mode is essentially that of the experiment: A homogenous group of persons experiencing the same problems in the labor market is divided into an experimental group and a control group. The experimental group is given a specific set of manpower services under controlled conditions, while the control group is left to its own devices. At some point after the experimental group has completed the program, a set of economic, social, psychological, and educational measures are taken of both the experimental and control groups. These measures are compared with similar measures taken prior to the enrollment of the experimental group and the preenrollment and post-program measures compared for the two groups. If differences are noted, the analyst develops a probability statement which indicates the extent to which the differences can be attributed to the manpower services. The analyst should also estimate how long these differences might be expected to persist into the future and then compare a derived estimate of the future stream of benefits to the total costs of the manpower services provided. The result is known as a cost/benefit ratio.

The difficulty in obtaining reliable control groups is the principal limitation on the widespread use of this form of impact evaluation. One chief limiting factor is the necessity that the control group be drawn from the same population as the experimental group in order for the comparison to have statistical validity. The statistically ideal approach would be to contact all persons eligible to enter the program prior to implementation. Then, on a purely random basis, persons would be designated for the experimental or the control group. At this point an appropriate random sample would be drawn from each group and extensive preenrollment interviews given. The experimental group would be enrolled in the program, while the control group would be left to its own devices. One year after completion of the program, follow-up interviews would be taken of both the experimental and control group samples. Sufficient resources would be available to contact a reliable proportion of both groups for the follow-up interview.

The result of this process would be a statistically reliable control group. The reasons for the rare use of statistically valid control groups are obvious. Aside from the money resources required, the legal problems involved in denying service to an eligible person, the preselection problems, the time period involved, and any number of other substantial problems have all served to limit attempts at impact evaluation, using a statistically valid control group.

Numerous alternatives to random control groups have been suggested and tried. Retrospective control groups are the most commonly used nonrandom alternative. The analyst uses those persons who qualified for a program but who did not enter. However, the size and direction of the bias introduced by this technique is unknown. Other studies have attempted to retrospectively match former enrollees with persons who never applied for the program — which again results in unknown biases. Finally, some studies have employed the "before and after" device on the enrollee group itself; in effect, using the experimental group as its own control. Again the sources of potential bias are substantial. However, if care is taken to make adjustments for prevailing wage and employment trends and to take into consideration other evidence as to change in the levels of economic activity so as to estimate what would have occurred in absence of the program, before and after comparisons can give reasonable control guidelines at low cost. Finally, another approach to the control group problem has been to develop "paper" control groups by matching enrollee characteristics to records of persons with similar characteristics in Social Security and other agency files. The problem here has been the lack of sufficient matchable characteristics to ensure that the experimental and the paper control groups are really from the same universe.

Practical solutions to these problems have not yet been found. The simple rejoinder — that the local grantee select a control group from the eligible applicant population — is neither satisfying nor appropriate at this point. It is certain, however, that practical solutions to this problem should be placed high on the priority list of manpower research. Meanwhile, the evaluator must do whatever possible to assure that what is being measured is actually a change which the program caused.

Even with the control group problem solved, however, the requirements of an impact analysis would be only partially achieved. To measure total impact, the planner would have to know what happened to other members of the labor force, the labor market, and its institutions.

Outcomes Analysis

Outcomes analysis offers the state and local planner an intermediate approach to impact assessment. This kind of analysis is basically an extension of relative cost/effectiveness analysis. Extensive pre- and post-program labor market experience interviews are taken from a statistically valid sample of program participants. The sample would generally be chosen at program entry. The size of the sample depends upon the statistical confidence level desired and the size of the groups for which the planner wishes to make evaluative statements. The proportion of the total enrollee population sampled increases as the desired confidence level goes up and the number of population subgroups under analysis increases. If preprogram interviews are to be conducted at program entry, the planner is required to develop rough estimates of the number of entrants who will be enrolled in each strategy from each population subgroup under analysis. These estimates are then used to determine the sampling proportions required for specific confidence levels.

The interviews are designed to collect information on changes in employment stability and intensity, as well as changes in income, dependency, and other relevant indicators of social and economic well-being. These measures of change are combined with program cost data to generate estimates of the relative cost effectiveness of alternative service strategies and occupational training areas over the time period. The most common form of outcomes analysis involves the comparison of the change in pre- and post-program income with program costs. This form of outcomes analysis requires the calculation of three important measures on each service strategy or subgroup from sample data collected in the pre- and post-program interviews. The first term, a measure of average employment intensity, is defined as

$$\text{Average employment intensity} = \frac{\text{Sum of weeks employed}}{\text{Sum of weeks out of the program}}$$

This term provides an average measure of the proportion of potential working time actually worked by the group. The planner would next construct an estimate of weighted hourly earnings defined as

$$\frac{\text{Weighted average}}{\text{hourly earnings}} = \frac{\text{Sum of period of employment} \times \text{hourly earnings}}{\text{Sum of weeks employed}}$$

This term provides an average hourly earnings figure which is adjusted for the differences in the amounts of time worked by individual members within the group.

The third key term is a post-program estimation of average annual income which is calculated by multiplying the average employment intensity term by 2,000 hours to estimate the proportion of available working time during a year which each group can be expected to be employed and then multiplying the result by the average hourly earnings figure.

Table 9-7 illustrates data abstracted from the post-program interviews needed for the development of outcome measures for a single service strategy. From the data in the table the planner can calculate the three key outcome measures as follows:

$$\text{Average employment intensity} = \frac{1,130}{1,300} = 0.87 \qquad (1)$$

$$\text{Weighted average hourly earnings} = \frac{2,997.15}{1,131} = \$2.65 \qquad (2)$$

$$\begin{array}{l}\text{Estimated average annual} \\ \text{post-program income}\end{array} = 0.87(2.65) \times 2,000 \qquad (3)$$
$$= \$4,611.00$$

These measures are calculated for each service strategy or group under study. A set of equivalent measures is then calculated from data on the same population from the preprogram period. The pre- and post-program measures are then compared. For example, the planner might compare changes in employment intensity or annual income and note differences between the strategies or groups. A more useful analysis would be to combine the changes

Table 9-7
Base Data for Calculating Key Outcome Measures

Participant (A)	Period out of Program (Weeks) (B)	Period Employed (Weeks) (C)	Average Hourly Earnings (Dollars) (D)	Weighted Earnings (C×D=E) (E)
A	26	15	$3.15	$ 47.25
B	26	20	3.05	61.00
C	26	10	2.85	28.50
D	26	24	2.95	70.80
.	.	.	.	.
.	.	.	.	.
.	.	.	.	.
.	.	.	.	.
N	26	21	3.20	67.20
TOTAL	1,300	1,131		$2,997.15

in the key measures with program cost to get a form of the now familiar cost/effectiveness ratio.

Using change in estimated average annual income as a measure of relative effectiveness the cost/effectiveness ratio can be defined as

$$\text{Cost/effectiveness ratio} = \frac{\text{Change in estimated annual average income}}{\text{Average cost per enrollee}}$$

Table 9-8 illustrates the calculation of cost/effectiveness indices for six service strategies with information obtained in the pre- and post-program interviews. In rows 8 and 9 of the table the cost/effectiveness ratio is indexed by dividing each ratio by the average ratio and multiplying the result by 100. For comparative purposes, row 10 shows the cost/effectiveness indices developed for the same set of service strategies from the example of alternative effectiveness assessment. A comparison of the ranking of the two sets of indices shows the effect of the inclusion of follow-up data and estimated annual income change in the evaluation design.

With the addition of a control group, the outcomes cost/effectiveness measure can assist the planner in determining the impact of the service strategies on the measured employment, wage, and income changes.

The development of cost/effectiveness indices based on outcomes data can assist the local manpower planner in identifying which of the alternative service strategies was the best investment on behalf of the target group. The planner should be cautioned, however, by the tentative nature of the income estimate. This estimate looks at expected change over the first post-program year. Without continuing follow-up, the planner cannot determine how long an earnings differential resulting from a service strategy will last. However, if it results from a basic improvement in an enrollee's employability, the differential should endure over an extended period.

Outcomes assessment offers the local manpower planner an evaluation tool well suited to his or her needs. Although it can be improved by use of control groups, it is not dependent upon them. The outcomes assessment cost/effectiveness measures are not cost/benefit measures. Relative cost/effectiveness analysis seeks to answer the question: "Given the mission, what is the least cost

Table 9-8
Cost/Effective Comparison of Changes in Estimated Annual Income

Row Number	Category	Service Strategy					
		Mechanical Repair (1)	Assembly Operator (2)	Machine Operator (3)	Various Occupations (4)	Sales Occupations (5)	Health Occupations (6)
1	Average intensity of employment	0.87	0.74	0.89	0.62	0.80	0.93
2	Weighted average hourly earnings	$2.65	$2.58	$2.83	$2.45	$2.50	$2.60
3	Estimated average annual income (post-program)	($4,611.00)	($3,818.40)	($5,037.40)	($3,038.00)	($4,000.00)	($1,836.00)
4	Preenrollment average annual income	$2,400.00	$2,350.00	$2,399.00	$2,320.00	$2,365.00	$2,328.00
5	Average increase in annual income	($2,211.00)	($1,468.40)	($2,638.40)	($718.00)	($1,635.00)	($2,508.00)
6	Average cost per enrollee	($1,267.06)	($1,343.07)	($1,602.87)	($1,301.84)	($1,067.79)	($1,621.18)
7	Cost/effectiveness ratio	(1.74)	(1.09)	(1.65)	(0.55)	(1.53)	(1.55)
8	Average cost/effectiveness ratio (all strategies)	(1.35)	(1.35)	(1.35)	(1.35)	(1.35)	(1.35)
9	Cost/effectiveness index—outcomes assessment (Ranking)	128.89 1	80.74 5	122.22 2	40.74 6	113.33 4	114.81 3
10	Cost/effectiveness index—alternatives assessment (Ranking)	109.49 2	98.02 4	99.69 3	86.56 5	120.12 1	86.12 6

means to achieve it?" That is, given the funds for manpower purposes, what is the best manpower use of the resources? Cost/benefit analysis tests whether an activity was worth undertaking. Did its benefits exceed its costs? Should the resources spent on manpower programs have been put to other uses? Relative cost/effectiveness considerations are the state or local manpower planner's primary evaluative concern.*

Uses of Evaluation

Evaluation, of course, is but the means to an end. For the state or local manpower planner, that end is optimal results from available resources. How efficiently are the services being delivered? Are the right services going to the right people? Is there a mix of services and a service strategy that would be more effective for the target group? Is the agency delivering the services functioning efficiently? Or would some other agency do a better job?

The only purpose of the evaluation step, therefore, is to modify the program as indicated by the results of the evaluation. No simple, overall evaluation of program worth will suffice. Ideally, every cross classification of target group, service mix, and delivery system should be evaluated separately. Whom to serve is primarily a political and value judgment. What services should be provided and who should provide them is a technical and, it is hoped, objective measurement decision. Politics may intervene, but if it violates the rule of effectiveness, the cost of that violation should be clearly recognized.

References

Borus, Michael E.; and Tash, William R. *Measuring the Impact of Manpower Programs.* Ann Arbor; University of Michigan–Wayne State University. November 1970.

Burack, Elmer H.; and Walker, James W. Editors. *Manpower Planning and Programming.* Boston: Allyn and Bacon. 1972.

U.S. Department of Labor, Manpower Administration, Office of Policy, Evaluation and Research. *Evaluation of Manpower Programs at State and Local Levels: A Guide for Manpower Revenue Sharing Grantees.* Washington, D.C.: U.S. Department of Labor. June 1973. Mimeographed draft.

---

*For a further introduction to the mechanics of outcomes assessment, see U.S. Department of Labor, June 1973.

10
The Politics of Planning

Identifying problems, choosing objectives, examining alternatives, and implementing, monitoring, evaluating, and modifying programs — the classical planning steps — for the manpower planner breaks down into the tasks of determining whom to serve and what jobs to seek for them, identifying the barriers which stand between them and satisfactory employment, deciding what mix of services will have the best probability of surmounting the barriers, choosing the most effective delivery of those services, and monitoring and evaluating the program. It remains to discuss the environment within which all of this must occur.

The Political Environment

Planning, as for nearly everything else encompassed by the manpower field, is a means, not an end. The goals are clear and relatively uncluttered: (1) a successful and satisfying working career for the individual, and (2) efficient use of available manpower resources for the economy. This book has concentrated on planning for the needs of those individuals who face various disadvantages in obtaining satisfactory employment — and therefore the job is the thing. With the goal of a satisfactory working career clearly in longer range focus, the planner knows that an immediate job or preparation for it is the beginning objective. Planners must assess

291

the strengths and weaknesses of their position in pursuing that objective and must perceive realistically roles to be played within the prevailing environment which will maximize influence over the manpower system.

Sources of Influence

Manpower planners for state and local prime sponsors operate in an amorphous political environment. They have no political power of their own but must depend for influence and "clout" upon the power of governors, mayors, or county executives to whom they are ultimately responsible. However, their distance from, contact with, and influence upon any elected official will differ widely by circumstance and issue. In some cases the distance will be great, yet little can be accomplished without at least the appearance of power. Power in politics is counted in votes, dollars, patronage jobs, and public services. Manpower planners have direct control over none, but can have some impact upon each, and from that must garner whatever influence they are to exercise.

An anomaly of the centralized manpower concept is the negative political reward system. It is assumed that local politicians have a better fix on the needs of people and labor markets within their jurisdiction than is possible from a national or even a state level. This is undoubtedly true, but with two reservations: Does the politician have (a) the incentive to care, and (b) the expertise to do anything about it? As noted earlier, the customers for manpower services to date are a group not large enough or cohesive enough to reward significantly political officials who serve them particularly well. At the same time they may be able to do the officials damage if the officials do not serve the customers well enough. Yet doing a good job for the disadvantaged is as likely to bring negative as positive marks from the remainder of the populace.

It is for this reason that most mayors did not choose to take over community action agencies when the Green amendment to the Economic Opportunity Act authorized them to do so. They didn't want to be responsible for unpopular and perhaps unsuccessful programs. For the same reason, several governors have encouraged local units to accept CETA prime sponsorship when they might have easily been convinced to join a statewide consortium. Mayors rarely enjoy the latter luxury because refusing to participate would appear an abrogation and a refusal to accept needed and available funds. Serving the unemployed in general and such special groups as veterans can be more politically rewarding. There will be fewer people receiving manpower services in the future than in the past, but to whom they owe any gratitude for service will be more clear.

The manpower budget is a significant amount of money when focused upon a limited target group in a particular jurisdiction. Planners, of course, influence the distribution of funds among agencies first and citizens thereafter. However, the service delivery agencies are what planners are most interested in being able to influence. The planner's power to reallocate funds, and therefore to exercise clout through the budget, again reflects back to relationships with the political executive. The planning councils upon which both agency and target group representatives normally sit are customarily advisory in nature, with the staff reporting ultimately to the executive rather than to the council as such. The planner's ability to direct the allocation of funds among agencies is measured by his or her influence, relative to theirs, over his or her principal.

The planner's impact upon staff slots in the planning office is a strength, but these are few compared to the staff jobs in the service delivery agencies. This influence over the ultimate jobs in the labor market toward which the clients are being directed is limited to those which subsidization can provide. Employers are jealous of their hiring prerogatives, and only the unions (by labor market power) and governments (by regulation) have been able to wrest away any job control. Manpower planners have no market power to win job control. They can only plan to prepare people to compete successfully for available jobs, to persuade employers to accept a civic duty, or to "bribe" them by subsidizing private or public employment. Yet eventually the manpower clientele must learn to face labor market forces and compete successfully with other claimants for the same jobs.

Planners cannot exercise influence in the labor market by expertise in the provision of labor market services. Their expertise is to plan, to review, and to evaluate, not to deliver. Delivery of services is the expertise of service agencies which the planner must involve by alliance. The manpower planner purveys a product considered substandard and passed over by the potential customer — the employer. He deals in the economics of misery and wrestles daily with residual problems, left over from a long line of attempts to solve the same set of problems.

Yet the manpower planner, like most others in the manpower field, is driven essentially by compassion. Why else operate in a field of uncertain tenure, deep-seated and complex problems, and limited public praise? The only explanation is a desire to make life better for one's disadvantaged unemployed or ill-paid fellows. The motive is the personal welfare of others. The stock in trade is to perceive need and then parlay limited resources and limited influence into effective programs of employability and employment. The politics of that assignment are at least as important as the planning.

A unique aspect of the CETA legislation is that it gives the state and local manpower planners (or, more accurately, their principals) some control over no more than two-fifths of the funds available for employability and employment programs, and expects them to plan for the whole of it and more. Coordinated planning encompassing the full range of available services and resources for the disadvantaged is essential to success. Yet the only incentive for participation by controllers of non-CETA resources is conviction that the results can be better for all.

Non-CETA manpower programs avoid some painful decisions by tending to be limited by law to a narrowly prescribed service population — the physically and mentally retarded, welfare recipients, and the like. CETA, on the other hand, uses terms such as "the disadvantaged," "the unemployed," and "those most in need of manpower services." But these are very inexact definitions, applicable to populations many times larger than available budgets can serve, and offering no clue as to the reasons for unemployment and poverty.

CETA may prove to be disadvantageous to the disadvantaged or, more accurately, to minority groups. Community action agencies and racially and ethnically oriented service organizations emerged from the conviction that old-line agencies could not and would not serve the poor, particularly the minority poor. These new community-based organizations, on the whole, never became particularly effective as deliverers of services, but they had a major impact on local and even national politics by giving control of budgets to the formerly powerless. The older agencies profited from the experience by changing to meet the unfamiliar competition.

Under CETA, the power will rest with offices of elected officials, and the services will be provided primarily by the old-line agencies. Community organizations will likely have no significant representation on state and local manpower councils, unless they vigorously pursue it. There will be representatives of target populations, but that representation has rarely involved significant power. Community organizations like the Opportunities Industrialization Centers and SER will be sufficiently influential to get their "piece of the action" in some places, but for the most part, that may be more crumbs than slices.

A direct loss will be the numbers of minority people who had access to staff slots but now will face all the merit system obstacles of government employment. The minority community and community-based organizations can gain a voice in the planning process if they demand it. But it will be a major responsibility of the planner in planning, monitoring, and evaluating to assure that the commitment to equal employment (and other) opportunity is not weakened. The planning staff through their distribution of service delivery assignments and their contracting authority can manipulate fiscal and delivery systems by requirement or policy. The compliance of the most obdurate agencies can be radically modified if the anxiety of agencies to win in the competitive contracting environment is exploited fully — and if the elected official will back the planner.

Support for the Planning Strategy

Change does not occur in a vacuum. For this reason the astute planner understands that he or she must possess more than competent analytical skills to bring off any needed change in the existing service delivery system. The support and confidence of higher political or administrative leadership is essential to the planner seeking to act as change agent.

For example, assume that from a series of evaluative studies or analyses of administrative procedures the planner determines that a consolidation of the present intake system could "free up" the services of several intake workers, who could then be reassigned to job development teams which the planner's analysis has found to be understaffed. The intake units are presently under contract to a community-based group, while the job development teams are under contract with the metropolitan office of the state employment service. The planner's proposal would consolidate three small intake units in neighborhood centers into two centers and transfer four intake workers to two existing job development teams.

The planner brings the proposal before the metro manpower council; the city manager is chairman of the meeting, and the metro employment service director and the director of the community-based organization are members. Two pages into the proposal and the employment service director and the community organization director have raised half a dozen questions, running the gamut from merit system problems to a "sellout" of the people search. The city manager tables the proposal, perhaps sets up a subcommittee, and is wondering if the planner he hired six months ago is the right man for the job. The planner in turn has added new "evidence" to his long-standing file on bureaucratic imperialism and gutless city managers.

The problem goes beyond simplistic human relations. Of course the groundwork should have been laid before the meeting started; the council chairman should have been involved long before that; and the directors of the affected agencies should have been given advance notice and the opportunity for a critique and for proposing alternatives to the proposal. But beyond these surface processes lies the need for the planner to understand and respect the simple realities of the conduct of public business and bureaucratic manners.

Too often the planner sharpens his technical skills to the neglect of his bureaucratic ones. Perhaps this is the result of the long ego-destroying years of the CAMPS experience or the inexperience of the novice fresh from graduate school. Whatever the reason, a thorough study would probably show that at least as many sound proposals for change have been mismanaged by the planner in the decision-making process as have been stopped purely by bureaucratic turf fighters.

The novice planner might say . . . "Who needs them?" Under CETA, the city has the money. "If they don't knuckle under we'll drop both their contracts; set up our own system." The reality is that there are probably very few places in the country where such an action would bring better results. The prime sponsor controls the smaller fraction of the manpower resources in almost every community. The employment service has a continuous flow of target group persons, as well as the largest source of job orders, and a substantial amount of employer contact. School officials control most of the training capacity. Unions control key access points to a significant number of the "good" jobs, and community organizations often have the only real bureaucratic access to key target groups. The rehabilitation service generally provides the only intensive client assessment units, and day-care access is generally the province of welfare agencies.

The effective planner seeks to maximize the coordination of all of the available manpower service resources in order to create an integrated, effective, and efficient set of manpower services in the community. The prime sponsor's CETA dollars are generally best used as a catalyst for bringing about coordination and for "filling in" those services needed to create a complete system. Dollars spent duplicating services or facilities that would be provided from other sources should be kept at a minimum. Each case of duplication must be considered a failure in planning. Although planners are not fully to blame in every case, they must share part of the blame nonetheless.

What then, exactly, is the notion we are trying to convey? The lesson is simply this: The astute planner must make the study of his or her bureaucratic environment, its decision-making mechanisms and institutions, and the cultivation of the confidence and respect (if not friendship) of its leadership a prime professional activity at least on a par with his or her technical competences. In many ways more important than the plan is the planning process. In fact, it might be argued that the main product is the ongoing process, with the plan as a byproduct. At least as much effort should go into laying the bureaucratic foundations necessary to implement a proposal for change as was allocated to developing the technical proposal. The planner who follows this admonition will find the rewards substantial and the numbers of "pretty but unused" proposals on the mythical planner's shelf fewer. All of these are key components in the service delivery strategy.

The Payoff for Manpower Planning

Despite the limited political payoffs from directing manpower programs, there are positive gains for most actors on the manpower scene. Evidence is ample that most participants in most of the categorical programs of the past have ended up better off for the experience. Their payoffs depended upon their own situations, the state of the local economy, and the nature of the program. Possible payoffs were: (1) improved employability, (2) job access, and (3) transfer payments. Only training, education, and work experience could have direct impact on the first. Either a favorable economy or subsidized jobs was a prerequisite for the second, but those were ordinarily not efficient. Some other barrier — personal or institutional — was ordinarily present to be removed or surmounted. Equal employment opportunity efforts, placement services, and subsidized jobs were some of the tools. Several programs seemed to provide little more than income maintenance, but that was not unattractive or unimportant to those who were poor.

Employers have rarely been hurt, though no more than modestly aided, by manpower programs. Their available work force has been expanded. They have generally been compensated for any services rendered. Perhaps the greatest loss was occasionally the autonomous discretion to discriminate. Labor unions have had the least to gain since their memberships have rarely been serviced. Yet their political stance has been surprisingly supportive.

Agencies have gained new budgets and expanded assignments. Staffs have gained employment and advancement. Impressive has been the "Tammany Hall" effect. New, community-based organizations have emerged to serve under federal financing. Patronage jobs, staff advancement, budgets, and a base for political activity have been provided to previously disfranchised people. From program participant to staff member and up and out into a new career in public or private employment has been a frequent experience.

From the decategorized and decentralized programs, the enrollees should gain no less, unless decentralized administration becomes a vehicle for discrimination. Employers and unions should be similarly unaffected. The old-line agencies of government will likely be relative gainers and community-based organization losers in the new funding pattern. With that loss will tend to disappear the spontaneous upward career ladder of the unstructured organizations.

There will be less total dollars for the service agencies to receive, but that is a consequence of shifting priorities, not of the decentralized approach. Agencies will lose guaranteed access to those funds which are available as state and local political authorities gain the power to choose among alternative service deliverers. Employment service offices see themselves in danger of losing manpower program money, though basic employment service support funds are guaranteed from the Social Security Act. Educational institutions lose any guaranteed access to manpower funds and are likely to follow community-based organizations as the greatest losers. Apart from those losers and status quo maintainers are some new winners. The governor, the mayor, and the county commissioner now have access to new budgets and new sources of patronage and power. Local officials can now take credit, for what it is worth, for services to those who would previously have owed gratitude to federal sources or to state agencies.

But will the recipients know and note that the largesse now comes from more politically responsive hands if the same agencies still have the delivery assignment? The new decentralized manpower budgets do offer opportunity, through public service employment and prime sponsor staff slots, to subsidize state, city, and county personnel budgets. Manpower planning also provides the opportunity to link manpower budgets into economic development activities or whatever else is the community's highest priority. It may also be a route to positive alliance with the minority community — if jobs for the poor is its priority interest. Above all it gives the political leader authority as well as responsibility for action occurring on local turf. Old equities will be destroyed and new ones created, but the system will once again accommodate and settle into workable stability.

As noted in chapter 1, manpower planning is implied but not required by decategorization and decentralization. There remain categories of service just as there were (and still are) categorical programs. The essence is not eliminating categories but leaving to local decision makers the choice among alternative categories. But it is easier to repeat last year's categories with this year's budget than to reexamine need, social and economic parameters, and performance in the derivation of a new plan. Prime sponsors can gain political patronage without manpower planning; service deliverers are likely to prefer the status quo (except for those left out of last year's assignments); busy federal reviewers may approve plans which follow the proper form but encompass no new planning. The planner remains the one actor totally committed to and dependent upon the planning function — he or she and the manpower client, if the planning is effective. It is to the planner's interest to convince all other actors of the value of planning.

The Care and Feeding of Manpower Councils

To the manpower planning staff will fall the responsibility for making effective use (or failing to use) the prime sponsor planning councils and state services councils. Typically, members of such councils serve most vigorously if they must defend themselves and their interests from potential incursions by council, planner, or executive decisions. They serve less defensively and less vigorously, but still with interest, if they perceive direct gains, and only apathetically to the extent their position is an objective (disinterested) one.

To derive plans unconstrained by extraneous kibitzers might be a planner's paradise, were it not that the planning function has in it little intrinsic satisfaction if the plans are not ultimately implemented and tested in practice. The political executive is likely to have too many demands on his attention to focus long on manpower issues. The planner must take the initiative for implementation, monitoring, and evaluation while maintaining access to the executive, when needed, for clout.

The planner, whether for a local or a balance-of-state prime sponsorship, remains aware that CETA encompasses only 40 percent of the funds of traditional manpower programs (if programs aged a dozen years or less can be called traditional). Keys to the other 60 percent are primarily in the hands of state agencies. If those funds are to be accessible and to be encompassed within manpower plans, the employment service and public welfare, vocational rehabilitation, vocational education, and other such agencies must also be engaged in the planning process. They are unlikely to commit or relinquish their resources unless they are party to the decision. Theirs is also the long-term relationships with state legislatures, employers, unions, and the public, which are unlikely to be matched in the short run by the manpower planner. The state manpower services council is the designed route for access, but there is equal reasons for its representatives to sit on the prime sponsor planning councils.

Access to employers is equally vital, depending upon the nature of the planning objectives. If basic employability is to be enhanced and people placed through normal competitive channels, the previous manpower services received are likely to be of no interest to the employer. If direct access to jobs for manpower clients is contemplated, employer cooperation is necessary. Generally, there is no one who can speak for all or even most employers in a community, but even the appearance of a trusted fellow employer on the planning body may bolster confidence, and a management participant may warn the council against pitfalls in dealing with his or her fellow participants. Unions are certain to be affected and become edgy about any incursion of manpower clients into unionized jobs. More centralized representation of organized labor is possible, and planning participation may avoid or quiet opposition.

Participation of client representatives is more problematical. Like employers, no one can speak for all. Most "community leaders" are self-appointed. Yet cosmetics are important, forecast of client group reactions may be obtained, and at best, two-way communication between the planners and the planned-for may be achieved. The last is a reward worth struggling for.

All of this participation is complicated by the requirement that one-third of state services council members be representatives of prime sponsors. That may be few or many, depending upon the state. Yet that membership may be doubly important. The state manpower services council was not conceived as a planning body but as a device through which prime sponsors could gain access to services available from state agencies. State planning was to be limited to balance-of-state prime sponsorship, except in states of minimum population where statewide consortia might emerge. But this is probably unrealistic. While there are political incentives, in some cases, for "going it alone," there are strong economic ones for at least coordinated planning. It is a rare city that can successfully plan autonomously. Many persons' residences and jobs are not within the same political jurisdiction. They live in the suburbs and rural areas but work in the city.

The labor market is the only viable planning scope in the longer run. (But that is an argument for consortia or cooperative planning among cities and counties, not necessarily for state-level planning.) However, progressive decentralization of industry makes consortia more difficult to contain and maintain. Relating manpower development to economic development will require broader geographical contexts. Relocation assistance is a manpower tool so far largely ignored in CETA manpower planning discussions. Statewide prime sponsor consortia are unlikely and probably unwise, except in the Intermountain West and other states of small populations. Some planning aspects must and will emerge as a state-level responsibility, and the state manpower services council is the logical entity for assuming that function, except where the balance-of-state prime sponsor encompasses the bulk of the population as well as territory.

The usefulness of manpower councils does not answer the question of how to use them, however. They inevitably will complicate the planner's life. Throughout this book we have used, rather loosely, the generic term "manpower planner" in contrast to the program operator. Since for the most part we were addressing why and how to plan, this created no communication problems. When one addresses the structure of manpower planning councils, however, further differentiation is necessary.

A manpower prime sponsor is responsible for planning *and* delivery of manpower services, monitoring and evaluation, and the handling of the allocated federal funds. Any of those functions may be delegated, but generally a prime sponsor will delegate most service delivery to available and experienced agencies and reserve the other functions for itself. To deliver services would require hiring extensive staff — always a sensitive thing for an elected official to do for his own office — and duplicating ability already available in the agencies and private organizations. The principle of separating planning and operations is also well accepted. Not only does operation absorb energy and attention, it puts full accountability upon the elected official, with no buffer of blame upon a delegate agency.

Thus a typical prime sponsor staff will include a staff executive director, who reports directly to the chief elected official, and a variety of staff members. Among the latter will be planners, program monitors (who deal directly with the delegate service delivery agencies), and financial controllers. Most often the staff will report to the executive director and through him to the elected official. The council is ostensibly advisory to the elected official, but in fact is more often in a semiadvisory, seminegotiating relationship to the executive director. Occasionally the staff will be considered responsible to the council, and the council to the elected executive, but that relationship is becoming rarer, since the interests of agency representatives may often diverge from those of the elected executive.

In the planning process, the planners may (1) prepare a plan for executive approval and submit it to the council for information or advice, or (2) do the same, but give the council power to approve or disapprove. The council may also be integrally involved in the planning process. For instance, a subcommittee, whose chairman is the vocational education representative, assisted by staff members might make and recommend to the full council all decisions relating to classroom skills training and so forth. The plan once completed would become the creation of the council, but completing and reaching agreement on the plan would likely be a lenthy and complex process with little executive input. Staff preparation of the plan to be submitted for council advice or approval generally moves with greater dispatch and achieves more coherence.

A further level of complexity involves the nexus between planning and operation. The prime sponsor can contract with one prime contractor (for instance, the employment service) for all operations, leaving it to that entity to subcontract to other agencies for specialized services. The prime sponsor may prefer to act as its own general contractor, subcontracting all delivery of services to specialized agencies but assuming the entire coordinating and monitoring responsibility.

Whatever approach is chosen, the prime sponsor staff must maintain the façade of involvement by the chief elected official, maintain contact with that power source, and be able to get his or her attention and give reality to his or her involvement when a crunch arrives. The staff must then deal effectively with agency representatives who are its advisers on the manpower planning council, its subcontractors at the service delivery level, and the subjects of its monitoring and evaluation efforts. It must attract the involvement of agencies controlling non-CETA manpower funds and under no compulsion to participate in comprehensive planning. The tenuous nature of that relationship is apparent from the description. The staff must obtain advice from, choose among, cajole, supervise, evaluate, reward, and punish the same entities while maintaining responsibility, accountability, and reasonable good will. If the staff's planning is to have meaning, there must be the clout to get it implemented. If planning and operations are to be separated, the planners are dependent upon the operators (though the limited possibilities of competitive assignment may maintain some discipline). If the planners are to be accountable, they must evaluate, feed back, modify, punish, and reward. If the agencies are to be advisers, there must be good will. Meanwhile, every agency has its independent political base, while the staff has only its access to the elected executive ear. The "care and feeding" of planning and service councils is a critical component of a manpower planner's skills. It is not surprising that employer, labor, and target group representatives often get little attention vis-à-vis the agency role.

Structural Issues in Manpower Planning

The viability and quality of manpower planning are inevitably dependent upon the structure, quality, and commitment of state and local governments. Accustomed to the leadership of a single federal government in the manpower field, even though a highly pluralistic one, those with limited state and local political experience may overlook the diversity of governments at that level. In many states, the concept of a governor as chief of state is a myth, though there is a slow tendency to strengthen the gubernatorial role. State agencies funded from the federal budget, lead by directors chosen and supervised by commissions and advisory boards and staffed by merit system employees, may have limited susceptibility to a governor's directives. Some cities may be governed by mayors with strong executive powers. But in others the mayor may be a part-time chairman of a city council in a city run by a professional manager. Or he may be a "tie breaker" among coequal commissioners, each with unchallenged executive authority over various city services. County governments may be equally diverse in structure. Some states are nearly blanketed with city jurisdictions, and others encompass vast unincorporated territories. A few cities are metropolitan, but most are central city or suburban fragments of a metropolitan labor market, with no cohesive government. Some counties have, in effect, replaced cities as the primary source of public services, and provide metropolitan government. Others are responsible for maintaining public roads and supporting a sheriff's office. Councils and associations of government exert varying degrees of authority. Almost universally, public education has been established as an autonomous government of its own with separate elective and appointive processes, taxing powers, and decision-making practices — and those who have been designated by federal law as manpower prime sponsors are most often forbidden by their own constitutions to make education decisions.

Intermingled with these general governments are innumerable special units — sanitary districts, animal control districts, special improvement districts, mosquito abatement districts, elective cooperatives, and so on — all with some degree of governmental authority and all employers of manpower and impacters on the local labor markets. Every general government will react differently to its manpower planning responsibility, and every special unit will have its impact, all of which the manpower planner must understand and use or offset. The people to be served and the jobs to be had are rarely within the same political jurisdictions — often not even in the same states. Political boundaries are almost never economic boundaries. The successful manpower planner must be at least an amateur political scientist and a practical politician.

Technical Assistance and Training

Ten years of gradually increasing state and local manpower decision-making authority have provided a substantial nucleus of manpower planning experience. No one knows the shape of the learning curve in manpower planning and administration. Certainly the inexperienced will learn, but sound technical assistance and staff training can shorten the time and lower at least the human costs.

There is at present considerable question about whence that support will come from the federal agencies. Each federal agency recognizes its dependence upon local service delivery agencies and governmental units. Often the need for technical assistance and training is given no more than lip service. When attempts are made to meet those needs, the federal agency normally and naturally perceives the need from its own vantage point. Therefore, as in the manpower planning case, the tendency is to train the local practitioner primarily in how to meet the requirements of federal law, comply with the federal regulations and guidelines, and fulfill the reporting requirements of the federal funding agency. Training and technical assistance in the substantive task at hand take a lower priority. And all too often there are not the resources, energy, and commitment to carry the technical assistance and training function beyond the procedural to the substantive.

The state and local manpower planning staffs will want to take full advantage of any effective assistance from any source. The Area Manpower Institutes for the Development of Staff (AMIDS) sponsored by the Division of Manpower Development and Training of the U.S. Office of Education have been the only staff training capability not beholden primarily to the needs of the federal agency. This was accomplished by contracting the function to private training organizations and giving them a free hand to contact manpower agencies, perform needs assessments, and cooperatively design workshops and seminars attuned to the needs of the local units. However, that activity was MDTA–funded and its future under CETA is obscure.

A few universities have also taken the initiative to develop and sponsor training programs for manpower staffs, usually of a degree-granting nature. The Office of Research and Development in the Labor Department provides institutional grants of three or four years' duration to one university in each federal region, along with schools in other specially designated categories, to build their capability as manpower service institutions. For the fiscal years 1975 to 1978, these grantee institutions are to concentrate on the training of state and local manpower staffs. Most of these universities will themselves have to learn the arts of manpower planning and administration before they can teach it; but linked into a nationwide network, they should not have to individually "re-invent the wheel." Those manpower planning organizations which recognize the upgrading needs of its staff should be able to find the needed assistance.

Strengths and Weaknesses of Decentralized Planning

As noted in chapter 2, CETA is a fruition of ten years of groping toward a system combining federal resources and enforcement of accountability with delivery of manpower services adapted to local labor market needs and realities. But there are no unmixed blessings. Decentralized planning and delivery of manpower services, combined with decategorization among manpower services, offer new opportunities but include inherent threats. It is important to review the strengths and weaknesses in order to build upon the former and avoid the latter.

Potential Contributions

The key element, of course, is the possibility of identifying local needs, setting local goals, and designing programs which are realistic and desirable within the realities of local labor market conditions. There is no guarantee that it will be so. Local planners can still ignore or never discover those needs and realities. Programs can be designed in prejudice or inertia, or in accord with political pressures, more easily than by knowledgeable and objective analysis. The best conceived plans can fail in delivery, and vice versa. One can only be certain that such adaptation was impossible with nationally uniform manpower services. Whether the change will be an improvement is, at this point, a matter of faith.

A possible consequence and corollary of adaptability is responsiveness. The locally planned system does have the potential capability to respond to changing or newly recognized needs, almost impossible to do with nationally directed programs. But the potential is not necessarily the actuality. It remains the line of least resistance to do this year what was done last year and to follow this year's plan to the end, regardless of changes which may occur during the period.

Accountability also becomes a possibility but may never achieve reality. It requires that objectives be clear and progress measurable, that some force monitor progress and reward or punish good or bad performance. Until now, primarily, a contractual relationship has existed between federal agencies and state and local public and private institutions. But there were never the resources and the energy to monitor and evaluate performance in a meaningful fashion. Overall, national program evaluations could assess whether a program had been useful on the average. Each program's total impact on the social and economic system was too small to be measurable, but it was possible to judge whether the average enrollee was better off for the participation. It was not possible, or at least not done, to hold local service deliverers accountable for their stewardship.

The basic notion of CETA is that state and local politicians will be held accountable by their voters for their stewardships. The flaw in this argument is the low level of visibility of manpower concerns among the many pressures impinging on a local political executive and the usually weak organization of the manpower constituency. The manpower planner is in a key position to act as conscience of the program in a local community to see that the appropriate people are served. It is not realistic to expect the "feds" to monitor and evaluate any significant number of individual programs. In fact, it has been the painful experience that federal plan approval and monitoring tend to enforce the wrong things. It is relatively easy to determine whether prescribed procedures are being followed, but nearly impossible to determine whether a plan or program fits current need or has the elements of success. Success can be determined after the fact, if objectives are measurable, but retroactive reward and punishment are politically difficult concepts. The tendency of such monitoring is to limit flexibility rather than enforce responsiveness. Monitoring and evaluating must also be a planner's responsibility. It won't get done unless planners do it. They can be objective about evaluation of individual service deliverers, but can they be objective about the planning function or the overall manpower activity?

A promising potential advantage of decentralized and decategorized planning is the coupling of both services and service deliverers in ways that were rare under national programming. It was not only because of legislated categorization that clients were required to fit programs, rather than the programs fitting the clients. With each agency often responsible for only a particular category of service, interagency cooperation was necessary for an appropriate mix of services. With a functional hierarchy extending from the national through a regional, state, and local level, there was little incentive and considerable disincentive for such cooperation. MDTA training is an example. Even within one piece of legislation, institutional training was an educational responsibility, with the employment service primarily responsible for on-the-job training. The latter agency had capability for employer contacts, and job training contracts got written. It had none for designing, recognizing, or enforcing training quality, and there was always the question of how much actual training occurred. A stereotype of on-the-job training evaluations was the trainee interviewed in a follow-up survey, who responded, "What training program? I've never been a trainee!"

An attractive training format would have been an initial period of general skills training in a classroom or lab, followed by on-the-job training for practice and more specific skills, perhaps followed by another institutional stint, and then back to the job training. Coupled programs were always rare because of the bilateral requirements. The local labor market planner could solve the problem of this example. The plan could call for the employment service to solicit and vocational education to monitor on-the-job training. The plan could direct alternate periods of institutional and on-the-job training, with the relevant employment service and schools responding as subcontractors. The prime sponsor can now marshal, by contractual assignment and through council participation, the varied expertise and resources of private and public education, employment service, vocational rehabilitation, minority and community organizations, day-care facilities, welfare and family services, employers, unions, housing and transportation agencies, and so forth. There is, of course, no guarantee that it will be done; only the possibility that it can be.

Related is the end to agency monopoly of particular services. The planning arm has the authority, if politically able to exercise it, to assign a task to the most competent provider of that service, irrespective of past history. In all probability, the traditional agency for that service will be the most capable of delivering it. But potential competition keeps not only private businesses alert to consumer needs; actual competition may invoke duplication of capacity, but potential competition is a relatively cost-free goad.

The Dangers

The threats of decentralization are equally serious. Perhaps the most fearful is the slackening of equal employment opportunity emphasis. It was certainly easier for a minority group to marshal sufficient national power to influence legislation and administrative fiat than to cause an impact upon all local political scenes across the land. The locations where minorities are majorities are usually resource- and opportunity-starved locations. Mayors in many large cities may be vulnerable to minority political power. Governors, county commissioners, and mayors of modest-sized cities almost never are. When prime sponsors continue to emphasize service to minorities and to the most disadvantaged, it will be more likely because they believe it to be right than because they feel pressured. Political power is a more dependable currency than moral commitment. It is reassuring to have both on the same side. The manpower planner is in a unique position to keep them in parallel.

Whether or not it is a likely consequence of decentralization, CETA has been the occasion for a substantial cut in manpower funding. Including both dollar cuts and inflation, available resources dropped about 30 percent in the transition from MDTA and the Economic Opportunity Act to CETA (see Table 10-1). There is no tradition of local funding for manpower services. Not until continuing and recurrent education for adults is recognized as great

Table 10-1
Manpower Budget Summary
(Millions; 1973–75)

	Actual 1973	Estimated 1974	Estimated 1975
Program			
Comprehensive manpower assistance training	$1,388	$1,398	$1,902
Emergency employment assistance	1,005	631	
Work incentive training and placement	177	197	200
Veterans programs	292	337	339
Employment service	431	428	424
Vocational rehabilitation	636	715	770
Social services training	58	41	61
Other training and placement programs	276	282	260
Employment-related child care	433	502	584
Program direction, research, and support	209	220	219
Other supportive services	48	58	71
TOTAL	$4,952	$4,808	$4,831

SOURCE: U.S. Office of Management and Budget

an educational responsibility as education for youth will there be any significant state or local investment. There is no likelihood for other manpower services. There is undoubtedly a tendency to make larger aggregate appropriations to several programs than to one consolidated one. These threats were clear to decentralization advocates. They thought the prize worth the cost, but hoped to avoid the latter.

A program of labor market manpower planning should be able to encompass and influence the total flow of resources on behalf of determined objectives. It is not a criterion of decentralization but only a fact of political life that CETA encompasses only two-fifths of the federal manpower budget allocated to employability and employment problems. The three-fifths remains outside the planning requirement. However, by their nature, the non-CETA manpower programs are not categorized as to the services they are allowed to deliver. Programs like the Work Incentive Program and vocational rehabilitation are categorized by service groups at least as free as CETA in choice of mix of services. The problem is to bring them under the labor market planning umbrella. Mingled in planning though kept separate in financial control, they serve an overlapping clientele and add to total resources.

CETA also suffers the threat of excessive decentralization. Under political pressure from local governments, sub-labor market areas become potential prime sponsors. The financial incentives for consortia are weak, relative to the political advantages of independent prime sponsorship. Yet consortia are forming. The lack of congruence between residence and job source is probably the most effective goad. The net result remains to be seen.

The lack of staff competence for manpower planning is obvious. Yet the assumption that federal staffs are more competent than their local or state counterparts is not justified. There may be an upward selection process, but there is also a growing desire for a life-style that cannot be offered in the national capital. The fact is that there was no such function or skill as labor market manpower planning ever required or present at the national level. The demand for manpower planners is a new one, and the competence would have to be developed anew, whether in Washington, regional offices, or at the state and local levels. It might as well be where the action is.

Problems of political influence and patronage are aggravated with decentralization. Not that there are none in the federal government. They are there, but they will continue in legislating, appropriating, and administering. State and local politics will be added to the total. However, one cannot simultaneously argue for local adaptation and local political responsibility and decry local political maneuverings.

Whether the advantages outweigh the disadvantages of decentralized planning and administration remains to be seen. We think they do. However, it took twelve years to bring federal manpower policy competence to its present relatively satisfactory level. There is as much to learn at the local level, but there is a base of experience in most sizable communities, federal capability to draw upon, and a body of technical assistance and training competence in and out of government. The long learning process can be shortcut, but only if the lessons of past experience are identified, codified, disseminated, and heeded, and if the available talent is marshaled and magnified through development of technique and training in its use. It will happen if there is aggressiveness from both suppliers and demanders of manpower planning competence.

Glossary

Accessible jobs — Specific job openings and entire occupations which, by nature of their training requirements, normal ports of entry, and lack of discriminatory barriers, afford the client a ready opportunity for employment.

Accessions — The total number of permanent and temporary additions to the employment roll of individual establishments, including both new and rehired employees.

(1) *New hires* — Temporary or permanent additions to the employment roll of persons who have never been employed in the establishment (except employees transferring from another establishment of the same company) or of former employees not recalled by the employer.

(2) *Other* — All additions to the employment roll which are not classified as new hires, including transfers from other establishments of the company and employees recalled from layoff. Generally not published as a separate figure but included in total accessions.

Algorithm — A rational, sequential procedure for searching or computing a decision. The procedure may take the form of a "tree" (i.e., branching out) or a list.

Allocation — An apportionment of resources among specific sets of objectives, activities, persons, geographical areas, or agencies.

Area of substantial unemployment — A specific geographical area with an unemployment rate in excess of 6.5 percent. This classification is sometimes used in determining eligibility for public employment programs and other federal manpower funding.

313

Assistant regional director for manpower — The executive officer of the Regional Manpower Administration for one of the ten federal administrative regions.

Balance of state — The geographical areas of a state which are not eligible for independent prime sponsorship of Labor Department–funded manpower programs and for which the state government serves as prime sponsor.

Bilingual — Communication in two languages.

Calibration — The process of estimating values for the parameters of a model under specific conditions.

Career education — A concept of education which brings together both general and vocational education in mutual support to assist the individual in the development and maintenance of a career throughout a working life.

Career ladder — The various skill or developmental steps, arranged from the lowest level to the highest, in a career area.

Categorical programs — Government programs designed to meet a specific need, with requirements and regulations specifically defined or legislated on an individual program basis.

Certification — The granting of a certificate which states that an individual has successfully completed a given course or a series of related courses and which indicates that the individual is qualified to perform a given function.

Civilian labor force — All persons employed and unemployed and not in the Armed Forces.

Client — An individual making use of the services of an agency.

Cohort survival technique — A technique for developing population projections characterized by the application of historical and forecasted vital rates (births and deaths) to a specific age, sex, and racial grouping of a population whose size and characteristics are known for some base period. Specific attention is given to adjustments for migration.

Community action agency — A local agency formed and funded by the Office of Economic Opportunity for the purpose of representing the poor and providing certain programs of assistance with a high degree of client control. Sometimes referred to as the community action programs.

Community college — A two-year educational institution with minimal entrance requirements, established to serve the post-secondary and remedial educational needs of a community.

Component — Any well-defined operating unit or service in a manpower service delivery system. A distinguishable portion of a service sequence.

Comprehensive manpower program — A pilot project established during fiscal year 1974 to test the decentralization and decategorization concepts in selected states, counties, and cities.

Comprehensive service approach — An approach to the planning and delivery of manpower services characterized by the availability of a broad array of well-integrated social and manpower services designed to assist persons in eliminating personal and institutional barriers to economic and social self-sufficiency.

Consortium — A group of independent units of a local general-purpose government organized for jointly planning and operating manpower programs in a single labor market area.

Cooperative Area Manpower Planning System (CAMPS) — A system established by federal agencies engaged in manpower development activities for the coordination of such activities at the local, state, regional, and national levels; superseded under the Comprehensive Employment and Training Act of 1973 (CETA).

Correlation analysis — A statistical approach to the measurement of the degree of relationship between variables.

Cost/benefit analysis — A comparison of the costs and benefits of a plan, activity, or program with the objective of determining the components which yield the greatest benefits per unit of cost. Characteristic of this approach is the attempt to quantify to the greatest extent possible all of the costs and benefits which may be financial as well as social, direct as well as indirect.

Coupled classroom — A program bringing work and classroom experience together, each reinforcing the other through a coordinated curriculum of activities.

Covered employment — Refers to employed persons who are working in jobs covered by public unemployment compensation programs. The principal groups generally not covered by unemployment insurance include agricultural workers, domestic service workers, employees of state and local governments, self-employed workers, and workers in nonprofit institutions. Persons who are covered but ineligible for unemployment compensation are generally those who have been unemployed long enough to exhaust their benefit rights and new workers who have not yet earned benefit rights.

Current Population Survey — A monthly household survey of a sample (sixty thousand) of the civilian noninstitutional population of the United States, conducted by the Census Bureau. The survey provides monthly statistics on employment, unemployment, and related subjects which are analyzed and published by the Bureau of Labor Statistics in *Employment and Earnings* and *Monthly Labor Force*.

Decategorization — The reduction of restrictive regulations on the use of federal manpower monies by state and local government, as well as a broadening of permissible activities, groups to be served, and possible administrative arrangements.

Decentralization — The delegation of greater authority and responsibility for the operation and planning of manpower programs to units of state and general-purpose local government.

Delivery systems — The linked array of administrative and planning structures, service providing units, component services, and associated client entry, exit, and transition points and mechanisms which, taken as a whole, constitute the community's system for the provision of manpower services to its citizens.

Delphi method — An intuitive method of invention which is characterized by a formal framework of questions used to obtain the perceptions of a selected panel of informed persons, a systematic feedback mechanism, and the development of a consensual viewpoint by the panel.

Dictionary of Occupational Titles — A classification scheme used for the systematic definition of jobs. The dictionary is published by the Labor Department and used extensively by public and private manpower planners and program operators. It is generally more detailed than the classification scheme used by the Census Bureau.

Disadvantaged — A person or persons who possess age, racial, educational, physical, or mental characteristics which set them at a competitive disadvantage in the job market. These characteristics are usually combined with income guidelines and current labor market status indicators in definitions designed for administrative and planning purposes.

Discouraged workers — Persons without work who make no overt attempt to find a job because they feel no work is available to them. Often referred to as the "hidden unemployed," they are not included in the unemployment estimates. The withdrawal of these persons from the labor market during periods of high unemployment results in an underestimation of the severity of unemployment.

Dropout — One who leaves school or a training activity before completing a specified program.

Economic Opportunity Act — Federal legislation of 1964 which set up the Office of Economic Opportunity with the avowed purpose of eliminating poverty by opening to everyone the opportunity for "education, training, work, decency, and dignity."

Employment

(1) *Actual* — number of people at a point in time who did any work and were paid for it; includes self-employed persons, persons who have jobs or businesses, and those who were temporarily absent due to illness, strikes, vacations, or personal reasons; excludes persons working in the home without pay and those working as volunteers in nonprofit organizations.

(2) *Actual full time* — The number of people employed at a point in time who worked 35 hours or more a week.

(3) *Actual full-time equivalent* — Total number of hours worked by all people employed, divided by 40.

(4) *Actual part time* — Number of people employed at a point in time who worked from one to 34 hours a week.

(5) *Nonagricultural payroll* — The total number of employees on nonagricultural payrolls who worked or received pay during the pay period that includes the 12th of each month. As a result of multiple job holding and payroll turnover, some workers are reported by more than one employer. Therefore the count is not of the number of different individuals but of jobs. Includes all corporation officials, executives, and other supervisory personnel, clerical workers, wage earners, persons on paid vacations, pieceworkers, part-time and temporary workers, and so forth. Excludes self-employed and unpaid family and domestic workers, workers who neither worked nor received wages during the pay period which includes the 12th of each month (as a result of strikes or work stoppages, temporary layoffs, or unpaid sick or vacation leave), and individuals who worked during the month but who did not work during the specific pay period which includes the 12th of each month.

Employment Security Automated Reporting System (ESARS) — The basic employment service reporting system which collects, organizes, and reports on key indicators of employment service workloads, performance, and use of resources. ESARS reports are developed for major local areas and states.

Evaluate — To assess the degree to which the objectives of a program, activity, or service delivery unit are achieved. There are four basic forms of evaluation of importance in the context of state and local manpower planning:

(1) *Alternatives effectiveness assessment* — The periodic evaluation of the success and costs of achieving specific manpower plan, program, and program component objectives in the intermediate time frame. The focus of alternatives effectiveness assessment is the comparison of the relative effectiveness of alternative strategies for achieving intermediate measures of success.

(2) *Impact assessment* — All of those analytical activities designed to measure the long-term changes attributable to a manpower program which impinge upon participants, the labor market, and the community. Impact assessments seek to determine the extent to which long-term objectives are being met.

(3) *Operational control and assessment* — The periodic monitoring of current operations for compliance with a preestablished model of efficiency and general principles of prudent management through the use of quantitative and qualitative program performance targets generally expressed in a time-phased operational plan.

(4) *Outcomes assessment* — The evaluation of post-program changes in the employability and labor market success of participants in manpower programs; control groups and the examination of change in the community or the local labor market are generally not included in outcomes assessment designs.

External labor market — That market lying outside the particular firm or craft. It is relatively free of administrative rules governing the pricing and allocation of labor and restrictive ports of entry.

Feedback — Information on past experiences or system performance; used for improving or correcting present and future system performance.

Follow-up — Contacts made by representatives of a manpower service delivery agency with former program clients to determine additional services needed by the client or to collect information on the client's current labor market status for evaluative purposes.

Fringe benefits — Monetary rewards or benefits provided by an employer, in addition to salary or wage payments.

Full employment — Theoretically, the employment of all persons willing and able to work. Practical goals aiming for "full" employment without excessive inflationary tradeoffs have ranged from 95 to 97 percent employment of the labor force.

General Aptitude Test Battery (GATB) — A set of tests designed to measure aptitudes in nine areas, including mental and physical abilities. The GATB is closely integrated with the *Dictionary of Occupational Titles* and is widely used in manpower counseling.

General education development diploma — An academic diploma awarded to high school dropouts who successfully complete a formal program of basic education. Educational development is measured by satisfactory performance in a formal instructional program and through standardized tests administered by authorized individuals. Generally accepted in lieu of a high school diploma.

Government authorized representative — The local representative of the Labor Department.

Gross national product — The market value of all goods and services produced by a nation for the marketplace.

Hands-on experience — One that uses actual equipment normally used on the job; also can mean close simulation of tasks as a training method.

Heuristic — Short-cut procedures based on experience and intuition used by planners and administrators to handle complex situations.

Hold harmless clause — A policy decision or legislative provision for protecting a manpower agency or prime sponsor from sharp reductions in funding through the application of allocation formulas. A hold harmless provision would guarantee the adversely affected party a specified percentage of some previous year's funding for a specified number of future planning periods.

Human resource development — The development of human beings into economic producers through education, training, and employment services.

Intake — The process, procedures, services, and organizational units assigned to bring persons into a manpower service delivery system.

Internal labor market — That labor market within a particular industry, firm, or plant in which the pricing and allocation of labor are governed by administrative rules and procedures.

Institutional program — A training program conducted within an educational institution as differentiated from on-the-job training which takes place at or near the work site.

Intervention — A predetermined strategy for brining about change; may relate to the prescription of services to an individual client or, in the context of manpower planning, the prescription of a set of services or policies designed to bring about a specific change in a group of persons, an institution, or a local labor market.

Job leavers — Persons who quit or otherwise terminate their employment voluntarily and who immediately begin looking for work.

Job evaluation — The process of dividing a job into its major components to facilitate analysis for the purpose of establishing rates of pay and training procedures.

Job losers — Persons whose employment ended involuntarily, who immediately begin looking for work, and persons on layoff.

Job opening — An unfilled paid position for which an employer is actively seeking a worker.

Journeyman — A craftsman qualified to function in a trade without supervision.

Labor force — All persons classified as employed or unemployed, plus members of the Armed Forces.

Labor force participation rate — The number of persons in the labor force, expressed as a percentage of all persons sixteen years of age and older.

Labor market — For purposes of state or local manpower planning, the geographical area within which most workers are secured. For some occupations, this may be a given community, while for others, it may be nationwide. The geographical area over which a worker can roam in search of a job, within reasonable commuting distance of his place of residence.

Linear equation — An algebraic equation of the first degree in which only one value of each unknown will satisfy the equation.

Linear programming — A mathematical method for the optimization of an objective function, expressed as a linear relationship, within the bounds of a set of constraints also expressed as linear equations. One of a set of techniques coming under the more general rubric of mathematical programming.

Manpower coordinating councils — Councils of federal officials from various agencies at the national and regional levels, organized to coordinate federal manpower programs.

Manpower Development and Training Act (MDTA) — Federal legislation of 1962 authorizing manpower services. Initially used to retrain persons possessing obsolete skills and later redirected to emphasize training for disadvantaged persons and youth.

Manpower planning councils — Councils at local and state levels representing a cross section of the community, including elected and appointed officials, clients, business and labor representatives, organized to plan and coordinate manpower activities.

Manpower revolution — The period of the 1960s in which technological changes and problems became apparent, producing a series of corrective manpower programs.

Manpower services councils — The state manpower advisory bodies created under CETA to monitor and coordinate manpower programs in each state. One third of the membership of these councils must be representatives of local prime sponsors.

Markov process — A mathematical technique for portraying a set of events in which the probability of any one event taking place is dependent upon the probability of the previous event.

Matrix — A structure of cells formed by rows and columns in which variables may be located. Matrix algebra provides rules for operations on mathematical matrices.

Minorities — Those ethnic groups constituting a minority in the total population who experience special problems of assimilation into the dominant economic and social system.

Model — A representation of a system by another system.

New entrants — Persons who have never worked at a full-time job lasting at least two weeks.

Objective — A specific and measurable aim toward which activity is directed. In manpower planning, objectives are set on the basis of more general goals and policy choices, and operational alternatives are selected and implemented which will meet chosen objectives. Progress in reaching desired objectives can be measured at specified time intervals.

Occupational cluster — A grouping of closely related job functions or occupations having a common core of skills and learning.

On-the-job training — The usually informal training that is a part of learning a job at the employment site, as compared with classroom and apprenticeship programs.

Open entry/open exit — A particular approach to the operation of a training facility characterized by an admissions policy which permits a student to enter training with a minimum of qualifications and exit the program at various levels of job-capable skills. Also may refer to a continuous intake policy.

Outreach – Reaching out into the community and offering manpower services to clients, rather than waiting for clients to come into an office.

Parameter – A variable which takes on a constant value in a particular case.

Personal income – That income an individual receives from all sources, the major components of which are wage and salary disbursements, proprietor's income, property income, and transfer payments from business and government. This figure is net of personal contributions to Social Security and does not include transfer payments between private individuals. This income is estimated primarily from required payroll reports submitted to the employment security agencies by employers who are covered by unemployment insurance and from government and uninsured employers who voluntarily submit payroll reports.

Placement – The placing of persons on a job by an educational or employment agency.

Prime sponsor – A public or private corporate body eligible under federal criteria to contract directly with a federal agency for the operation of manpower programs in a given locality. The most common prime sponsors under CETA are local governments of a hundred thousand and over population and recognized Indian tribes. CETA also provides for consortium prime sponsors, composed of one or more independently eligible units of local government and other nearby units of local government not independently eligible. Such consortia are designed to plan and coordinate manpower services in substantial portions of labor market areas. A prime sponsor can provide services through its own agencies as well as subcontract with other agencies for the delivery of manpower services.

Prime sponsor advisory councils – The mandatory local policy advisory bodies, composed of labor, business, and client representatives authorized by CETA, to advise local prime sponsors.

Productivity – The output per unit of input, usually expressed in units per man-hour.

Professional – One who works in any profession (such as law, medicine, engineering, and the like) implying training at the four-year college level.

Projections – Conclusions reached about the future from facts collected in an earlier period.

Public Employment Program – The temporary program established by the Emergency Employment Act of 1971 to subsidize jobs in the public sector of the local and state levels of unemployed and underemployed persons.

Public service employment — Subsidized employment in the public sector authorized under Title II of CETA.

Reentrants — Persons who previously worked at a full-time job lasting at least two weeks but who were out of the labor force prior to beginning to look for work.

Referrals — Those persons referred to an agency or employer for service or employment.

Relocation — The process of moving, usually from an area of labor surplus to an area of labor shortage.

Reporting unit — Any firm, organization, division, or the like, for which data are separately identified on the unemployment insurance employer contribution or supplemental report. An individual or company which maintains two or more separate establishments located within the same county and engaged in the same industrial activity is counted as a single reporting unit.

Salary — Payment to a person by the week, month, or year for work rendered.

Scenario — A planning method for generating alternative future states from the present state by the systematic development of a complete range of alternatives and successive events or conditions flowing out of each alternative.

Seasonal adjustments — A statistical technique designed to minimize regularly occurring fluctuations in numerical time series.

Separation — Terminations of employment classified according to cause: quits, layoffs, and all other separations such as death, retirement, and so forth.

(1) *Quits* — Terminations of employment initiated by employees, including failure to report after being hired and unauthorized absences if on the last day of the month the person has been absent for more than seven consecutive calendar days.

(2) *Layoffs* — Suspension without pay lasting or expected to last more than seven consecutive calendar days, initiated by the employer without prejudice to the worker.

(3) *Other* — Terminations of employment due to discharge, permanent disability, death, retirement, transfers to another establishment of the same company, and entrance into the Armed Forces, for a period expected to last more than thirty consecutive calendar days.

Standard industrial classification code (SIC) — A scheme for the classification and description of employing establishments by the type of industrial activity in which they are engaged. The SIC is published by the Office of Management and Budget and regularly updated.

Standard metropolitan statistical area (SMSA) — A widely used Census Bureau concept for defining urban areas: a county or group of contiguous counties which contain at least one city of fifty thousand inhabitants or more, or "twin cities" with a combined population of at least fifty thousand, and such additional contiguous counties which meet criteria demonstrating their metropolitan character and economic and social integration with the central county or city.

Subprofessionals and paraprofessionals — Persons trained to perform work to assist professionals but requiring less than baccalaureate education and training.

Supportive services — Services provided clients of manpower programs in support of training and employment services, such as day-care, health care, and transportation allowances.

Turnover — The gross movement of wage and salary workers into and out of employed status with respect to individual establishments. Turnover is divided into two broad categories: accessions (rehires and new hires) and separations (including all types of terminations of the employment relationship).

Typology — A scheme for the differentiation of a larger set of items into classifications based on some characteristic attribute or feature.

Underemployment — Includes persons working full or part time, with inadequate incomes, including those working part time because full-time work is unavailable, those working full time with earnings that do not raise family income above the poverty or near-poverty level, and those working full time at jobs that require lower levels of skills and abilities than other jobs for which they are qualified.

Unemployment — Includes persons available for work but without a job and in the process of looking for work, as demonstrated by specific job-seeking efforts made within the last four weeks. Also includes persons on layoff who are waiting to be recalled or who are waiting to report to a new job starting within thirty days.

Unemployment rate — The number of persons unemployed, expressed as a percentage of the civilian labor force.

Universe of need (UON) — The total number of different individuals, both unemployed and underemployed, who may need manpower training or related services during the course of the planning year according to some predetermined criteria.

Upgrading — The improvement of job skills undertaken to enable persons to move into occupations or positions requiring greater skills than those previously held.

Wages — Payment by the hour for work rendered. Total wages for statistical purposes include all renumeration paid to workers, including commission, bonuses, cash value of meals, lodging, and other gratuities, when furnished in connection with the job.

Work force — Total number of persons employed, based on establishment data rather than census data. Because these statistics are derived from surveys of employment establishments, they differ from labor force statistics that are based on household data, because persons who work for more than one establishment may be counted more than once. Private household workers, self-employed persons, and unpaid family workers are excluded, but workers less than sixteen years old may be counted in the work force. The difference between work force and labor force statistics is particularly significant when data are being compared for places where workers commute between areas.

Index

327